Student's Book

MORE! 4

Gerngross · Puchta · Holzmann
Stranks · Lewis-Jones

General course

HELBLING LANGUAGES

Mit Bescheid vom 28. August 2012, GZ: BMUKK-5.028/0014-B/8/2011, hat das Bundesministerium für Unterricht, Kunst und Kultur das Unterrichtsmittel „MORE! Student's Book 4 General Course" von Gerngross u.a. antragsgemäß in der vorliegenden Fassung gemäß §14 Abs. 2 und 5 des Schulunterrichtsgesetzes, BGBl. Nr. 472/86 und gemäß den derzeit geltenden Lehrplänen als für den Unterrichtsgebrauch an Hauptschulen und an allgemein bildenden höheren Schulen für die Klasse 4 im Unterrichtsgegenstand Englisch (1. lebende Fremdsprache) geeignet erklärt.

Zeichenerklärung:

- 1 CD 1 – Dazu gibt es eine Tonaufnahme auf CD (Obere Zahl: Tonspur / Untere Zahl: CD Nummer)
- SbX – Dazu gibt es eine interaktive Übung im Internet (SbX)
- MP3 – Dazu gibt es für die SchülerInnen eine Audio-Aufnahme als Gratisdownload im Internet (www.helbling-ezone.com)
- DVD – Dazu gibt es einen Film auf DVD.
- 2 CHOICES – Auswahlangebote zur inneren Leistungsdifferenzierung (Grundlegende und vertiefte Allgemeinbildung)
- ★ – anspruchsvolle Aufgabenstellung
- CYBER HOMEWORK 15 – Dazu gibt es eine Hausübung im Internet (www.helbling-ezone.com) siehe Teacher's Book
- WB p.15 – Dazu gibt es passende Übungen im Workbook (auf Seite 15)
- 1 – Diese Übung gehört zum Kernstoff und sollte nicht ausgelassen werden.
- 2 – Diese Übung kann bei Zeitmangel im Sinne eines "Fast track" durch die Unit ohne Probleme ausgelassen werden.
- BiSt – Diese Übung bietet eine spezielle Vorbereitung auf die Bildungsstandards-Prüfungen.

MORE! STUDENT'S BOOK 4 – GENERAL COURSE

by Günter Gerngross, Herbert Puchta, Christian Holzmann, Jeff Stranks, Peter Lewis-Jones
adaptation for the Neue Mittelschule in collaboration with Andrea Köstenbauer, Monika Haring, Roswitha Kemmer

Edited by Johanna Günther

Design and layout by Amanda Hockin and Carmen Zingerle

Printed by Athesia

First published 2013

Second edition 2013, third print run 2015

ISBN 978-3-85272-599-4

Schulbuchnummer: 160.405

www.helblinglanguages.at

Contents

UNIT 1 Welcome to Ireland

Vocabulary About a country

SbX 1 **Make sure you know what these words / phrases mean. If necessary, ask your teacher.**

What's … in German?

- capital (city)
- people
- a member of the EU
- the weather
- official language
- be fluent in a language
- a part of the United Kingdom

1 CD 1 ★ 2 a **Do the Ireland quiz in pairs. Then listen and check your answers.**

Do you know Ireland?

		T	F
1	The capital of the Republic of Ireland is Belfast.	☐	☐
2	There are about four million people in the Republic of Ireland.	☐	☐
3	The official languages of Ireland are English and Irish.	☐	☐
4	More than a million Irish people are fluent in Irish.	☐	☐
5	Irish is spoken primarily in the west of Ireland.	☐	☐
6	Ireland is not a member of the EU.	☐	☐
7	The Irish money is the pound.	☐	☐
8	The Republic of Ireland is part of the United Kingdom.	☐	☐
9	Ireland exports a lot of software.	☐	☐
10	Northern Ireland is not part of the Republic of Ireland.	☐	☐
11	The capital of Northern Ireland is Derry.	☐	☐
12	Most Irish people in the Republic are Catholics.	☐	☐

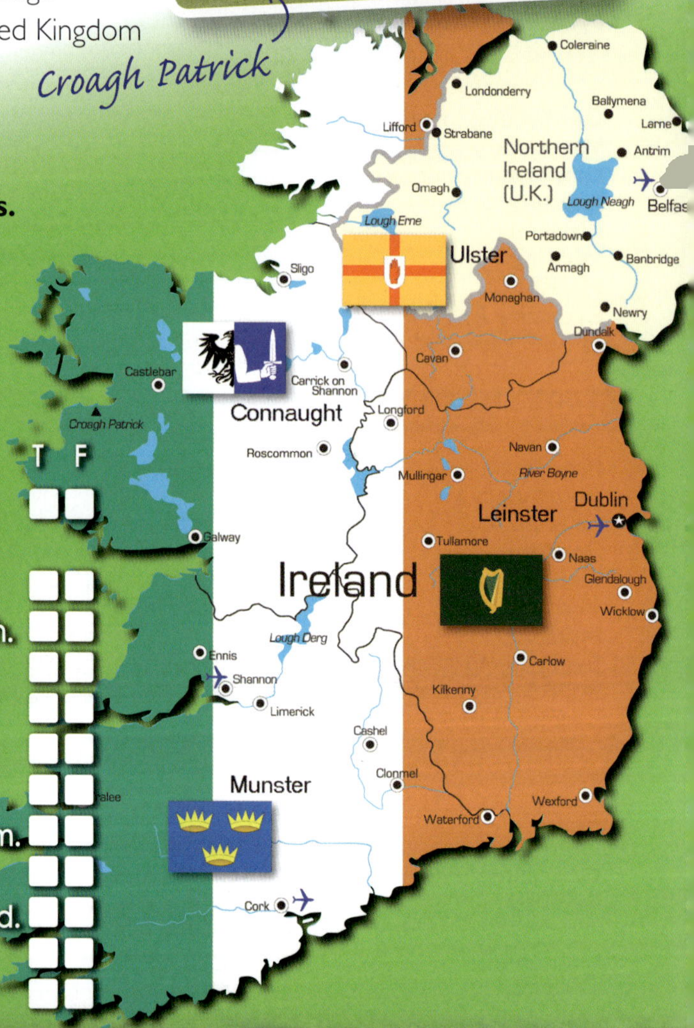

Get talking Expressing surprise / Asking your partner to say something

b **Work in pairs. Tell your partner three things that surprised you from the quiz.**

I wasn't aware that …
I didn't know that …

How about you?

I had no idea that …
I didn't know that …

3 CHOICES

a AN IRISH STORY

Vocabulary

1 Say which words go with the pictures.

servant
knife
cellar
brick
lantern
village
spoon
fork

2 Look at the picture and say what you think the story is about.

3 Read and put the paragraphs in order. Then listen and check.

☐ So Mary went to cook for the farmer. She always put two plates, spoons, forks and knives on the table. One for the young farmer and one for his mother's ghost. And when she brought the meat and the vegetables, she always asked, "Meat, vegetables, madam?" But the ghost never answered.

☐ A long time ago a girl called Mary lived with her parents in a small village in Ireland. Everybody knew Mary because she was not afraid of anything. One day a rich, young farmer came to Mary's house. He said, "Last year my mother died. But her ghost often comes back at dinner time. I have had five servants since last year. All of them ran away. They were afraid of the ghost. I've heard that you're not afraid of anything. Please come. I will pay you good money."

☐ "Pick up those bricks," the ghost said. Mary did so and she saw two bags. "The big bag is for my son," the ghost said. "The small one is for you because you are a brave girl." Then the ghost disappeared and Mary was alone in the dark cellar. She picked up the bags. While she was climbing up the stairs, she heard a noise. Somebody had left the house. When Mary was in the kitchen, she opened the bags. They were full of gold coins.

☐ One day the farmer had to go into town for two days. When Mary was reading in the evening, the ghost of the farmer's mother appeared. "Come into the cellar with me," the ghost said. "Don't bring a light." Mary followed the ghost, who shone like a lantern.

☐ The young farmer scratched his head. He liked pretty Mary who was never scared. "Will you marry me, Mary?" he asked. Mary laughed. "Yes, I will," she said. And she thought: "Then the small bag *and* the big one will be mine!"

☐ When the farmer came home the next day, Mary told him what had happened. "The big bag is for you and the small one is for me," she said.

▶ WB p. 5

MP3
BiSt
★

b A VERY SHORT HISTORY OF IRELAND

The Battle of the Boyne 1690

1 Look quickly at the text. What kind of text do you think it is?

a a story **c** a news report
b a diary entry **d** a magazine article

2 Quickly go through the text and find out what happened in these years.

1845 1916 1922 2007

3 Read the full text. Sum up in one sentence what the main idea of the text is.

Why do Irish football fans never support or cheer for England? History is the answer. For many centuries the Irish fought against the British and hundreds of thousands of Irish people were killed.

In September 1845, the situation of the people in Ireland was dramatic. A fungus destroyed the potato crop. The following year, there were no potatoes again. Many poor people in Ireland were starving, but at the same time Protestant Irish landlords sent badly needed grain and cattle to England to sell it there. The British government didn't help either. One official said in 1846, "It is not our intention at all to import food for the use of the people of Ireland."

There were about eight million people in Ireland in 1850. While they were trying to find food, one million of them died and another million fled to the USA, Australia and New Zealand.

In 1916, the "Easter rebellion" of the Irish was put down by the British and the leaders of the rebellion were shot. A guerrilla war followed. In 1922, the Irish Free State was founded. But the Irish had to pay a price. The province of Ulster, where the majority of the people were Protestant, did not become part of the Free State. And there has been trouble in Northern Ireland ever since.

However, since peace talks in 2007, things are looking a lot better. The troubles seem to be over.

Dublin Memorial to the Famine of 1846

Vocabulary

4 Match the words / phrases and the definitions.

1 put down	☐	a man who owns land
2 army	☐	all the potatoes produced in a year
3 intention	☐	becoming ill or dying because you do not have enough food
4 majority	☐	a hundred years
5 starve	☐	cows and bulls
6 cattle	☐	shout as a way of showing you're happy
7 cheer	☐	use military power to stop something
8 century	☐	most people
9 potato crop	☐	a plan to do something
10 landlord	☐	people trained to fight in a war

▶ WB p. 6

3 CD 1 ★

4 **a A group of British students are going on a school trip to Glendalough in Ireland. Look at the pictures and answer the questions.**

1 Do you think this is a good place for a school trip? Why / Why not?
2 What kind of places for school trips do you like best? Give your reasons.

The Bell Tower – an ideal place to hide from attackers.

There are two beautiful lakes in the valley.

Glendalough is great for hiking.

b Read the questions. Listen and take notes. Then compare your notes.

1 What would the boys like to do at the lakes? Is it possible to do these things? Why / Why not?
2 How do they boys feel about the trip? Give examples.
3 How do the boys try to be funny? Give examples.
4 What does the teacher say about the bell tower that you can see in one of the photos?

A song 4 U *Will you remember? (The Cranberries)*

4/5 CD 1

5 **Listen to the song. Cross out the four lines that do not belong to the lyrics.**

Will you remember the dress I wore?
Will you remember my face?
Will you remember the lipstick I wore?
This world is a wonderful place.

Will you remember the black limousine?
Will you remember champagne?
Will you remember the things that we've seen?
I will return here again.

Will you remember the things we said?
Will you remember my voice?
Will you remember the stories we told?
I know there is no other choice.

Will you remember the flowers in my hand?
Will you remember my hair?
Will you remember the future we planned?
The world is not waiting out there.

I won't remember the dress I wore.
I won't remember champagne.
I won't remember the things that we swore.
I will just love you in vain.

Will you remember?
Will you recall?
Will you remember?

Did you know … ?

Ireland is famous for music. There's live music in pubs and there are famous singers and groups. Among them are *U2, Boyzone, Enya, Sinead O'Connor, The Cranberries, Paddy Casey* and many others.

CD 1 6 BiSt

6 **Read the questions below, then listen to the interview and take notes. Use your notes to answer the questions.**

1 Where is Anna from?
2 What's she doing in Dublin?
3 Why has Anna come to Dublin?
4 What does the interviewer think of Anna's English?
5 What does she like about Dublin?
6 What doesn't she like about Dublin?
7 What is LUAS and what does Anna think about it?
8 What is her favourite place in Dublin?
9 What does she think about the weather?

Sounds right Elision

CD 1 7 ★

7 **Listen to the dialogue. Pay attention to the underlined parts. Then listen and repeat.**

Alan I'd like to visit Dublin.
Brenda Why?
Alan My friend went there. He loved it. It must be a great city.
Chris I'd rather go to Spain.
Brenda Why Spain?
Chris Because it's hot there. Where would you like to go?
Brenda Guess!
Chris I haven't got a clue.
Brenda Nowhere. I don't like travelling.

Get talking Expressing interest

BiSt

8 **Work with a partner. Ask and answer questions. Talk about a place you'd (not) like to visit and give your reasons.**

I'd love to visit …
I'd never go to …

I've got no interest in going to …

Would(n't) you? How come … ?

★ **9** **a What do you think the headline of the newspaper article means?**

a The foxes have escaped from the zoo.
b Foxes are having problems with visitors to the zoo.
c Foxes are cleverer than people working at the zoo.
d Foxes are scared of visitors' dogs.

BiSt **b Read the article and find out.**

ZOO STAFF ARE OUT-FOXED

Two clever foxes were making life difficult for the staff of Dublin Zoo last week. The problem was that the foxes were killing some of the zoo animals. Five exotic animals were already dead by last Friday. The zoo director said the foxes came from the grounds of Phoenix Park which surround the zoo. "There's a healthy population of urban foxes there," the director said. "Because there's a lot of building activity at the zoo, we think a gate was open and this is how the foxes got in."

The foxes have now killed three more South American Maras (which look a bit like big rabbits), a penguin and a peacock. Two days ago one of the two foxes was shot, but the other one is still around. "We even got a fox whistle and a trained dog, but we're out-foxed by this fox," said the director.

★ **10** **Find words or phrases in the text that mean:**

1 people working at the zoo
2 something strange from another country
3 to be everywhere all around something
4 all the people or animals living in an area
5 an instrument that you hold to your lips to make a high sound
6 to make a fool of someone

Get talking

★ **11** **Work in pairs. Start a conversation about the text. Use the language to help you.**

FOX KILLED

Do you think it was right / wrong that they shot …?

Some people say … should (not) be allowed.

What's your opinion?
What do you think about it?

Why? Why not?

In my opinion it's (not) okay that …

Yes, I think so, because …
I don't think so, because …

Why do you think so?

I think it's wrong, because …
I think it's right, because …

DVD The Mag 1 The competition

1 **Watch the story. Then tick T (*True*) or F (*False*).**

	T	F
1 Liam wants to be a journalist on the Mag.	☐	☐
2 Nick and Liam decide to have a competition.	☐	☐
3 Lucy chooses more of Liam's photos than Nick's photos.	☐	☐
4 Liam took all of his photos off the net.	☐	☐
5 Lucy didn't know about Nick and Liam's competition.	☐	☐
6 Lucy agrees to give Liam a second chance.	☐	☐

2 **Complete the sentences with not more than four words each.**

1 Liam is new at the school and wants to join …
2 When Nick hears that Liam is also a photographer, he isn't …
3 Lucy wants five photographs from each of them so she can …
4 Nick suggests to Liam that the one whose photos gets picked should …
5 Liam's photos are brilliant, but the others find out he got them …
6 Lucy says Liam can't …

Everyday English

3 **Complete the dialogues with the phrases from the box.**

Whatever. Piece of cake! How does that grab you? What a nerve!

WB p. 7

Writing *for your Portfolio*

BiSt **Do one of the two writing tasks.**

a Write an email to tell a friend about a place where you would like to go for a holiday. Write 40 – 70 words and do not take more than 10 minutes.

Tell your friend:
- where you would like to go
- what you would like to do there
- why you think it would be a great place to go.

★ **b You have been invited to write a story for your school magazine. The story should be about a holiday adventure. It should be about 120 – 180 words. Do not forget to use paragraphs and do not take more than 20 minutes.**

In your story, say:
- where you went
- who went with you
- what the ending of the story was.
- what happened
- how you felt and why

SbX

Grammar Past continuous (Revision)

When Mary **was reading** in the evening, the ghost of the farmer's mother appeared.
While she **was climbing** up the stairs, she heard a noise.

Form: *past tense* von *be* + *-ing*-Form des Verbs.

Complete: Du verwendest oft das [1].. , um eine längere Handlung in der Vergangenheit zu beschreiben, die durch eine kürzere unterbrochen wird. Für die kürzere Handlung verwendest du das [2].. .

Du verwendest das [3].. auch, wenn du über eine länger andauernde Handlung in der Vergangenheit sprichst oder schreibst.
Many poor people in Ireland **were starving**.

While his mum was reading, Johnny gave her a surprise.

MORE fun with Fido!

▶ WB p. 8

8 CD 1 BiSt

1 **Listen to the dialogue and fill in the missing words and phrases.**

Tony	Hi Nadia. Did you go to New York [1]...................................?
Nadia	Yes, I did.
Tony	Did you go with your [2]...................................?
Nadia	No, [3]................................... with my mum. My dad had to look after my grandmother.
Tony	Did you [4]................................... it?
Nadia	Yes, I did. It was fantastic.
Tony	How long did you stay there?
Nadia	[5]................................... for a week.
Tony	What did you like most?
Nadia	The shops on 5th Avenue.
Tony	Did you [6]................................... a lot?
Nadia	No, I didn't. Just a few souvenirs.

8 CD 1

2 **Now cover up the dialogue. Listen again and correct what is wrong in each sentence. Then look at the dialogue and check.**

1 Nadia went to New York a week ago. ....
2 Nadia went with her parents. ....
3 Nadia's mum had to look after her mother. ....
4 Nadia didn't enjoy New York. ....
5 Nadia stayed there for three weeks. ....
6 Nadia liked the museums on 5th Avenue best. ....
7 Nadia bought lots of clothes. ....

BiSt **3** **Ask four people in your class about their holidays. Use the questions below.**

Where did you go on holiday?

I went to …
I stayed at home.

Did you like it?
Did you … go with your …?
What did you do there?
Did you make some friends?
Was there something you didn't like?
What did you like most?

Yes, … / No …
Yes, my … / No, I …
We went / swam / snorkelled / walked / played …
Yes, I … / No, I …
Yes, I didn't like the … / No, everything was fine.
The …

Martin went to …
He went with …
He didn't like …
He liked … a lot.
A typical day was like this.
First … Then …

4 **Make a class survey.**

How many students went to Croatia? ☐
How many students did some sports? ☐
How many students went to Italy? ☐
How many students like their holiday? ☐
How many students went to another country? ☐
How many students hated it? ☐
How many students stayed at home? ☐
How many students made some friends? ☐
How many students travelled with their family? ☐
How many students spoke English during their holidays? ☐
How many students went to a camp? ☐

WB p. 9 CYBER HOMEWORK 2

UNIT 2 The Curious Case of the Locked Room

★ **1 Read the beginning of the murder mystery and the notes in 2 and complete the police crime report.**

SCENE 1 *(At police headquarters)*

Sgt Jenkins Excuse me, Inspector.

Inspector Fell What is it, Jenkins?

Sgt Jenkins Bad news, I'm afraid. We've just got a call from Murdoch Towers.

Inspector Fell The offices of the computer king?

Sgt Jenkins That's right. There's been a murder. John Murdoch is dead. He has a deep wound in his chest.

Inspector Fell I don't believe it! Five thirty on a Friday! Let's hope this is an easy one. Come on, Jenkins. Get your coat!

POLICE CRIME REPORT

Victim –

Crime – murder

Weapon –

Date – Friday 19th May

Time of report –

Reporting officer –

Investigating officers –

Suspects –

John Murdoch

SCENE 2 *(At Murdoch Towers)*

Sgt Jenkins Inspector, this is Detective Ward. He's the reporting officer.

Inspector Fell Okay, Ward. So, what have we got?

Detective Ward Well, sir, Murdoch was holding a small office party for just four of his employees. Nobody else was in the building. All the other employees had left.

Inspector Fell Good. So we know that it was one of them.

Sgt Jenkins Most probably. But which one?

Inspector Fell That's what I'm going to find out.

Detective Ward There is one other thing, Inspector.

Inspector Fell What?

Detective Ward Well, it's very strange, but the room where Murdoch's body was found was locked from the inside. All the witnesses …

Inspector Fell You mean suspects.

Detective Ward Yes, sir. All the suspects told me the same thing.

Inspector Fell So you've already questioned everyone?

Detective Ward Yes, sir. But only very quickly.

Inspector Fell What about the murder weapon?

Detective Ward We haven't found it.

Inspector Fell Aha! Can I see your notes?

★ **2** **Read Detective Ward's notes and write the names of the people under the pictures.**

Jasper Ford / 40 years with the company / knew Murdoch's father / office clerk
Oliver Wilson / nephew / computer programmer
Isabel Miller / project manager / attractive / was working with Murdoch on top secret project
Charles Dunning / head salesman / bit of a playboy / very good-looking

Name				
Motive				

★ **3** **a Read Scene 3.**

b Make notes of Inspector Fell's theories about each suspect's motive in the box in 2.

SCENE 3 *(Sgt Jenkins and Inspector Fell are looking at Detective Ward's notes.)*

Sgt Jenkins Jasper Ford. 40 years with the company. He's a lot older than the others.

Inspector Fell And he doesn't have such a good job as all the others. He's just a clerk. All the others at the party have very good positions in the company. What was he doing there, I wonder?

Sgt Jenkins He's probably a friend of the family.

Inspector Fell Or perhaps he had found something out about his boss.

Sgt Jenkins Do you think he was blackmailing Mr Murdoch, sir?

Inspector Fell Perhaps. He probably needs money for his old age. Keep an eye on him.

Sgt Jenkins OK. And what about Oliver Wilson, sir? Have you got any ideas there?

Inspector Fell The nephew. Hmm, that's difficult. Did John Murdoch have any children?

Sgt Jenkins No, sir. Why?

Inspector Fell Well, now that Murdoch's dead, he might be the one who gets the company.

Sgt Jenkins Right. And the other two – Charles Dunning and Isabel Miller?

Inspector Fell Isabel Miller. Hmm. Ward's notes say that she's very pretty. And Murdoch was rich! Maybe she had fallen in love with Murdoch.

Sgt Jenkins But then, why would she kill him?

Inspector Fell I'm not sure. Perhaps the secret project is the key. Let's see.

Sgt Jenkins And Dunning?

Inspector Fell Good-looking and a bit of a playboy. Well, maybe he needs money for gambling, or perhaps he's in love with Isabel Miller and he was angry about her relationship with Murdoch.

Sgt Jenkins Well, we've got a lot of ideas then.

Inspector Fell Yes, let's start the interviews.

▶ WB pp. 12, 13

9 CD 1 ★

4 Listen to the interviews with Jasper Ford and Oliver Wilson. Tick the correct answer.

SCENE 4 and 5

What Jasper Ford said:

1 Mr Murdoch went to his office to …
(a) ☐ call his wife. (b) ☐ get some papers.
(c) ☐ answer a phone call. (d) ☐ write an email.

During the party:

2 Oliver Wilson went to …
(a) ☐ get some more drinks.
(b) ☐ Mr Murdoch's office.
(c) ☐ get a sandwich. (d) ☐ the toilet.

3 Isabel Miller went to …
(a) ☐ make a phone call. (b) ☐ the toilet.
(c) ☐ get a drink. (d) ☐ answer a phone call.

4 Jasper Ford went to …
(a) ☐ get some drinks. (b) ☐ his office.
(c) ☐ the toilet. (d) ☐ write an email.

5 Charles Dunning left to …
(a) ☐ get some drinks. (b) ☐ go to Mr Murdoch's office.
(c) ☐ get some food. (d) ☐ make a phone call.

6 His plan is to …
(a) ☐ retire. (b) ☐ work for Oliver.
(c) ☐ leave the country. (d) ☐ work less.

7 Jasper Ford believes that Oliver Wilson is going to …
(a) ☐ sell the company. (b) ☐ take over the company.
(c) ☐ buy a new company.
(d) ☐ give the company to him.

8 Jasper Ford does <u>not</u> have a good relationship with …
(a) ☐ Oliver. (b) ☐ Charles.
(c) ☐ Isabel Miller. (d) ☐ his sister.

What Oliver Wilson said:

9 Jasper Ford was going to …
(a) ☐ lose his job.
(b) ☐ work for another company.
(c) ☐ buy his own company.
(d) ☐ find a new job.

10 Mr Murdoch went to his office to …
(a) ☐ get some papers.
(b) ☐ call his wife.
(c) ☐ surf the web.
(d) ☐ read a book.

11 Jasper Ford …
(a) ☐ left the room for a few minutes.
(b) ☐ didn't leave the room.
(c) ☐ fell asleep.
(d) ☐ felt sick.

12 The person who broke the window and unlocked the door from the inside was …
(a) ☐ Charles Dunning.
(b) ☐ Isabel Miller.
(c) ☐ a stranger.
(d) ☐ Jasper Ford.

10 CD 1 ★

5 Listen to the next two interviews with Isabel Miller and Charles Dunning. Tick (a) or (b).

SCENE 6 and 7

What Isabel Miller said:

1 Isabel Miller put her hand through the broken window she …
(a) ☐ saw a knife.
(b) ☐ felt a key in the lock.

2 Isabel Miller left the party to …
(a) ☐ go to the toilet.
(b) ☐ go to Mr Murdoch's office.

What Charles Dunning said:

3 Two people left the room at the same time:
(a) ☐ Mr Murdoch and Jasper Ford.
(b) ☐ Mr Murdoch and Isabel Miller.

4 When Oliver left the room to get some drinks, someone went with him:
(a) ☐ Mr Murdoch.
(b) ☐ Isabel Miller.

5 The person who broke the window and opened the door was …
(a) ☐ Isabel.
(b) ☐ Oliver.

★ **6** **Inspector Fell has solved the case.**
Who do you think is the murderer and why?

Detective Ward Excuse me, sir. We've found something in the wastepaper bin. I think you might be interested.

Inspector Fell Thank you, Detective Ward. *(Reads paper.)* Excellent, that's what I thought. Jenkins, call in the suspects.

Sgt Jenkins All of them?

Inspector Fell Yes, Jenkins, all of them.

I think the murderer is …
The murderer must be … because …
I'm not sure … but it might be …
I'm certain the murderer is …

11 CD 1 ★ **7** **Listen to the ending of the story and see if you were right. Then answer the questions in 8.**

SbX ★ **8** **Inspector Fell presents the solution. Answer the questions.**

1 Who broke the window in the door of Mr Murdoch's room?
2 What did the murderer do after killing Mr Murdoch?
3 How did the key get into the lock on the inside of the door?
4 What motive did the murderer have?
5 What did Mr Ford try to hide and where did he hide it?
6 Why did Mr Ford hide it?
7 What did the murderer want from Mr Murdoch?

★ **9** **What is the purpose of the text *At Murdoch Towers* (Scene 2, page 16)?**

1 to warn about criminals
2 to give historical information
3 to entertain
4 to inform about the work of a detective

Get talking

10 **Think of a detective film you know. Work with a partner. Act out similar dialogues.**

A: Do you watch detective films on TV?
B: Yeah, a lot!
A: What's your favourite?
B: .... It's so …
A: What happened in the last one you saw?
A: Well, there was this …

A: Do you watch detective films on TV?
B: No, not very often.
A: Why not?
B: Because they're (not) … I'm not really into detective films.
A: What other films do you watch then?
B: I prefer … films.

▶ WB pp. 12, 13

Vocabulary Crime

★ **11** **Fill in the words from the box.**

blackmail
crime
evidence
suspects
victim
murderer
weapon
witnesses

1 What was the .... ? – Murder.
2 Who was the .... ? – John Murdoch.
3 Who were the .... ? – Jasper Ford, Oliver Wilson, Isabel Miller and Charles Dunning.
4 What was the murder .... ? – A knife.
5 Were there any .... ? – No.
6 Who tried to .... Murdoch? – Isabel Miller.
7 Who tried to hide the .... ? – Jasper Ford.
8 Who's the .... ? – The police don't know yet.

A song 4 U *Tango at the Blue Bar*

12/13 CD 1 MP3

12 **Listen to the song and sum up the story in one sentence.**

They are dancing in the bar and
someone says "They're out to get you."
But the boss just goes on dancing,
dancing with blonde Daisy Miller
and the boss, he doesn't care.

Chorus
Dangerous tango,
down at the Blue Bar.
Dangerous tango and
the danger's never far.

They are dancing. She says "Honey,
let's get out of here, I beg you.
I don't need the diamonds, honey.
I just want you to be safe, dear.
Jewels, gold? I just don't care."

Chorus

They are dancing in the bar and
he just holds her and he watches
the two guys with their guitars who
no one's ever seen before.
And he doesn't seem to care.

Chorus

They are dancing. They are dancing.
When the lights go out, there's screaming
and then some shots ring out as well.
And the band just goes on playing
and they don't seem to care.

Chorus

When the lights come on again,
there are two dead guys on the floor
and the boss just goes on dancing,
dancing with blonde Daisy Miller.
And they both just do not care.

Chorus

Sounds right /a:/ vs. /ʌ/

14 CD 1

13 **Listen and tick.**

	/a:/	/ʌ/		/a:/	/ʌ/
1 dance	✓		**4** just		
2 luck		✓	**5** son		
3 bar			**6** guitar		

15 CD 1

14 **Listen and repeat.**

We got in the car and drove to the park.
We played the guitar and danced in the dark.

CYBER HOMEWORK 3

MP3 SbX ★

15 **a Quickly read through the text and answer the following question: Who invented the locked-room mystery?**

The Locked-Room Mystery

What is it?

Inside the room lies the victim – there is no one else. When the murder happened, nobody could enter or leave the room unseen. Now the detective not only has to work out who committed the crime, but also how they did it.

Other popular ingredients for this 'impossible' crime are:

- The only door is locked from the inside with the key in the lock.
- There is no fireplace or chimney for escape.
- The only window is closed from the inside.
- Outside, there is fresh snow and there are no footprints.
- There is no secret door.
- There is usually no murder weapon.

Who invented it?

The first writer to use the locked-room mystery was the master of the American detective story, Edgar Allan Poe (1809–1849) in his *The Murders in the Rue Morgue.*

Two women were found dead in their bedroom. The police had no idea who the murderer was. The room was locked from the inside and the windows were shut. They thought it was impossible for the murderer to climb in through the window because the room was on the fourth floor. There was no motive because the two women lived alone, everybody liked them and the police found a lot of money lying around on the floor, so nobody stole anything. The police weren't able to solve the crime, but a clever man, Mr Dupin, could. He looked carefully at the window and discovered that something was broken. He believed that the killer was an excellent climber who had escaped through the window. Then the window closed automatically. When the police heard this, they laughed at Dupin's theory, but he found the murderer – it was an orang-utan that had escaped from a sailor!

b Read the full text and tick the correct sentences.

1 In a locked-room mystery the murder weapon

- **a** ☐ cannot usually be found.
- **b** ☐ is usually a dagger.
- **c** ☐ is something strange.
- **d** ☐ is taken away by the murderer.

2 In *The Murders in the Rue Morgue* by Poe,

- **a** ☐ the room was locked and none of the windows were open.
- **b** ☐ the police found money and broken glass on the floor.
- **c** ☐ a man and a woman were killed.
- **d** ☐ the police asked detective Dupin for help.

3 Dupin's investigation showed that

- **a** ☐ the killer was someone very unusual.
- **b** ☐ the police were looking for two killers.
- **c** ☐ the dead women knew their killer.
- **d** ☐ the murder was the work of a serial killer.

4 The killer in the Poe story

- **a** ☐ was not human.
- **b** ☐ was a sailor who had escaped from prison.
- **c** ☐ was a man who was an excellent climber.
- **d** ☐ planned his crime carefully.

c What does the text do?

a It gives information about the life of an American writer.
b It tells a funny story about an animal.
c It explains a special kind of crime story.
d It tells you about the most famous mystery stories.

DVD The Mag 2 The rivals

1 Watch the story. Then circle the correct words.

1 Stern writes *an article / a poem* for another school's magazine.
2 Lucy is *angry / happy* with Stern.
3 Stern went to a party and met Kate, the *reporter / editor* of another magazine.
4 Kate and Lucy fought about *Stern / a magazine*.
5 Stern gives Lucy chocolates and *flowers / a poem*.
6 Stern tells Jessica that he's interested in *her / Kate*.

2 Find and correct seven mistakes in the summary.

Lucy is angry because Stern has written an article for the Whiteoaks' school magazine. The Whiteoaks' school magazine is called *The Journal* and its editor is a girl called Katy Price. Stern met Katy at the disco and she asked him to write a story about life at St. George's School. Lucy was once a student at Whiteoaks. She and Katy Pimm had an argument about a boy and they stopped being friends. This is the real reason why Lucy was so upset. When Nick explains this to Stern he feels really bad about writing the story. He buys Lucy a teddy bear to say sorry. He also writes her a poem. When Lucy says she wants to put the poem in *The Mag*, Stern begs her not to. He is worried what his friends in the football team might think.

Everyday English

3 Complete the dialogues with the phrases from the box.

It's not the end of the world. How could you? Don't you dare! have you got a moment?

WB p. 13

Writing *for your Portfolio*

★ **16** **Look at the questions. Use the language to write a new story. Find a good title.**

Where was Inspector Fell when the phone rang?	*... on a holiday in ...*
What information did he get?	*The Inspector learnt that ...*
How did he feel about it and why?	*He wasn't very pleased because ...*
What did he see when he came to the crime scene?	*As soon as the inspector got to ..., he noticed ...*
Who were his assistants at the crime scene?	*His assistants were ...*
Who were the suspects?	*It was immediately clear to Inspector Fell that the main suspects were ...*
What possible motives did they have?	*... had a motive because ...*
What did somebody suddenly find and where?	*But Inspector Fell was wrong because ...*
Who was the murderer and why?	*Suddenly ... entered the room.*
How did Inspector Fell find the solution to the case?	*The murderer was ... because ...*
	A short while later Inspector Fell knew who ...

SbX

Grammar

Past perfect

Du verwendest das *past perfect*, wenn du betonen möchtest, dass eine Handlung vor einem bestimmten Zeitpunkt in der Vergangenheit geschehen war.

Nobody else was in the building. All the other employees **had left**.

Form: Person + *had(n't)* + *past participle* des Verbs

When Harry got up in the morning, he realised that he had put up his tent in the wrong place.

Circle the verbs in the past simple.
Underline the verbs in the past perfect.

1. The killer had escaped through a window. He was an excellent climber.
2. It was an orang-utan. It had escaped from a sailor.

16 CD 1 BiSt

1 Listen to the dialogue and fill in the missing words.

Nadia *(On the phone)* Hi, Tony. What are you doing right now?
Tony I'm [1].. my hamster and I'm also cleaning its cage.
Nadia Can you [2].. to my place?
Tony Why? What's going on?
Nadia Harry and I are playing a computer game, but we've got a problem with the computer.
Tony OK, give me ten [3].. .

(Ten minutes later)
Harry Is it a virus?
Tony I don't [4].. so. Nadia, how often do you run an anti-virus program?
Nadia Every day.
Tony I think there's something [5].. with the hard disk. Take it to the computer shop tomorrow.
Nadia OK.

16 CD 1

2 Now cover up the dialogue. Listen again and try to complete the sentences. Look at the dialogue and check.

1 Tony's feeding ....
2 Nadia and Harry are playing ....
3 Nadia has a problem with ....
4 Nadia runs an anti-virus ....
5 Tony thinks there is ....
6 Tony tells Nadia to take her computer ....

Vocabulary Computers

3 Fill in the missing verbs.

burn	run
check	save
click	send
~~create~~	surf

1 to ......create...... a backup of your files
2 to .... your hard disk for viruses
3 to .... an email to a friend
4 to .... your files on your hard disk
5 to .... a program
6 to .... with a mouse
7 to .... the Internet
8 to .... a CD

Vocabulary Free time activities

17 CD 1 **4 Listen and write in the numbers next to the pictures.**

Get talking Asking and answering questions about free time

BiSt **5 Talk to your partner.**

What do you do in your free time? How often do you do it?

I play … / I listen to … / I go … an hour a day / two hours a week / once a month …

Who do you play / do it with?

With my friend(s) / my brother / my sister …

6 Report to the class.

WB p. 16   CYBER HOMEWORK 4

UNIT 3 Kids speak out

1 CHOICES

a A STORY

Vocabulary Expressing emotions

18 CD 1

1 Listen and write the words.

giggle
cry
shout
laugh
whisper

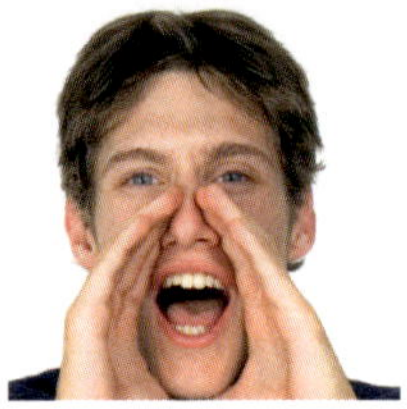

1 .... 2 .... 3 .... 4 .... 5 ....

19 CD 1 MP3 SbX

2 Emily thinks a boy is really nice. What's his name? Read the text quickly to find out.

3 Read the text carefully. Then listen.

Incident during a Maths lesson

Emily wasn't listening to the teacher.
She was looking at something.
A photo — a photo of a boy.
His name was Anthony.
Anthony from 4c.
Emily liked him a lot. She whispered his name.
"Show me what you've got there!"
That was Chris. Chris sat behind Emily.
Emily didn't want to give him the photo.
So Chris took it. Tore it out of her hands.
He showed it to all the other boys.
"Look – Emily's new boyfriend!"
They giggled and laughed and looked at her.
Emily got angry.
"Give me the photo back!" Emily shouted out loud.
"Stop it, Emily, will you!" the teacher said.
Now the teacher was angry with Emily.
The world can be unfair!

BiSt

4 What does the text do?

a It tells you about Maths lessons at schools in England.
b It tells the story of what happened to a girl in a Maths lesson.
c It tells you a joke to make you laugh.
d It tells you a story about a girl's hobby, photography.

5 Complete the sentences. Only one word is correct in each sentence.

1 It was during the .... lesson. (Maths / German / English)
2 Emily was looking at a .... of a boy. (letter / phone number / photo)
3 Chris took the photo and showed it to the other .... (girls / boys / children)
4 They all started to .... (cry / shout / laugh)
5 Emily .... , "Give me the photo back!" (whispered / said / shouted)
6 The teacher was .... (angry / sad / happy)

WB p. 19

MP3
BiSt
★

b AN INTERVIEW

1 Read the newspaper interview. What is the interview with Annabel about? Tick the correct box.

- ☐ Young people who want to become journalists.
- ☐ How to set up an online magazine.
- ☐ A 15-year-old student who is also a journalist.
- ☐ How to help teenagers who are being sent out of the UK.

THE DAILY NEWS

Annabel Speaks Out

An interview with Annabel Green from *Headliners*

INTERVIEWER Annabel, you do lots of interviews. How do you feel now that you're answering the questions, not asking them?

ANNABEL It's alright, I've been interviewed before.

INTERVIEWER Great. So, tell us a bit about yourself.

ANNABEL Well, I'm 15, I go to a comprehensive here in London and I spend most of my free time being a journalist.

INTERVIEWER A journalist? At 15?

ANNABEL Yes. On my own or with a friend, I do interviews for *Headliners*. It's an online magazine written by young people for everyone.

INTERVIEWER Who can write for *Headliners*?

ANNABEL Well, basically anybody. Last year more than 500 kids wrote stories and did interviews.

INTERVIEWER And what are you into?

ANNABEL I love doing interviews. A month ago my friend Aysha and I did an interview with two teenagers from Eritrea. Four years ago they came to Britain looking for asylum because of the trouble there. Next month they turn 18, and when they're 18, the British government could send them back to Eritrea. And they could be put in prison there.

INTERVIEWER And you interview these teenagers to let other people know about them?

ANNABEL Yes. I want people to be more tolerant. I want young people who have a good life to think about teenagers like this. That's why I do the interviews.

INTERVIEWER Is it all about people looking for asylum?

ANNABEL Oh, no. Only last week I talked to a young man who lives in Surrey and who's gay. Some people in his community are making life very difficult for him. They make fun of him and even beat him up. So wherever you look – you can do something for tolerance and understanding. So please tell your friends to check out our website so that we can all try to make the world a better place.

INTERVIEWER Thank you, Annabel, we certainly will.

2 Read the text again. Tick T (*True*) or F (*False*).

	T	F
1 Annabel works as a journalist for a newspaper.	☐	☐
2 *Headliners* is an online magazine.	☐	☐
3 Hundreds and hundreds of kids write for *Headliners*.	☐	☐
4 Annabel did an interview with two 10-year-old asylum seekers.	☐	☐
5 She wants people to be more tolerant.	☐	☐
6 Last week she talked to a young gay man.	☐	☐
7 Annabel thinks it's worth checking out *Headliners*.	☐	☐

▶ WB p. 20

Free flow

BiSt **2** **Work in pairs. One of you will play the role of a reporter for a school magazine (A), the other one will play the role of a teenager from another country (B). Take two minutes to prepare your discussion. Use the prompt cards to help you. Talk for four minutes.**

Prompt Card A

You are 14. You work for the school magazine. You are going to interview a boy or a girl who is at your school. He/she is from another country. You need to find out about:

- where he/she came from.
- why he/she came here.
- what he/she likes about being here.
- what he/she doesn't like.
- what he/she misses most about his/her country.

What other things are you going to ask about?

Prompt Card B

You are 14. You are a student from this school who came from another country some time ago. You have agreed to be interviewed by a magazine. Think about the following areas:

- where you came from.
- why you came here.
- what you like / don't like about being here.
- what you miss most about your country (food? / friends? / …?).

What other points do you think might be interesting?

MP3 SbX ★ **3** a **Read the story.**

Is it over?

Stevie May 14th

I've been seeing this girl, but we're not really having a relationship. I think she's kind of cool. Different. Not one of these girls who only talk to you if you're wearing the right clothes or if mum and dad are stinking rich. I don't know much about her, however. All I know is that we have the same taste in music. But not in films. I like a good adventure film now and again, but she's more into French films and stuff like that. Anyway, I kind of really like her and when I wake up in the morning, she's the first thing I think of. And the last thing, too.

Rachel May 15th

At first I didn't want to talk to him. He seemed so much like the other guys. A bit loud. Laughing that "haw, haw" laugh with his mates. But when he went up to the DJ and asked for a song and it was my favourite song, I got talking to him. And he was really nice. Not like most boys at these parties. "I want to show you my CDs some day," he said. "Whoa!" I thought. "What a line! Be careful, Rachel!" But when I went to his place one day, he really did show me his CDs. There were more than a hundred. And he talked about some of them. Why he liked the music or the lyrics. And because of that I really began to like him.

Rachel June 5th

I think I'm in love. The only problem is Mum. She's a bit funny about me having a boyfriend. "At fifteen?" she said. Anyway, when she sees Stevie, she'll think again. He's really sweet. I told her to stop worrying.

Stevie June 6th

We've been seeing each other every day. I just feel great. Next week I'm going to her place. Her parents asked me to come to dinner. She lives in an area where mostly rich people live. Do I have to buy flowers for her mother?

Stevie June 12th

It was OK. Mind you, I didn't really feel right there. I couldn't really relax. And her mother asked me questions about my future. What do I care about the future? I've got so much to do in the present.

Rachel June 12th

I think everything went fine. I want Stevie to come to our garden party next week. He's not really looking forward to it, but he said he'd come because he loves me. How sweet!

Stevie June 19th

It's over! Horrible garden party. She introduced me to her two cousins. Boy and girl. Twins. I really hated what they said to me. "So that's where you live? What's that you're wearing? How uncool!" And on and on and on. Rachel didn't say anything.
I left early. I hung around a bit in front of the house, but Rachel didn't follow me.

Rachel June 19th

How could he do that? OK, the twins are terrible, but why didn't he just laugh about them? I wanted to follow him when he left, but Mum wanted me to stay. He hasn't phoned me or anything. Should I phone him?

Stevie June 20th

I sent Rachel a long email. She hasn't answered yet. But she texted me. L8er. So here I am, in front of my PC. Waiting. Is it over?

BiSt

b Tick the one thing that does NOT happen.

- ☐ Rachel goes to Stevie's house to look at his CDs.
- ☐ Stevie didn't stay at the party long.
- ☐ They see a French film at the cinema.
- ☐ Stevie goes to a garden party at Rachel's house.

Get talking

★ **4 Get together in groups of 3 – 4 and talk about it. Is it really over? How could the story go on? What could they do to get together again? Tell the class about your solution.**

If she wants him to try and …
We think her mum has no right …
We think that her/his problem is really …
What they could do is …
We think … should / could …

20 CD 1 **5 Listen to an interview with four teenagers. Tick when you hear one of them talk about one of the following:**

- ☐ music
- ☐ fights
- ☐ mobile phones
- ☐ shopping
- ☐ getting help
- ☐ friends
- ☐ poor countries
- ☐ differences between boys and girls

▶ WB p. 21 ▶ CYBER HOMEWORK 5

20 CD 1

6 **Listen again to what they say. Tick T (*True*) or F (*False*).**

		T	F
Jonathan	**1** Boys do better at school.	☐	☐
	2 Girls watch different TV programmes.	☐	☐
Helen	**3** Girls talk more about things.	☐	☐
	4 Boys are better at problem solving.	☐	☐
Samir	**5** Boys don't have so many problems.	☐	☐
	6 Music helps you to relax.	☐	☐

Free flow

7 **Say what you think about the sentences in 6.**

It's true that boys … / girls …
It's not true that …

8 **Get together in groups and pick three of the topics from 5. Find out what your group thinks of these topics. Sum up your ideas and report to the class.**

- Take notes
- Decide on a speaker before you start working
- Keep your report short and simple

Two of us believe that …
All of us think that …
None of us likes …

9 **CHOICES**

Writing *for your Portfolio*

BiSt

You have received the following email from a friend in England. Read it carefully and answer it. In your email:

- tell Katie what you think about the situation
- tell her what she should do
- tell her who could help her.

Hi,
I hope you're OK. Listen, I want to ask you for some advice. Annie, a girl in my class, has fallen in love with a boy, but he isn't very interested in her. She keeps giving him presents and she hangs around in front of his house and waits for him in the mornings. We know that he and his mates laugh about her and that the guy wants her to leave him alone. Should we tell Annie that everyone is laughing about her? Or should we just wait and see what happens? What do you think? PLEASE let me know. Write soon!
Katie

a **Write 70 – 100 words. Make sure you use the phrases from the box.**

What's probably best … My suggestion is, that … Don't forget that she …
Even if it's really painful … Why don't you … You should talk to …

★ **b** **Write 100 – 120 words.**

- also tell Katie about a problem one of your friends has.

It is only fair to tell her …

▶ WB p. 22

Sounds right Final consonants

21 CD 1

10 **Listen and repeat.**

1 road – wrote | had – hat
cab – cap | made – mate
ride – right | bag – back

2 Ride on the right!
I made some new mates.
He had a hat on his head.
Put the bag back!

SbX

Grammar

Want someone to do something

So drückst du aus, dass jemand möchte, dass eine andere Person etwas Bestimmtes (nicht) tut.
I **want Stevie to come** to the garden party.
They **wanted me to organise** games for the kids.

Form: *want* + Person + *to* Infinitiv

Andere Verben, die dieselbe Struktur haben (Verb + Person + *to* Infinitiv):

tell: I **told her to stop** worrying.

ask: They **asked me to come** to dinner.

Connecting ideas

So kannst du Sätze miteinander verknüpfen. Beispiele:

Cause/Result (Ursache/Ergebnis)
Four years ago they came to Britain looking for asylum **because of** the trouble there.

Contrast (Gegensatz)
Although I enjoy reading, I also work at the church.
However, I also spend quite a lot of time at home.

Purpose (Absicht)
Check out our website **so that** we can all try to make the world a better place. I write poetry **in order to** deal with my problems.

WB pp. 23, 43, 44

22 CD 1 BiSt

1 **Listen to the dialogue and fill in the missing words and phrases.**

Tony Boy, I'm exhausted! Walking round the shops is [1]..!

Sally I know. That's why I like shopping online.

Tony Really? You shouldn't do a lot of online shopping, you know – it can be a bit [2].. .

Sally I don't think so. Well, I've never had a problem anyway. And [3]... online is so easy!

Tony That's true – anyway, I can't shop online.

Sally Why not?

Tony I haven't got a debit card.

Sally You ought to have a debit card. They're [4].. .

Tony Yes, I know. I'm getting one, but it hasn't arrived yet. Actually, it's taking a long time – we asked the bank for it two weeks ago.

Sally I think you should find out what's happening.

Tony Yeah, you're right.

Sally Oh, look – there's Asher! Hi, Ash!

Asher Hi, you two. Listen, there's a great new CD shop in Station Road – you should go and have a look. They've got a fantastic second-hand section.

Sally Second-hand? No chance! I don't want to buy things that someone else has used.

Asher Oh, come on, Sally – they're CDs, not [5]..!

Sally Well, maybe I'll go, but not now. I ought to go home.

Tony OK – see you, Sally! Now Asher – where's this CD store?

22 CD 1 BiSt

2 **Now cover up the dialogue. Listen again and tick the correct answer. Then look at the dialogue and check.**

1 Sally likes …
- **a** ☐ shopping online.
- **b** ☐ buying second-hand clothes.
- **c** ☐ walking around shops.
- **d** ☐ shopping with Tony.

2 Tony can't …
- **a** ☐ spend a lot of money.
- **b** ☐ pay in cash.
- **c** ☐ shop online.
- **d** ☐ get a debit card.

3 Sally thinks that Tony should …
- **a** ☐ find a credit card.
- **b** ☐ talk to his mother.
- **c** ☐ talk to the bank about his debit card.
- **d** ☐ get money from his mother.

4 Asher has found …
- **a** ☐ a good shop for CDs.
- **b** ☐ a good clothes shop.
- **c** ☐ an old shop for CDs.
- **d** ☐ an ice cream shop.

5 Sally is going …
- **a** ☐ to buy second-hand clothes.
- **b** ☐ to the CD store.
- **c** ☐ home.
- **d** ☐ to the movies.

Vocabulary Types of shops

3 **Write the words below the pictures.**

chemist's
bookshop
clothing shop
music shop
newsagent
baker's

1 ....

2 ....

3 ....

4 ....

5 ....

6 ....

Get talking Talking about shopping

23 CD 1

4 **Complete the dialogue. Then listen and check.**

At the second-hand shop.
Lots of clothes.
£12.
I've been shopping.
Yes, that's right.
Look, here they are.

A What have you been doing?
B 1 ....
A What did you buy?
B 2 ....
A How much were they?
B 3 ....
A Only £12?
B 4 ....
A Where did you buy them?
B 5 ....
A Show them to me.
B 6 ....
A Oh, they look great

5 **Work in pairs. Do a short role play. You are meeting a friend. He's / She's been shopping. Ask and answer questions: *What …? Where …? How much …? Why …?***

UNIT 4 Beautiful Boston

MP3 SbX BiSt

1 a What American cities can you name? What do you know about them?

b Read the text and write the phrases A – E in the gaps.

A where you can try some
B but Boston does
C and always a popular place with visitors
D one of the oldest in the USA
E along the streets of the downtown area

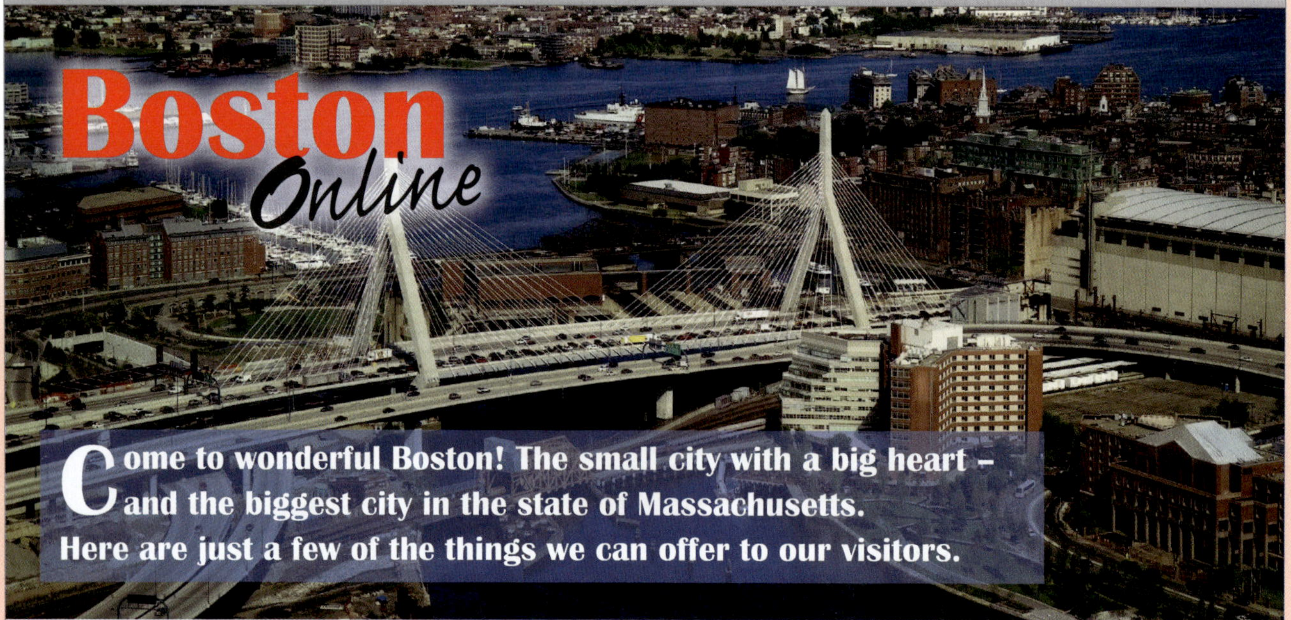

Come to wonderful Boston! The small city with a big heart – and the biggest city in the state of Massachusetts. Here are just a few of the things we can offer to our visitors.

History

There's been a city of Boston since 1630 – it's 1 .... – and the city played an important part in the American Revolution. So there are many historical buildings amongst the new ones. Walk along the Freedom Trail – there is a red line painted on the sidewalk and it leads you to all the historical sites in the downtown area. There's lots of history to see and feel in Boston.

Eating

Boston and Massachusetts are famous for seafood – especially lobster! And there are plenty of restaurants 2 .... Of course if you prefer other kinds of food, we can offer that, too. Italian, Japanese, French or whatever. Plenty of stuff for kids, too!

Sport

Boston is a great place for sports fans – there's something for everyone here. Not many cities in the USA have a top team in all four major sports, 3 .... So you can see top-class sport here at almost any time of the year. (Check websites for games and times.)

Relaxation

Want to relax? Take a Swan Boat out on the lake in the Public Garden in the summer. If you're here on December 31st, take part in the Grand Procession 4 .... See the Boston Marathon in April (or if you want to, run in it!). And we have theaters, cinemas and shops for everyone.

Outside the City

There are many other great places in Massachusetts. Why not take a trip to Salem? Salem is famous for the Witch Trials of 1692. It's only an hour away 5 .... If you want to go a little further away, you could visit the beautiful island of Martha's Vineyard, too.

c Now answer the following questions:

- What kind of buildings would you see along the Freedom Trail?
- What's the speciality in many restaurants?
- What event takes place in December?
- Why should people take a trip to Salem?

Free flow

BiSt **2 Look at the pictures in 1 again. Talk for 1 – 2 minutes about a possible trip to Boston. The questions will help you to think about the topic. Take one minute to prepare.**

Talk about:

- why you would / wouldn't like to go to Boston as a tourist
- which place would be of most / least interest for you and why
- which sports events you would like to see
- why you would / wouldn't like to go to Salem.

▶ WB p. 27

3 CHOICES

a BOSTON'S SPORTS TEAMS

1 What do you know about the sports in the photographs?

A

B

C

MP3 BiSt

2 Quickly find out which team each of the people in the pictures plays for.

1 THE BOSTON RED SOX

The Red Sox began in 1901 as the Boston Pilgrims. In 1908, they changed their name to the Red Sox. They won their first World Series championship in 1903 – and their second one in 2004.

Many great players have played for the Red Sox – one of them was Babe Ruth. Many people say he was the greatest baseball player of all time.

2 THE NEW ENGLAND PATRIOTS

At first they were the Boston Patriots. In 1970, they changed their name to the New England Patriots. They played for many years in Foxboro Stadium. In 2002, they moved to the new Gillette Stadium.

When they started, the Patriots were not very successful. But since 2001 they have won the Super Bowl (American football's big championship) three times: in 2001, 2003 and 2004.

3 THE BOSTON CELTICS

When the NBA started in 1946, the Celtics were there. Since then they have always played a role in the world of American basketball. They have won the NBA Championship 16 times – more than any other team. They have a record of eight championships in a row from 1959-1966. Their famous green shirts have a lucky clover on them. But their success is not a question of luck!

BiSt

3 Now read the texts carefully.
Tick the sentences T (*True*) or F (*False*).

	T	F
1 The New England Patriots played in a different stadium before.	☐	☐
2 The New England Patriots are a famous basketball team.	☐	☐
3 The Boston Red Sox got their new name more than 100 years ago.	☐	☐
4 Babe Ruth was a famous basketball player.	☐	☐
5 The Boston Celtics are the most successful basketball team in the US.	☐	☐

Free flow

4 Discuss in class. Do you have a team you support? (Which?) Do you often go to sports events? Say why / why not.

WB p. 28

24 CD 1 MP3 ★

b A DARK SPOT IN AMERICAN HISTORY

1 Look at the picture of a "witch trial" and quickly read the text to find answers to these questions.

- When did they happen?
- Where did they happen?

a witch

Puritans

a gallows

2 Now read the text below carefully and find the answer to this question: Why did the witch trials happen? Then listen and check.

The Salem witch trials

It was January 1692 in the town of Salem in Massachusetts. Salem was a Puritan village – the Puritans were people who at that time could be very superstitious because religion was important to them. The story goes that one night, two young girls – Betty Parris, aged 9, and her cousin Abigail Williams, aged 11 – started to do strange things. They threw things around the house. And they made strange noises. Their parents called the doctor. The doctor could not find anything wrong with them. So he said to the parents that the two girls were witches.

In the next few days, more and more "witches" were put into Salem prison: 150 men and women (and a 4-year old girl). In June 1692, the Salem Witch Trials began. 13 women and 7 men were hanged as witches on Gallows Hill. But they hadn't done anything wrong.

In October 1692, the Governor of Massachusetts stopped the trials. He said there had been a mistake. Only in 1954 – more than 250 years later – the American government said that the witch trials were a mistake. They said that all the "witches" were not guilty. We don't know what the real story is. But we know that those poor children and people were not witches!

Salem became very famous. Now, a million tourists go to Salem every year. They come to see the Witch Museum. And there are lots of shops where tourists buy witch souvenirs (pens and T-shirts and key-rings, etc).

BiSt **3 Where is the text from?**

a a diary
b a newspaper
c a brochure
d a magazine

4 Read the text and answer the questions that follow it.

1 What examples are given of how the two girls started to "behave strangely"?
2 Who said that the two girls were "bewitched"?
3 How many people were hanged as witches?
4 Why are the Witch Trials important in Salem now?

Vocabulary

5 Match the sentence halves to get sentences about the story.

1 Two girls in Salem started to do	☐ into Salem prison.
2 The doctor couldn't find	☐ hanged as witches.
3 So he said the girls were	☐ strange things.
4 150 people were put	☐ the witch trials.
5 20 people were	☐ witches.
6 In 1692 the Governor stopped	☐ anything wrong with them.

Free flow

6 Discuss these questions. Say what you think.

1 Do you find this text interesting? Why / Why not? Give reasons.
2 How many reasons for the girls' behavior can you think of? Name them.
3 What other stories about witches have you heard or read about? Give examples.
4 Would you like to visit the museum in Salem?

Writing *for your Portfolio*

BiSt **4** **Imagine that you are spending a two-week holiday in Massachusetts with your family. You have been staying for three days now. Write an email (120 – 180 words) to a friend at home. Do not take longer than 20 minutes.**

Write about:

- where you are right now
- where you have been staying so far
- what places you have visited so far
- what you like / don't like about Boston
- your plans for the next days.

WB p. 27

25 CD 1 SbX ★

5 **a Listen and answer the following questions:**

- Who is the person you hear first and last?
- Who is the person who does most of the talking? Why is she talking?
- Who are the people who interrupt her? Why do they interrupt her?

b Listen again and fill in the missing information.

THE BOSTON TEA PARTY

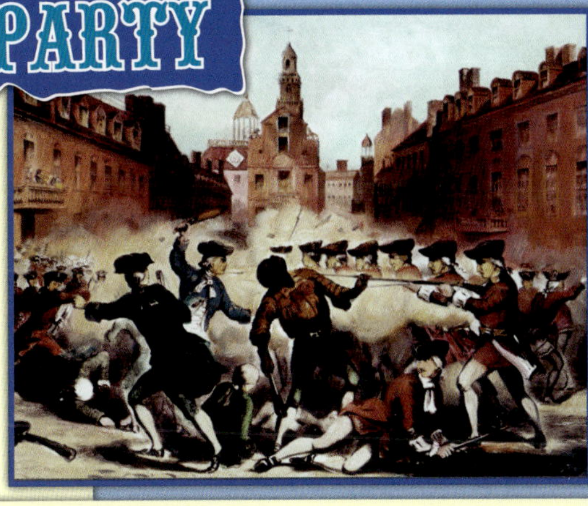

Background

- *In the 1700s, Boston was a very important port.*
- *America was still a colony of Britain.*
- *Americans had to pay taxes to Britain.*
- *In 1770, in "The Boston Massacre", British soldiers killed ¹.................................. American men.*

The Tea Party

- *It happened on the night of the ².................................. of December, ³17..................... .*
- *There were ⁴.................................. ships in Boston Harbour with tea.*
- *Three groups of ⁵.................................. men ("The Sons of Liberty") went on to the ship.*
- *They threw ⁶.................................. boxes of tea into the sea.*

25 CD 1 ★

6 **Listen again and circle the correct options.**

1 The Americans were *not happy about / scared of* paying money to Britain.
2 The tea on the ships belonged to *the British government / a British company*.
3 The men who went on the ships *were Indians / were dressed like Indians*.
4 *British soldiers / People in the town* watched the men throw the tea into the sea.
5 They *cheered / cried* when the tea went into the sea.
6 After the "Tea Party", the British government closed *Boston harbour / shops in the city*.

The Mag 3 Stern gets worried

1 **Watch the story. Then tick T (*True*) or F (*False*).**

	T	F
1 Jessica and Stern aren't going to the cinema any more.	☐	☐
2 Mr Ricks runs a theatre group at the school.	☐	☐
3 Liam goes with Jessica to interview Mr Ricks.	☐	☐
4 Linda is Stern's new girlfriend.	☐	☐
5 Stern thinks Jessica likes Liam.	☐	☐

2 **Answer the questions and say what you think.**

1 Stern says he and Jessica should not hang out with each other so often. Why does he say that?
2 How does Jessica react and how does she feel about it?
3 What happens when Lucy wants an interview with Mr Ricks, their teacher?
4 One day Stern's mum wakes him up in the middle of a rather bad dream. What was it about?
5 How does Stern feel when he hears that Liam has a new girlfriend, Linda?
6 Why does Stern ask Jessica at the end of the episode if she is disappointed?

Everyday English

3 **Say the missing words. Practise the dialogues.**

what are you up to? by the way Let's get cracking! Are we still on for

WB p. 29

Grammar Reported speech (statements)

SbX

Wenn du etwas weiter erzählst, was eine andere Person zu einem früheren Zeitpunkt gesagt hat, und das *reporting verb* im *past* steht (*He/she said … He/She told me …*), dann werden die Zeitformen in der indirekten Rede meist verändert.

- "I'm cold," said Tom (He said it yesterday.) → Tom said he **was** cold.
- "We made a mistake," the governor said. (He said it a few days ago) → The governor said that they **had made** a mistake.
- "I've lost my keys," Anna said. (She phoned my last week.) → Anna told me she **had lost** her keys.
- "I'll phone you tomorrow," Mandy said. (She said this two days ago.) → Mandy said she **would phone** me the next day.

Beim Berichten wirst du möglicherweise die folgenden Zeitausdrücke brauchen:

the day (week/month/year) before, 3 days before: She said John had phoned her **the day before**.

the next/following day (week/month/year) 3 days later: Tom told me he was leaving **the following day**.

Aber: Wenn am gleichen Tag berichtet wird, dann ändern sich die Zeitbezüge nicht!

"John phoned me **yesterday**," said Lisa. (She said it this morning).
Lisa said John had phoned her **yesterday**. (NOT: ~~the day before~~)

Tom said, "I'm leaving **tomorrow**."
(Tom told me a few hours ago).

Tom said he was leaving **tomorrow**.
(NOT: ~~the following day~~)

say vs. ***tell***
Wenn du *tell* als Einleitewort verwendest, musst du die Person(en) nennen, zu denen etwas gesagt wird/wurde:
He **said** that the two girls were bewitched.
He **told the parents** that the two girls were bewitched.

When the boss said people couldn't write personal emails from the office, Bill decided to try a different kind of communication.

WB p. 29

26 CD 1 BiSt

1 **Listen to the dialogue and fill in the missing words and phrases.**

Asher

Greg

Emily

Emily Asher! Hi. What are you doing here?

Asher Hi, Emily. I'm 1 .... Pete. We're going to the match together.

Emily Oh, right. 2 ...., this is my friend Greg.

Asher Hi, Greg. How are you?

Greg Hey, Asher. Fine thanks, and you?

Asher Yeah. So, you're not from England, are you?

Greg No, I'm from the States. We live in Boston, but my dad's working in the UK for a year, 3 ....

Emily Greg's living in the house next door to us. He's only been in England for two weeks.

Greg That's right. There's a lot to learn – some things are really different here! I mean – what's in that bag? And what are those things?

Asher These things are cricket pads. 4 .... of cricket?

Greg I think so. It's a sport that you guys play in the summer.

Asher That's right. I love it. I'm not very good, though.

Emily It's a bit like baseball.

Asher Well, no, not really – 5 ....! But listen, Greg – do you play football?

Greg Absolutely. I've played football since I was six years old. I'm a quarterback.

Asher A what? Ah – I get it. Sorry, I'm not talking about American football – I'm talking about our football.

Greg Right – soccer. No, I've never played it – but 6 .... Are you in a team?

Emily OK, you two. That's enough about sport. Can we talk about something else, please?

26 CD 1

2 **Now cover up the dialogue. Listen again and correct the sentences.**

1 Asher is waiting for Emily. — *Asher is waiting for Pete.*
2 Greg's dad is working in Boston for a year. ....
3 Greg has been in England for a month. ....
4 Greg has seen cricket pads before. ....
5 Asher is very good at cricket. ....
6 Greg has never played American football. ....

Get talking Phone conversations

27 CD 1

3 **Listen to the dialogues. Then read the texts and match them to the pictures.**

Dialogue 1

Sally Hello, Steve. What are you doing?
Steve Hi, Sally. I'm doing my homework. And you?
Sally I'm not doing anything.

Dialogue 2

Duncan What are you doing, Monica?
Monica I'm writing an email to my friend in America.

Dialogue 3

Joanna Hello, Andy. What are you doing?
Andy Hi, Joanna. I'm waiting for the bus. And you?
Joanna I'm buying new clothes for the party on Saturday.

4 **Make dialogues like the ones in 3. Use the pictures.**

Progress Check Units 1–4

Listening

28 CD 1 BiSt

Listen to the conversation. Tick the correct answers.

1 What kinds of books does Monica like to read?
- a ☐ Love stories.
- b ☐ Crime stories and thrillers.
- c ☐ Science fiction.
- d ☐ Animal stories.

2 Monica has …
- a ☐ never read anything by Agatha Christie.
- b ☐ never seen any Agatha Christie films.
- c ☐ read everything by Agatha Christie.
- d ☐ doesn't like Agatha Christie.

3 Monica thinks that Harlan Coben's thrillers …
- a ☐ are not easy to read.
- b ☐ are too scary to read at night.
- c ☐ are very silly stories.
- d ☐ are so good that she wants to read them all night.

4 Monica gets lots of crime stories …
- a ☐ from the library.
- b ☐ from her dad.
- c ☐ from her aunt Betsy.
- d ☐ from her English teacher.

5 She also gets a lot of book tips …
- a ☐ from her teacher.
- b ☐ from a youth magazine.
- c ☐ from a chat group.
- d ☐ from her mum.

☐ 5

Reading

Read the text. Are the sentences T (*True*) or F (*False*)?

Friendship

Friendship is very important to young people. It comes right after family for most kids from ages 13–16. Friends are important because they make you feel safe. Going to school together and enjoying your free time – everything is easier if you have friends.

Talking to each other is very important. Kids share secrets, hobbies and interests that they don't share with their parents. A group of kids, for example, often like the same kind of music. But their parents usually don't like that kind of music at all! If you ask kids what they want from a friend, they say things like "Good friends don't hurt you. They listen to you and they try to understand you. Good friends help you with problems. They respect and trust you and they care about you. Finally, they are still your friend when nobody else is." For young people friendship is much more important than for other age groups.

	T	F
1 Friends make you feel safe.	☐	☐
2 Your family and friends often like the same kinds of music.	☐	☐
3 Good friends always try to understand you.	☐	☐
4 Real friends are not always there for you.	☐	☐
5 Friendship is not very important for young people.	☐	☐

☐ 5

Grammar

Circle the correct options.

1 I didn't hear the telephone because I *listened / was listening* to music.
2 I *went / was going* to Canada last year.
3 I *want her to / want that she* pick us up a bit earlier.
4 As soon as I saw the first scene I knew I *saw / had seen* the film before.
5 I want *that everyone leaves / everyone to leave* the room quietly.
6 I didn't want to call you while you *slept / were sleeping*.
7 She said she *doesn't want / didn't want* to go to Salem.
8 I went to Boston last summer. I *hadn't been / wasn't* there for years.
9 John said that he *was running / had run* the Boston marathon twice.
10 She made me a sandwich but I *didn't eat / hadn't eaten* it.

☐ **10**

Vocabulary

Match words and definitions.

1 motive	☐	a crime when somebody kills another person
2 murder weapon	☐	person who might be the criminal
3 witness	☐	person trying to find the criminal
4 suspect	☐	a reason for doing something
5 evidence	☐	instrument used to kill somebody
6 investigation	☐	something that helps you to prove a crime
7 inspector	☐	the person who is killed
8 murder	☐	a case that is like a puzzle and difficult to solve
9 victim	☐	when the police look into a crime to find out the truth
10 mystery	☐	a person who has seen something important

☐ **10**

Dialogue

Match the sentences to make a dialogue.

1 What's your favourite TV show ?	☐	I'm going next summer.
2 What's it about?	☐	It's *Spenser: For Hire*.
3 Do you want to go to Boston some day?	☐	Because my dad has a summer job at Harvard University.
4 Why are you going to Boston?	☐	Sure. I want to see the Boston Red Sox play.
5 Will you go to a baseball game?	☐	It's about a cool detective in Boston.

☐ **5**

How did you do?

	☺	😐	☹
Listening	4-5	2-3	0-1
Reading	4-5	2-3	0-1
Grammar	8-10	4-7	0-3
Vocabulary	8-10	4-7	0-3
Dialogue	4-5	2-3	0-1
Total	25-35	12-24	0-11

UNIT 5 A working life

Vocabulary Professions

SbX **1 Match the words with the pictures.**

1 doctor	11 soldier
2 cook	12 accountant
3 website designer	13 bank clerk
4 flight attendant	14 farmer
5 tour guide	15 travel agent
6 shop assistant	16 waiter
7 factory worker	17 teacher
8 dentist	18 receptionist
9 secretary	19 mechanic
10 nurse	20 electrician

Sounds right /ə/

1 CD 2 **2 Listen. Pay attention to the underlined sounds.**

Don't want to be a secretary.
A waiter's life is not for me.
A flight attendant, that's my dream.
Be an accountant? No – I'd scream!

3 People often talk about the areas they work in. Which of the people above could say:

I work in
- computing.
- health care.
- finance.
- education.
- sales and marketing.
- the travel / the hotel / the food industry.

Free flow

BiSt ★ **4 Work in pairs. Each of you picks two jobs that you'd like to do. Then ask each other about these jobs and why you picked them.**

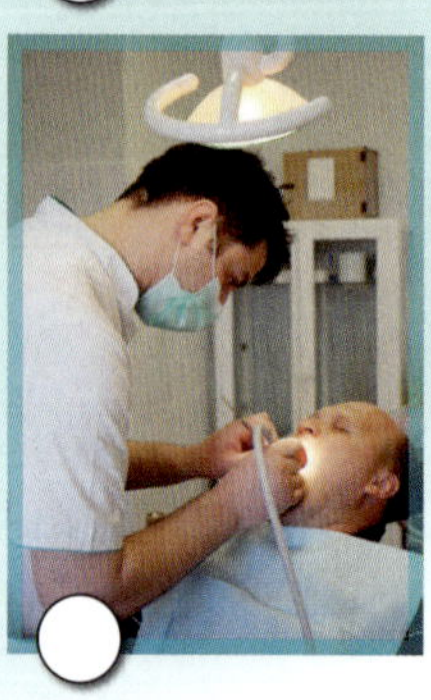

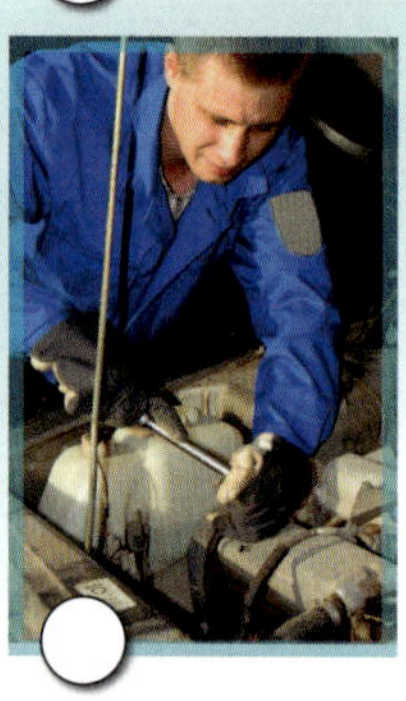

▶ WB p. 33

5 **Look at the two photos. Work with a partner. Say what you think.**

I think he / she wants / doesn't want to work outdoors.
I think Philip / Mandy wants to be a …
I think Philip / Mandy likes / doesn't like to …
I think Philip / Mandy is interested in …

Mandy

Philip

2 CD 2 SbX

6 **Listen to Philip and Mandy, two teenagers. Tick the correct box/boxes.**

	Philip	Mandy
1 I want to be a dancer.	☐	☐
2 I want to be a soldier.	☐	☐
3 My dad is a dentist.	☐	☐
4 My dad hasn't got a job at the moment.	☐	☐
5 Men and women should get the same money for the same job.	☐	☐
6 I'll give up work when my children are young.	☐	☐

7 CHOICES

2 CD 2 BiSt

a Listen again. Tick the correct answers.

1 Philip's family

- ☐ think he should become a singer.
- ☐ think he should become a teacher.
- ☐ don't like his dancing.
- ☐ like his dancing.

2 Some of Philip's friends think that

- ☐ his dancing is cool.
- ☐ he is not a good dancer.
- ☐ it's not normal for a boy to dance.
- ☐ dancing is for boys.

3 What does Mandy say she doesn't want to be?

- ☐ a waiter
- ☐ a dancer
- ☐ a soldier
- ☐ a teacher

BiSt ★

b Answer the questions.

1 Why does Philip want to be a dancer?
2 What do his family and friends think about his dancing?
3 What jobs does he think only men should do?
4 Why does Mandy want to be a soldier?
5 What do her friends think about her plans?
6 What job would Mandy hate to do and why?
7 What are her thoughts on having a family and working?

MP3

a A JOB PROFILE

1 Read the text.

So you want to be ... an Event Manager

A company has a big party with entertainment. A man and a woman are getting married but they have no time to organise the wedding. Who organises these things? Very often the answer is: an event manager.

Mona Stephenson from Glasgow is an event manager. She organises events for a professional basketball club, The Lions. Mona earns about £20,000 a year, and loves her job.

What does she do?

As event manager for The Lions, Mona manages all the club's events. She must make sure that The Lions are in the newspapers – she writes things about the club for the local media, for example. Mona says: "Basketball is not the most popular sport in Britain. I have to think of ways to keep the club in the news." We asked Mona to tell us about the pros and the cons of her job.

The "Pros"

"This is a dream job for me. It's a really great feeling when the media and the fans enjoy an event that I have organised. I love working with the other people."

The "Cons"

"Event management isn't a nine to five job. I work long hours. The events often happen in the evening or at weekends. And I have to be there."

2 Read the text again. Tick T (*True*) or F (*False*).

		T	F
1	Mona works for a sports club.	☐	☐
2	She doesn't like her job.	☐	☐
3	When people get married they sometimes have an event manager.	☐	☐
4	Mona has to write about herself in the news.	☐	☐
5	She dreams about getting another job.	☐	☐
6	She likes working with people.	☐	☐
7	Mona sometimes has to work evenings or weekends.	☐	☐
8	Event managers always work from nine to five.	☐	☐

WB p. 34

★ **b ABOUT JOB INTERVIEWS**

1 Rachel went for a job interview. She wrote an email to her friend after the interview. Complete the email.

Hi Annie,
Well, I had the interview today. I'm sure I won't get the job! Why? Well, I was late because I didn't [1]………… myself enough time to get there. Then I forgot to [2]………… hands with the interviewer. I tried to answer everything quickly, I didn't [3]………… my time – big mistake! I was so nervous – I just looked at the floor, I didn't [4]………… eye contact at all. Oh, and I [5]………… gum during the interview, too!
Another interview on Friday – I'm going to [6]………… for that one!
Bye!
Rachel

Get talking Interviews

2 Use these pictures to talk about how you should behave in interviews. Say:

- what they are doing wrong
- what they should / shouldn't do
- what you think are the two most important rules for job interviews.

He / She … and I think that was a bad idea!
It wasn't a great idea to …
He should never have …
It was a big mistake to …

I agree / I disagree …

3 CD 2 **9 Listen to two people talking about their job interviews. Who had to answer these questions? Write K (*Kelly*) or L (*Liam*) next to each one.**

Dialogue 1 – Kelly Dialogue 2 – Liam

1 Do you like working with people? …………
2 What's your ambition? …………
3 Where have you worked before? …………
4 Have you had any experience of journalism? …………
5 Why do you want to work here? …………
6 When can you start? …………

WB p. 34 CYBER HOMEWORK 9

Get talking

BiSt

a Talk to a partner for 3 – 4 minutes. The prompts will help you to think about the topic and ask questions. You have one minute to prepare.

JOBS

- What do you want to do when you leave school …? I'd like to be a …
- What qualifications do you need for this job?
- You have to … … study hard … pass lots of exams …
- Why are you interested in this job?
- You need to be … … patient … … able to speak two foreign languages … … polite …
- … it's an outdoor job. … the money is good. … work with other people … it's not boring. … my mum thinks it's a good job. … work long hours. I would … I could …
- Do you know somebody who is a …? What's his / her day like?
- I wouldn't like to be a … because …
- I'd like to be a … most because …

Free flow

BiSt ★

b Work in pairs. One of you will play the role of a career advisor (A), the other will play the role of student (B). Take two minutes to prepare your part of the interview. Use the prompt cards to help you. Talk for four minutes.

Prompt Card A

You are a career advisor. You are going to interview a student and recommend a job for him/her. Before you make your recommendation you will need to find out:

- what he/she most enjoys doing.
- what he/she doesn't like doing.
- how important money is for him/her.
- if he/she wants to work long hours.
- what his/her personality is like (shy/sociable etc).
- if he/she wants to go to university.

What other things would it be good to ask?

Prompt Card B

You are a school student and it's time to think about what job you might do when you leave school. You are going to see a career advisor. Think about the following things:

- the things you most enjoy doing.
- the things you really don't like doing.
- how important money is to you.
- how hard you want to work.
- how you would describe yourself.
- if you want to go to university.

What other things might be good to tell the career advisor?

Writing *for your Portfolio*

BiSt **11** **Do not take longer than 20 minutes to write a text (120 – 180 words) about your dream job. Do not forget to use paragraphs. Write about:**

- what kind of job it is
- what your dream job is like
- what you expect from it (money / stardom / good friends …)
- why you expect these things
- what is so fascinating about your dream job
- when you first heard about it
- who could help / support you
- what you will have to do for your future career.

SbX

Grammar

Questions in reported speech

Wenn du über Fragen berichtest, ändert sich die Zeit meist so wie in der indirekten Rede (siehe Unit 4). Außerdem verwendest du dann Fragewörter (*why / where / who / when / how* etc) oder *if*.

He asked me **why I had** a dog with me.
He asked me **where I had worked** before.
They asked me **when I could** start.
He asked me **if I liked** working with people.
They asked me **if I had** any experience of journalism.

Wenn du über Fragen berichtest, verwendest du kein *do, does* oder *did*.

She asked me **where I lived**.
(Not: She asked me ~~where did I live~~.)

WB pp. 35, 36

4 CD 2 BiSt

1 Listen to the dialogue and fill in the missing words and phrases.

Dad Sally, how did the interview go?
Sally It didn't [1]..................................... .
Dad Why not?
Sally They don't need a secretary for four weeks only.
Dad That's a pity. What did they ask you?
Sally How long I could do the job. How fast I could type. And then a man and a woman came in.
Dad What did they want?
Sally They wanted to talk to the boss.
Dad What about?
Sally They had a problem with designing their [2]................................ .
Dad Was that the end of the interview?
Sally Yes, it was. And then I went with the man and the woman.
Dad Why?
Sally Well, I helped them with the [3]..................................... .

The phone starts ringing and Sally answers it.

Dad Who was it?
Sally The boss. They don't need a [4]..................................... for four weeks, but …
Dad But what?
Sally They need someone to help them with their website!

4 CD 2 BiSt

2 Now cover up the dialogue. Listen again and tick the correct answer. Then look at the dialogue and check.

Which statement is NOT true?

- ☐ Sally went to do a job interview.
- ☐ Sally wanted to work as a secretary for 4 weeks.
- ☐ Sally thought the interview was great.
- ☐ Sally didn't get the job, but she got another one.

Sally's dad thinks …

- ☐ it's not a problem that she didn't get the job.
- ☐ she didn't get the job because she can't type fast.
- ☐ it's not good that she didn't get the job as a secretary.
- ☐ it was a mistake to go with the man and the woman.

Vocabulary Work places

3 **Match these people to the places where they work. Write the correct number in the box.**

☐ a gym	☐ a hotel	☐ a mine	☐ a factory	☐ an office block
☐ a warehouse	☐ a laboratory	☐ a prison	☐ a court	☐ a farm

farmer

miner

factory worker

scientist

judge

office worker

prison warden

warehouse worker

porter

aerobics teacher

4 **Choose one of the workers in 3. Mime an action that person might do for the other students to guess.**

You're milking a cow.
You're on a farm.

Get talking Talking about work places

5 **Read the dialogues and complete them with the words on the left.**

where
prison
criminals
factory

Dialogue 1

A What does your dad do?
B He's a warden. He works in a [1]................................ .
A What's that?
B It's a place where [2]................................ go.

Dialogue 2

A What does your mum do?
B She works in a [3]................................
A What's that?
B It's a place [4]................................ people make things.

5 CD 2 **6** **Listen and check. Then practise the dialogues with a partner.**

BiSt **7** **Work in pairs. Do a short role play. One of you is the reporter for a school magazine. The other chooses one of the jobs from page 46. Ask and answer questions about:**

- a typical day in the person's job
- what he/she likes about the job
- what he/she doesn't like about it
- the money.

WB p. 37 CYBER HOMEWORK 10

UNIT 6 Hungry?

Vocabulary Food

6 CD 2

1 Listen. Write the numbers next to the words. Then match the words and the pictures.

☐ chocolate	☐ yoghurt	☐ pork	☐ milk	☐ bread
☐ eggs	☐ orange juice	☐ tomatoes	☐ fish	☐ crisps
☐ carrots	☐ rice	☐ apples	☐ chicken	☐ cheese
☐ pasta	☐ beef	☐ spinach	☐ chips	☐ pizza

2 Look at the different kinds of food above.

a Show how much you like the food. Give it a number.

I don't like it / them 1 2 3 4 5 *I like it / them very much*

b Is the food healthy? Give it a letter.

It's / They're very healthy A B C D E *It's / They're unhealthy*

☐☐ yoghurt	☐☐ spinach	☐☐ eggs	☐☐ bread	☐☐ apples
☐☐ milk	☐☐ chips	☐☐ cheese	☐☐ chocolate	☐☐ chicken
☐☐ pizza	☐☐ tomatoes	☐☐ carrots	☐☐ rice	☐☐ crisps
☐☐ orange juice	☐☐ beef	☐☐ pork	☐☐ fish	☐☐ pasta

WB p. 40

3 **Compare your ideas in groups.**

For me chips is a 5. I like them a lot.

What number did you give to orange juice?

I gave it a 2. I don't like it.

What letter did you give to eggs?

I gave it an A. I think eggs are healthy.

Get talking

4 **What do you often eat for lunch / dinner? Is it healthy or unhealthy?**

5 **Talk about food in your family.**

My dad/mum/sister/brother likes … We never have … because …
Nobody in my family can stand … My … is a vegetarian. He/She never …

Oh, really?
Well, in my family …

6 CHOICES

MP3
BiSt

a A WEBSITE

1 **Read this website. Match the texts and the pictures. Write numbers in the boxes.**

Feed me better.com

☐ Many young people don't know what celery or zucchini taste like. And they don't know how to cook them. They don't learn about food at school and at home. Kids need lessons to teach them about food.

☐ A school dinner should have fresh food and also all the proteins, minerals and vitamins that kids need for health.

☐ What are young people in England eating for school dinners? Junk food! It's fattening and it's harmful. Young people need better food – now!

☐ Dinner ladies work hard. They cook the meals for the kids. Our dinner ladies have between 35p and 45p to spend on food per kid per meal. That's about the price of a bag of crisps. They need at least 70p per person to cook a healthy meal!

▶ WB p. 41

2 Read the texts again. Try to answer the questions.

1 Why don't most young people know how to cook things? ....
2 Why are dinner ladies important? ....
3 What should school dinners provide? ....
4 What is more money needed for? ....

★ b A FAMOUS CHEF

1 Look at the text for 10 seconds. How much can you find out about the man in the picture? Compare in class.

2 Now read the text about Jamie Oliver. What changes do you think he would make to this menu? Give reasons.

Note:
English: chef = cook
German: Chef = boss

Jamie Oliver
and Feed me better

Jamie Oliver is a world-famous English chef* who owns and runs his own restaurants and trains new chefs. He also does cookery programmes on television. A few years ago, he did a TV programme called *Jamie's School Dinners.*

Many schools in Britain give the kids a meal at lunchtime – the meals are called "school dinners" (even though they're lunches, not dinners!). There are people called "dinner ladies" who make the meals for the kids.

In his TV programme, Jamie Oliver found that a lot of school dinners are just "junk food". What's junk food? It's food that is filling, but not very healthy because it has artificial things in it. Since the programme, Jamie has been working to improve school dinners. He started a movement called *Feed Me Better.*

Fairview school Menu
Mon 12th October
Starters: Vegetable soup or Mini pizza
Main course: Hot dog and chips or Spinach lasagne
Dessert: Chocolate mousse or Fresh fruit salad

Vocabulary Words about food

★ 7 Match each word about food with a definition.

1 artificial	☐ has good effects on your body
2 harmful	☐ makes you become heavier
3 healthy	☐ tastes very, very bad
4 nutritious	☐ makes you feel full, feel that you have eaten a lot of food
5 fresh	☐ full of the natural things your body needs
6 tasty	☐ tastes very, very good
7 revolting	☐ not natural; man-made
8 filling	☐ has bad effects; doesn't do you good
9 fattening	☐ new; not frozen or in a tin

▶ WB p. 41

8 **Look again at the food items on page 54. Which words in 7 can you use to describe them?**

I think yoghurt is …

Free flow

BiSt **9** **Talk for two minutes about your eating habits. Talk about:**

- what you eat for breakfast / lunch / dinner
- what your favourites are and how often you have them
- what you totally dislike
- what your intake of healthy / unhealthy food is
- how much fresh food / freshly prepared food you eat
- if eating together with your family plays an important part.

SbX **10** **Read the information about hunger in the world. Where do you think these numbers should go? Use a dictionary for words you don't know.**

515 34 100,000 850 12 50 300 7

WORLD HUNGER
SOME FACTS

- The population of the world is around 6 billion people.
- The world can produce enough food to feed [1]....................... billion people.
- Every day, [2]....................... people die of hunger.
- Every [3]....................... minutes, somewhere in the world, a child dies of hunger.
- Around the world, [4]....................... million people do not have enough to eat. Of these, 34 million are in developed countries and [5]....................... million are in Asia (24% of the total population).
- Africa is very badly affected, too. In Liberia, 18% of the population are undernourished, including [6]....................... % of children below the age of 10.
- In black Africa, [7]....................... % of the population (186 million people) suffer from "extreme hunger", which means that each one of them only gets about [8]....................... calories a day.
- In the USA, adults have an average intake of 2,000 – 3,000 calories a day.

7 CD 2 MP3 **Listen and check.**

MP3 SbX ★

11 **Look at the text quickly to find the answers to these questions. Then read the text carefully and check.**

1 What problem does Shannon talk about?
2 Does Shannon still have this problem?

YOUR STORIES

Shannon

I was never really fat and I was never really thin. I was somewhere in the middle.

That's what I thought. Maybe I was a little overweight. When I was fourteen, I was invited to Rebecca's birthday party. When Rebecca ate the third piece of cake, I heard her sister say: "If you go on eating like that, you'll get as fat as Shannon!" That hurt. Most of my friends at school were thinner than me and being thin like a model was a topic all the girls talked about all the time.

Not long after the party, I started to throw up after eating. At first, I threw up only once or twice a week. But soon I felt that this wasn't enough. Whenever I ate something, I had the feeling it was too much. Whenever I had the chance, I looked in the mirror. And I didn't like what I saw. "Fat, fat, fat," I thought.

And there were times when I opened the fridge as soon as I got home from school. I stuffed myself with food and afterwards I felt so bad about it that I ran into the bathroom.

It was a terrible time. I often had stomach ache. I often felt very weak and I often felt sick. I didn't enjoy eating any more. It didn't matter what I ate. My friends knew that something was going on, but I never talked to them about my problem.

When we were on holiday in Italy, I tried to stop throwing up after eating. But I couldn't. When I looked in the mirror, I was sure I had gained 20 kilos, but of course I hadn't.

Then one day I collapsed in the gym at school. After the lesson my P.E. teacher told me to come to her room. She offered me a cup of tea and she talked to me. I couldn't tell her about my problem, but I promised I would talk to my mum.

So I wrote a letter to my mum and left it on the kitchen table one day before I left the house.

I was scared when I came home, but my mother hugged me and said, "We'll solve this problem together."

Every week I go to a meeting of a group of girls who have eating disorders. We talk about our problems and I feel much better. I eat regularly and don't throw up any more. And I don't look in the mirror all the time. I'm a little overweight again, but I have learned to accept it. At Rebecca's party for her fifteenth birthday, I met a boy. When he walked home with me, I knew I had finally beaten my problem. ●

BiSt ★

12 **What does the text do?**

a It tells you how a girl learnt to solve her eating problems.
b It tells mothers how they can help their children with problems.
c It tries to tell young people how they can lose weight.
d It tells you how to keep fit and eat well.

▶ CYBER HOMEWORK 11

BiSt ★

13 **Tick T (*True*) or F (*False*).**

	T	F
1 Her eating problem started when she was fourteen.	☐	☐
2 Right from the beginning she threw up after every meal.	☐	☐
3 She never tried to stop throwing up.	☐	☐
4 Her friends never knew what was going on.	☐	☐
5 She told her P.E. teacher about her problem.	☐	☐
6 She is happy that she can talk about her problems to others.	☐	☐

Get talking

BiSt

14 **Talk to a partner for 3 – 4 minutes. The prompts will help you to think about the topic and ask questions. You have one minute to prepare.**

FOOD

WHERE?
restaurant
school canteen
at home

QUALITY
minerals / proteins / nutritious /
fresh / tasty / fattening / filling
artificial / harmful
revolting

EATING HABITS
… miss breakfast …
Nobody in my family / My sister …
… is a vegetarian …
… family meals …
… eat out …

EATING DISORDERS
… allergic to …
overweight
keep a diet
gain / lose weight
throw up

LIKES / DISLIKES
I (don't) like …
I hate …
I can't stand …

WORLD HUNGER
food production /
too much … too little /
war /
die of hunger

COOKING
Who?
Can you cook?
… favourite recipe?

Sounds right /æ/ (apple) /ʌ/ (hungry) /e/ (egg)

8 CD 2

15 **Listen and repeat the rhymes.**

1 Eggs are healthy,
apples, too.
If you're hungry,
eat a few.

2 I love carrots.
Eat a ton.
I get angry
when there's none.

3 I'll eat anything,
can't get enough.
Bread and butter?
It's great stuff!

DVD The Mag 4 The meat debate

1 Watch the story. Complete the sentences with the words in the box. There are four you don't need.

animal	headmaster	Maths teacher	loves	handbag
sandwiches	pizza	pocket	police	hates

1 The school offers veggie burgers and veggie ....
2 Stern .... meat.
3 Vegans don't eat any .... products at all.
4 Mr Davis nearly got into trouble with the ....
5 Mr Johnson is the ....
6 Miss Chappell put the steak in her ....

2 Match the people with what they think.

1 Miss Chappell
2 Mr Davis
3 Nick
4 Jessica

☐ understands why the demonstrators are unhappy.
☐ used to demonstrate for animal rights.
☐ found it difficult to get good vegetarian food.
☐ enjoys cooking vegetarian food.
☐ thinks there's enough vegetarian food on the menu.
☐ feels healthier not eating meat.

Everyday English

3 Fill in the missing words. Practise the dialogues.

Beats me! Go right ahead. Between me and you Not as far as I know.

▶ WB p. 44

Writing *for your Portfolio*

Note:
English: a healthy diet =
German: gesunde Ernährung
But: I'm on a diet =
German: Ich bin auf Diät

BiSt **a Read what Paul Harris (14) eats. Do you think his diet is healthy?**

I often miss breakfast. I'm not very hungry in the morning. At school I eat some crisps and have a cola during the morning break. I have lunch at school – it's usually something with chips, a hamburger perhaps or some chicken nuggets. When I get home in the afternoon, my mum makes me something like a ham and cheese sandwich. In the evening we usually all have dinner at different times – I have something like sausages and chips, normally.

You have just read Paul's text in a youth magazine. Write an email to Paul. It should be 40 – 70 words and you should not take more than 10 minutes.

Write about:
- what you think of his diet
- what you eat
- your ideal meal.

BiSt ★ **b You have read about Shannon and her eating disorder. Write a letter to her (120 – 180 words). Do not take longer than 20 minutes to do this.**

Tell her:
- how you feel about her story
- what you think of her problem
- what your eating habits are like
- what your favourite food is
- what healthy food is
- what a healthy diet consists of
- what else she could do to stay healthy.

SbX

Grammar Past perfect (Revision)

Circle the correct options. Complete the rule.

James thought that perhaps he had forgotten something.

Du verwendest das *past perfect*, wenn du betonen möchtest, dass eine Handlung *vor / nach* einem bestimmten Zeitpunkt in der Vergangenheit geschehen war. Du bildest das *past perfect* mit [1]................................. und dem [2]................................. des Hauptverbs.

When he walked home with me, I knew I **had** finally **beaten** my problem.

Wenn du *before* oder *after* am Anfang eines (Glied-)Satzes verwendest, brauchst du meist das *past perfect* nicht zu verwenden.

My friends **left** before I got there.

MORE fun with Fido!

9 CD 2 BiSt

1 Listen to the dialogue and fill in the missing words and phrases.

Nadia Hello. Can I have chicken and chips, please?
Woman [1] ...., dear. Would you like cabbage, too?
Nadia Erm – yes, please!
Woman OK. Here you are.
Nadia Thanks.
Harry Cabbage? You [2] .... cabbage!
Nadia That isn't true. I eat cabbage every week. Well, almost every week.
Harry I hate cabbage. My father loves it – he eats it every Sunday.
Woman And for you, dear?
Harry Oh, sorry! Er – can I have fish, please? With potatoes.
Woman [3] .... tomatoes?
Harry No thanks. Just potatoes. Oh – and a yoghurt, too, please.
Woman OK. Here you are.
Nadia I hate yoghurt, but my mother loves it. She eats it every day. She always takes yoghurt [4] .... with her. Weird.
Harry Oh? I eat it about [5] .... a week. It's good for you!

9 CD 2 BiSt

2 Now cover up the dialogue. Listen again and tick the correct answer. Then look at the dialogue and check.

Why are Nadia and Harry talking to the woman?

- ☐ The woman is Harry's mother.
- ☐ They are telling the woman about their favourite food.
- ☐ They are complaining that there aren't any tomatoes.
- ☐ They are telling the woman what they want to eat.

Why does Harry eat yoghurt quite often?

- ☐ Because he likes weird food.
- ☐ Because he thinks it's better than fruit salad.
- ☐ Because he thinks it's healthy.
- ☐ Because his mother eats it every day.

10 CD 2

3 Read and listen to the dialogue.

Waiter Are you ready to order?
Girl Yes, I'd like tomato soup first. And then I'll have chicken with rice and vegetables.
Waiter Right. Anything to drink?
Girl Just water, please.
Boy I'd like cream of potato soup. And then I'll have the beef with potatoes and a salad.
Waiter And to drink?
Boy A cola please.

4 Look at the menu. Act out similar dialogues.

5 Work in pairs. Ask and answer.

Do you ever eat out?
What's your favourite restaurant?
What do you usually order there?
Do you ever try something new?
Do you like sweet foods or spicy foods?
What do you usually drink with your meal?
Do you often have dessert?

Yes, I sometimes / often … No, I never …
It's called … It's in …
I usually have … I often have …
Sometimes I have …
I like … best. I don't really like …
No, I don't like sweet food. I usually have …
Yes, my favourite dessert is …

WB p. 45 CYBER HOMEWORK 12

UNIT 7 Superheroes

1 Which of the superheroes and supervillains in the pictures do you know? What do you know about them? Add your own superhero / superheroine or supervillain and talk about him / her.

SbX **2 The Superman Fact File. Complete the list with information from the box.**

Steel
1938
enemies
Krypton
2007
reporter
Siegel

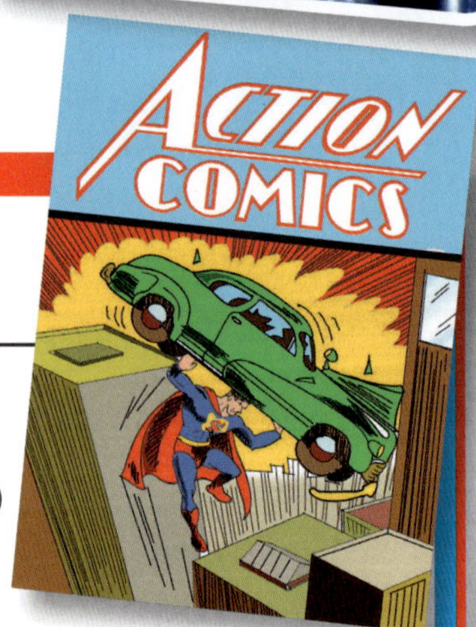

FACT FILE

Superman

Superman: also known as "The Man of 1 .... ".
Created by Joe Shuster and Jerry 2 .... in 1932.
First appeared in Action Comics #1 (June 3 ....)
Born on the planet 4 ....
Works as a 5 ....
Loves a fellow reporter and marries her in the 90s.

Has superpowers: He can fly. He's very strong. He's very fast. He can see through things. He has a super memory and he hears perfectly.
Some 6 .... are Lex Luthor, Doomsday and Bizarro.

There are many *Superman* films and TV series. In 7 .... David Zucker's funny version (*Superhero*) was released.

11 CD 2 MP3

3 a Listen to the radio show and check your answers.

★ **b Now listen again. Take notes of any more information you hear and compare your notes in class.**

A song 4 U *Superman (R.E.M.)*

12/13 CD 2

4 Listen to the song.

Chorus
I am, I am, I am Superman
and I know what's happening.
I am, I am, I am Superman
and I can do anything.

You don't really love that guy
you make it with now, do you?
I know you don't love that guy
cause I can see right through you.

Chorus

If you go a million miles away,
I'll track you down, girl.
Trust me when I say I know
the pathway to your heart.

5 Put the lines in the correct order to get a summary of the song. Write numbers 1 – 6.

- ☐ He knows how to win her back.
- ☐ He knows what she is thinking.
- ☐ The boy thinks he is Superman.
- ☐ He will find the girl even if she goes far away.
- 1 The song is about a boy. His girlfriend has left him.
- ☐ He thinks the girl doesn't love her new boyfriend.

Get talking

BiSt **6 Say what you think about the song. Use the language below.**

☺ I really like this song.
I think the tune is catchy (great / cool …)
I like the lyrics. They tell a real story and the story makes me think of …

☹ I don't like the song at all.
I think the tune is a bit boring / too simple / …
I find the lyrics a bit boring / difficult to understand / …

Talking about the band:

What do you think?
For me, … are one of the greatest bands.
Another great song by … is …
I really like it because …

I don't find … very interesting.
I think their songs are too … /
My favourite band / singer is … because …

Agreeing / Disagreeing with what someone says:

I can understand why you say that …
I completely agree with you.

I'm not sure I agree with you. I think …
I completely disagree with what you say about … . I think …

Vocabulary

7 Look up the words on the left in your dictionary. Then do the matching exercise.

1	pleasant	☐	when you're very ill and can't see, speak or feel anything
2	result	☐	a straight beam of light
3	breakthrough	☐	something that makes an illness go away
4	nightmare	☐	when you study something carefully
5	ray	☐	finding an important new thing
6	research	☐	make food or drink go down your throat
7	swallow	☐	the consequence of something
8	cure	☐	enjoyable or attractive
9	coma	☐	a frightening dream

8 CHOICES

14 CD 2

MP3

SbX

a A COMIC

1 At Alderhurst High School the 14-year-old students of the drama class have created a comic called "Nightmare over the City". Look at the characters and say what you think about them.

THE CHARACTERS

2 Now listen to the comic. Look at the pictures and find out which character in 1 does not appear. Then listen again and fill in the words.

check	evil	scientist	help
lab	dream	laughed	hospital

4
All the kids had bad dreams about Superkid.
What does that mean?
I don't know. I think Superkid should .... it out ...
Just be careful, Matt. Please be careful!
5
Don't be afraid. I'll .... you.
No, go away. You're bad. Go away.
Superkid always helps young people in trouble.
6
Here's your little girl.
Mummy! He's bad!
But young people don't like Superkid any more.
7
There was an interview in the school magazine with a ....
Dr Morgan?
Yes. Let's find him!
8
Let me check it out. I'll be back soon.
Be careful, Superkid!
9
Not much to look at, is it?
Oh, my goodness. This looks like a ....
10
Take him to .... quickly! He's taken sleeping pills. And he's destroyed his dream machine.
OK!
I'm so sorry.
11
He's at the hospital. We can go home.
Why did he do that?
He's not an .... person. First he wanted to give people nice dreams. So he built a dream machine, but people .... about him. So he gave us bad dreams.
Oh, Matt. I'm so glad it's over.
Me too. And, of course, so is Superkid!

MP3
SbX
BiSt
★

b TWO TEXTS

1 Look at the texts quickly. Are they:

☐ film reviews? ☐ film summaries? ☐ biographies? ☐ short stories?

CHRISTOPHER REEVE

"People say Christopher Reeve is their Superman. Well, he's my Superman as well," says Brandon Routh, who played the superhero in *Superman Returns* (2006). And it's true – everybody still agrees that there was no one like Reeve in his double role of Superman and the reporter Clark Kent.

He was 26 when Richard Donner, director of the 1978 *Superman* film, asked him to play the hero in blue and red, making him the youngest actor ever to play the part. Reeve worked next to some big names in the film industry and everybody loved him. Reeve went on to do three more *Superman* films, but none of them were as good as the first one.

In 1995, everything changed for Reeve, the successful Hollywood star, when he fell off a horse. He was paralysed and in a wheelchair until his death in 2004. He was only 52 and much admired for the way he lived with his disability. Reeve showed people that there is more than one way to be a superhero.

HALLE BERRY

Halle Berry (born 1966) was the first African-American actress to win an Academy Award. She won it in 2002 for her role in *Monster's Ball*. However, she also won a "razzie" – an award for the worst acting! And she got it for a female superhero role – her 2004 role as *Catwoman* in the film of the same name. Berry's Catwoman is not the only comic book character she has played. She was also Storm in the three *X-Men* movies. Storm is a mutant who can control the weather and one of the strongest African-American characters in comics. Halle Berry herself has always been interested in political and racial issues. She once said: "I've learned to realize that the best thing about me is that I don't have blonde hair and blue eyes and that I do have brown skin … I do not think that we live in a color-blind society, […]. But I believe that it is possible that things are moving in that direction and I believe that one day, color and race won't matter. I hope I am here to see it, but it hasn't happened yet."

2 Read the texts again. Write R (*Reeve*) or B (*Berry*). Which of the two actors …

1 was born in 1952? ....
2 won an Academy Award? ....
3 was in a wheelchair for many years? ....
4 played the role of Superman? ....
5 played the role of Catwoman? ....
6 is an African-American? ....
7 died in 2004? ....
8 believes that colour and race won't matter in the future? ....

Writing *for your Portfolio*

BiSt **a Write a blog entry of 60 – 80 words. Create your own superhero.**
You can also add a picture. Write: his / her name, what he / she looks like, where he / she lives, what his / her superpower is, why he / she is your superhero.

★ **b Your favourite newspaper is organising a writing competition. The topic is "Superheroes". Write a text of about 120 – 180 words and do not take more than 20 minutes to do it. Do not forget to use paragraphs!**
Describe • your superhero's size, typical features, costume and logo
• what superpowers she/he has • one of his/her great adventures.
Say • what her/his job is • who her/his enemies are and what they want to do.

SbX

Grammar

Adverbs of manner (Revision)

Mit dem Adverb der Art und Weise drückst du aus, wie jemand etwas macht oder wie etwas geschieht.
He hears **perfectly**.
We've got find him as **quickly** as possible.
I **completely** agree with you.

Complete: Regelmäßige Adverbien werden mit dem .... + -ly gebildet.

Beachte die Ausnahmen:
good – **well** fast – **fast** hard – **hard**
[hardly = kaum, e.g. I **hardly** slept at all last night.]

Bei einigen Zeitwörtern (look, sound, feel, taste, smell, find) werden Adjektive und nicht Adverbien verwendet.

Things **look** really **bad**. That doesn't **sound good**.
This food **tastes awful**.

Question tags

Um die deutschen Fragen *oder?* bzw. *nicht wahr?* zu bilden, verwendest du im Englischen sogenannte *question tags*. Hierbei gelten folgende Regeln:

Bei bejahenden Sätzen verwendest du einen verneinenden *tag*, bei verneinenden einen bejahenden.

Z.B.: And we still haven't found Morgan, **have we**?

Im *question tag* wiederholst du das Hilfsverb (*be* oder *have*) bzw. das *modal verb* (z. B. *can / must / should / will / might*).
It**'s** easy, **isn't it**? We**'ve** been here before, **haven't we**?

Wenn im Satz kein Hilfsverb oder *modal verb* vorkommt, verwendest du eine Form von *do* im *question tag*:
I think Ann interviewed him, **didn't she**?

Das Nomen wird durch ein Pronomen ersetzt.
Morgan hasn't come yet, has **he**?

MORE fun with Fido!

15 CD 2 BiSt

1 **Listen to the dialogue and fill in the missing words and phrases.**

Mum Look. It says here if we book early, we'll get [1].. .
Sally What for?
Mum A holiday in Lake Windermere in the Lake District.
Harry I don't want to go there. There's too much rain. I'll stay with grandpa and grandma.
Sally Well, if he stays with grandpa and grandma, I'll go and stay with Lisa.
Dad No way. [2].. going mountain climbing in Scotland?
Sally No, not again! I hate mountain climbing.
Mum Why [3].. to Norway?
Harry It's always cold there.
Mum OK. Harry, you stay with grandpa and grandma. And you, Sally, you stay with Lisa.
Sally And what about you?
Dad Mum and I will go to Florida.
Harry [4].. . We'll come with you.
Sally Yippee! This summer we're going to Florida!

15 CD 2 BiSt

2 **Now cover up the dialogue. Listen again and tick the correct answer. Then look at the dialogue and check.**

What is the dialogue about?

- ☐ holidays in the Lake District
- ☐ where the family should go on holiday
- ☐ how parents are unfair to their children
- ☐ how the weather is important when you're on holiday

Why does mum think it's a good idea to book their holiday now?

- ☐ Because she wants to go to Norway.
- ☐ Because it's cheaper to book now.
- ☐ Because mum and dad want to go on holiday without the kids.
- ☐ Because dad likes mountain climbing.

What is the main reason why mum says the children should stay with grandma and grandpa / Lisa?

- ☐ She would like to go on holiday just with dad.
- ☐ A holiday for 2 people is cheaper than for 4.
- ☐ Mum and dad make suggestions, but the children don't like them.
- ☐ She thinks Florida in the summer will be too hot for the kids.

Which statement about Sally is NOT true?

- ☐ She has been mountain climbing before.
- ☐ She doesn't like mountain climbing at all.
- ☐ She doesn't want to stay at her grandparents' with her brother.
- ☐ She doesn't want to go to Florida.

Get talking Talking about alternatives

16 CD 2

3 Listen and repeat.

Girl Let's go to the park.
Boy But what if it snows?
Girl Then we'll watch TV at your place.
Boy OK.

Man Let's go swimming after work.
Woman But what if the pool is closed?
Man Then we could play cards at my place.

4 Work with a partner. Look at the pictures, then match the phrases from columns A, B and C and make dialogues.

1

2

3

4

5

6

	A	B	C
Let's	- take the bus ...	- the bus is late	We'll go and see another film.
	- go to the cinema ...	- the computer doesn't work	We'll write the letter.
	- use the computer ...	- it is too hot	We'll take suncream and hats.
	- go to Africa on holiday ...	- there are no more tickets	We'll take the next train.
			We'll take a taxi.

UNIT 8 Travelling down under

Get talking

1 Work in pairs. Look at the questions below and take a guess at the answers.

I've no idea.
I haven't got a clue.
What do you think?
Have you got any idea?

I know that …
I'm pretty sure the answer's …
I'm not 100% sure.
I've got a feeling the answer's …

1 When did people first come to Australia?
- **a** ☐ 10,000 years ago
- **b** ☐ 20,000 years ago
- **c** ☐ 40,000 years ago
- **d** ☐ 2,000 years ago

2 Where did the Aborigines come from?
- **a** ☐ from America
- **b** ☐ from Asia
- **c** ☐ from Europe
- **d** ☐ from Africa

3 How big is Australia?
- **a** ☐ As big as the US without Alaska.
- **b** ☐ As big as Austria.
- **c** ☐ As big as North and South America together.
- **d** ☐ As big as South America.

4 How many people live in Australia?
- **a** ☐ 50 million
- **b** ☐ 20 million
- **c** ☐ 12 million
- **d** ☐ 30 million

5 What is the capital of Australia?
- **a** ☐ Brisbane
- **b** ☐ Canberra
- **c** ☐ Melbourne
- **d** ☐ Sydney

6 Name three animals that we can only find in Australia.

- a ☐ kangaroo, koala, wombat
- b ☐ kangaroo, koala, tiger
- c ☐ kangaroo, koala, rattlesnake
- d ☐ kangaroo, wombat, pelican

7 Name the three biggest cities.

- a ☐ Sydney, Melbourne, Canberra
- b ☐ Melbourne, Adelaide, Brisbane
- c ☐ Melbourne, Sydney, Darwin
- d ☐ Sydney, Melbourne, Brisbane

8 What time is it in Sydney when it is 3 p.m. in Vienna?

- a ☐ 12 a.m. (midnight)
- b ☐ 10 p.m.
- c ☐ 4 a.m.
- d ☐ 7 p.m.

9 How many states are there and how many territories?

- a ☐ 8 states and 1 territory
- b ☐ 7 states and 5 territories
- c ☐ 5 states and 3 territories
- d ☐ 6 states and 2 territories

17 CD 2

2 Listen to the quiz programme and check your answers.

18 CD 2 MP3 SbX

3 Listen to Amy's blog. In what order does she visit the following places?

Sydney Opera House Ayers Rock Rottnest Island Broome Sydney Aquarium Perth

SbX BiSt

4 Read the text quickly and find the answers to the questions.

1 Where are they flying on the second day?
2 What was the instrument Simon was playing?
3 How long is the beach at Broome?
4 What was the last stop in their trip?
5 How long did the bridge climb take in the end?

TravelBlog www.travelblog.org

Ryan and Amy

Heathrow Airport

Hurray! We're going to Australia next Friday. We leave London at about 9 p.m. on Friday and arrive in Perth at 00.30 on SUNDAY. What a long flight! We'll watch all the films they have on the plane.

Perth

Days 1 and 2: Perth

It's winter here, but it's not cold. Perth is a great city with lots of parks. Went by boat to Rottnest Island off the coast. Hired bikes there and went round the island. Saw some funny animals called Quokkas.

Dad and mum said we have to see Ayers Rock. So we're flying into the centre of Australia tomorrow, to Alice Springs.

Rottnest Island

Quokka

Days 3 – 5: Alice Springs

Ayers Rock

Dad rented a car and we went to Ayers Rock. We were driving for hours and suddenly there was this big red mountain there. We didn't climb Ayers Rock because the Aborigines don't like that. So we just took photos. First we went to an information centre of the Aborigines. A guy called Simon told us how the Aborigines lived a long time ago. We saw examples of tents made of small trees, tree bark and leaves. Later we watched Simon playing the didgeridoo. Simon told us that most Aborigines live in or near cities now. Most have forgotten how to hunt.

Didgeridoo

Another trip by plane tomorrow. We leave Alice Springs at 10 o'clock. Back to Perth. Two boring hours at the airport and then we fly off to Broome.

Days 6 – 7: Broome

Broome

Broome has got the most beautiful beach. It's 22 km long. Mum, Jack and I wanted to swim and lie on the beach, but dad wanted to drive into the Kimberley Wilderness to camp there. But we got lucky. In the evening we talked to two tourists, Eve and Jeremy, at the hotel. When they had told us their story, dad was happy to stay in Broome!

Eve and Jeremy's story

Eve and Jeremy

Saltwater crocodile

My girlfriend and I were camping near the Pentecost River. During the second night something started shaking our tent. We were in a panic and we crawled out of the tent and ran to the car. Fortunately the car wasn't locked and the key was in the car. I started the car and put the headlights on – and I saw a big crocodile. It was trying to drag the tent into the river. After a while, the crocodile gave up and went back into the water. We watched it for a long time. Suddenly our headlights went out. It was the battery – it was flat. We were too scared to go back to the tent, so we slept in the car. In the morning we could still see the crocodile near the river bank. The next morning a car came. We jump-started our car and left.

Day 10
We've got a nice tan. Three days on the beach, swimming, snorkelling and playing frisbee. We say good-bye to Broome today. We are on our way to Sydney.

View of the harbour

Days 11 – 13: Sydney

Day 11
We went around the Harbour on a boat, did a tour through the opera house and some shopping. Bought three presents and six T-shirts.

Day 12
We spent the morning at the aquarium. I liked watching the sharks best. In the afternoon we did some more shopping.

Day 13
We did the bridge climb – 3 ½ hours!!! We climbed to the highest point of the bridge. There's a wonderful view from there. But if you're scared of heights, don't do the climb.
Tomorrow we fly back to London at 5 p.m. A great holiday!

View from the Harbour Bridge

WB pp. 55, 58, 59

5 **Look at the map on page 72. Draw the route of the trip.**

6 **a Answer the following questions.**

1 How long did the flight take from London to Perth?
2 What did they do on Rottnest Island?
3 How did they spend their time at Ayers Rock?
4 How did they get from Alice Springs to Broome?
5 What did they like best about Broome?
6 Why didn't they go camping in the Kimberley Wilderness?
7 What sights did they visit in Sydney?

BiSt

b Tick the correct answers.

What is the purpose of the text? To ...

- ☐ sell holidays in Australia
- ☐ tell you how to book flights in Australia
- ☐ give information about holidays in Australia
- ☐ tell you about different countries

What does 'tan' (Day 10) mean?

- ☐ hotel on the beach
- ☐ person who sells drinks on a beach
- ☐ skin that is brown from the sun
- ☐ swimming pool

Vocabulary

19 CD 2

7 **Listen. Write the numbers into the pictures. Then match the pictures and the words.**

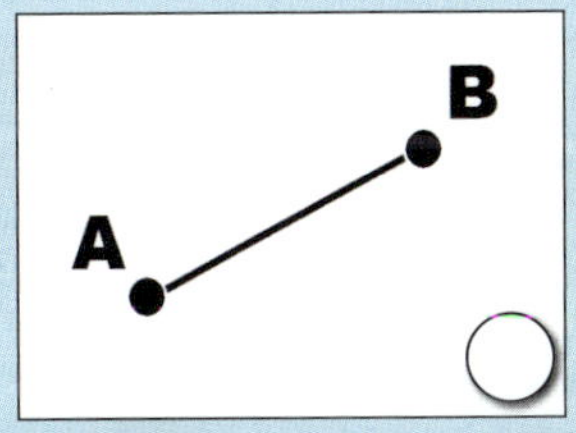

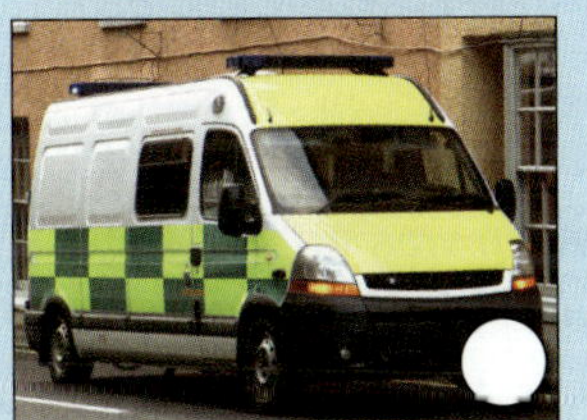

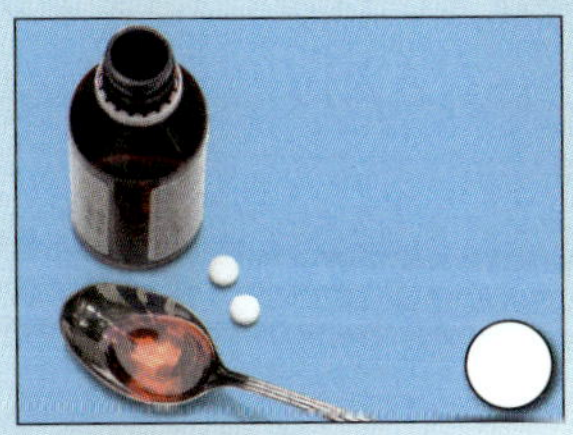

- ☐ distance
- ☐ ambulance
- ☐ European Union
- ☐ twice
- ☐ drugs
- ☐ bandage

20 CD 2 SbX ★

8 **Pauline works as a pilot for Australia's Flying Doctors. Listen and circle the correct word(s).**

1 That's the problem with illnesses in Australia. The *distances* / *problems* between doctors and patients are great.

2 There are *farms* / *airports* that are more than 500 km away from the nearest town.

3 The Royal Flying Doctor service is for people who live *far away from* / *near* towns.

4 There are about 450 people who *fly planes for* / *work for* the Royal Flying Doctors.

5 On a typical day the doctors make about *twenty* / *a hundred* landings.

6 A hundred years ago doctors had to travel by horse or by camel to get to their *families* / *patients*.

7 In 1917 a young man had an idea. He *solved* / *spoke about* the problem of the great distances.

8 Most people living far away from towns have a *cupboard* / *box* with drugs, bandages and other first aid material.

▶ WB p. 57

Vocabulary

9 **Match the words with the pictures. In pairs, create a story using the words.**

1 gun
2 load a horse
3 feed a horse
4 leaves
5 die of thirst
6 tracker

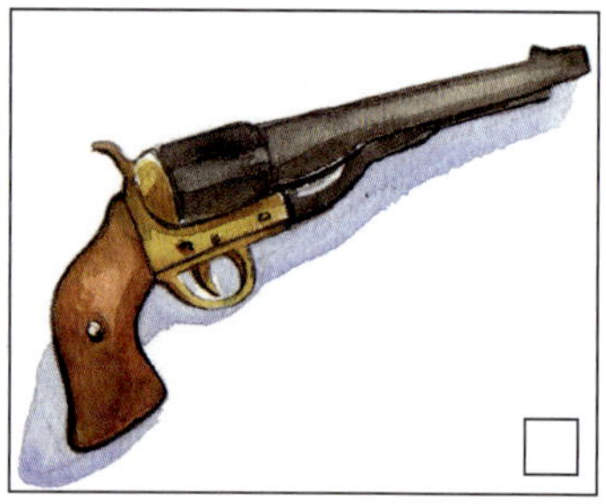

MP3 SbX ★

10 **Read the story and find the answers to the questions.**

It was the year 1884 in Milparinga. Inspector Saunders was writing a report at the police station when there was a knock at the door. It was the bank manager. An Aborigine had heard four men talking in the bar the night before. They wanted to break into the bank to steal the 30 kg of gold that was there. "The Aborigine told me that the men have guns," the bank manager said. "You have to take the gold to Wilcannia for me. Help me, please!"
It hadn't rained for a year. Saunders knew that it was almost impossible to do the trip of more than 300 km on horseback. It had been so hot that there was no grass for the horses and no water in the rivers. Saunders also knew that he wouldn't have a chance against four men with guns. So he thought up a plan. He sent for an Aboriginal tracker, who was a very strong, clever man. The tracker got three horses and loaded them with food, bags of water and the gold. They left the same evening.

Because of the heat, Saunders and his tracker only rode at night. During the day, they rested. They did not take the straight track to Wilcannia. They had enough water and food for the first few days, but not for the whole trip. When they ran out of food and water, the tracker knew some waterholes where he hoped they would find enough water. But when they got there, they saw there was very little water in the waterholes, hardly enough for the two men and their horses. There were also some small bushes. The two men fed all the leaves from the bushes to the horses – it was the only food they could get.

On the last day of the journey, when they wanted to leave the waterhole, the tracker suddenly heard a noise. Carefully, Saunders and the tracker checked out where it had come from. Not far from their camp, they found two men who were too weak to speak.

When Saunders had given them some water, the men said that the group of four men had followed Saunders and the tracker, but the water holes were dry when they got there. It was too late to return to Milparinga. Two men in the group and all their horses died of thirst. Saunders left them some water in a bag and rode on with his tracker. The next day they reached Wilcannia. They put the gold into the bank there and then rested for a day. Saunders and his tracker loaded their horses with bags of water and food and rode back. When they came to the place where they had left the two men, they only found pieces of clothes.

1 Why did Saunders go to Wilcannia?
2 Why did Saunders and his tracker only travel at night?
3 Who died and why?

11 CHOICES

Writing for your Portfolio

BiSt **a Write a short text of 40 – 70 words for English-speaking tourists about the place / town where you live. Take about 10 minutes for it. Write:**

- the name of the place / town
- how many people live there
- what the main attractions for tourists are
- what you like best about your place / town and why.

★ **b Look at the pictures and write the story (120 – 180 words). Take about 20 minutes and make paragraphs.**

Write about:

- what the place is like
- why people go there
- who the people in the story are
- what happened and to whom
- how other people reacted
- how the story ended.

DVD The Mag 5 Australia

1 Watch the story. Cross out the incorrect word(s) and correct them.

1 Lucy's family's moving to ~~Perth~~. Sydney
2 Liam has forgotten his old friends. ....
3 Lucy doesn't like Australian music. ....
4 Lucy wants Stern to be the new editor. ....
5 Liam gives Lucy a present. ....
6 At the end Lucy is happy because she's not going to Australia. ....

2 Put the events in the order that they happen.

- ☐ Liam tells Lucy about his experiences of moving.
- ☐ Stern talks about all the great things there are in Australia.
- ☐ Lucy tells the team she's not moving any more.
- ☐ Lucy decides she's really looking forward to moving.
- ☐ Nick gives Lucy a goodbye present.
- ☐ Lucy tells the team that she's moving to Australia.
- ☐ Jessica promises to look after the magazine.

Everyday English

3 Say the missing words. Practise the dialogues.

I know how you feel. How come? Not on your life! it's not really my scene.

▶ WB p. 59

Get talking

★ 12 **Work in pairs. One of you will play the role of a travel agent (A), the other will play the role of a tourist (B). You have one minute to prepare your discussion. Use the prompt cards to help you. Talk for four minutes.**

Prompt Card A

You are a travel agent. You are going to talk to someone interested in going to Australia.

- Give some general information about the country. (Use the information in this unit to help you.)
- Find out what kind of holiday he/she is looking for.
- Think about the different places you can recommend (use the information in this unit to help you).

Prompt Card B

You want to go on holiday to Australia. You are going to talk to a travel agent.

- What do you want to know about the country?
- Think about what kind of holiday you want (cities / wildlife / beaches / sport).
- Ask for recommendations for places to visit.

SbX

Grammar

Present simple for future

Du verwendest oft das *present simple* für Handlungen, die in der Zukunft stattfinden, wenn etwas fest vereinbart ist (Fahrpläne, Flugpläne, usw.). Zum Beispiel:

We **leave** London at about 9 p.m. on Friday and **arrive** in Perth at 00.30 on Sunday.

Our plane to Alice Springs **leaves** at 8.30 tomorrow.

Today we **say** goodbye to Broome in the early afternoon and **fly** to Sydney.

The train leaves at eight. Bruce is worried he hasn't got time for a cup of tea.

MORE fun with Fido!

21 CD 2 BiSt

1 Listen to the dialogue and fill in the missing words and phrases.

Tony I [1]............................ great film on Channel 5 yesterday.

Sally Really? What was it like?

Tony It was great. It was about kids who got these [2].......................... phone calls. Their mobile rang, they answered and then they heard a strange voice. It said: "Your [3]............................ ."

Sally Oh, come on. That's an old trick. That's not scary.

Tony That's what the kids thought, too. They believed it was a trick but each time something really bad happened to them. One boy fell off a building, a truck hit a girl. They had all kinds of [4]............................ .

Sally Were you [5]..........................., then?

Tony Yes, it was so real. Then my phone rang at midnight. I got quite a shock.

Sally What was the title of the film? Not *The Phone*?

Tony Yes, it was!

Sally That film's rubbish.

(Sally's mobile rings)

Sally Hang on! Yes?

Voice Your end is near.

Sally Ha, ha, very funny.

Voice Your end is near.

Sally I said stop it. [6]............................ , Harry? *(getting more nervous)*

Voice Yes, it is. Listen, Sally. I saw a great film on Channel 5 yesterday.

Sally Oh no. Don't tell me about it!

21 CD 2 BiSt

2 Now cover up the dialogue. Listen again and tick the correct answer. Then look at the dialogue and check.

What is the dialogue about? A scary film called …

- ☐ *Your end is near*
- ☐ *All kinds of accidents*
- ☐ *The Phone*
- ☐ *Channel 5*

Why did Sally get nervous at the end when someone phoned her?

- ☐ Because it was midnight.
- ☐ Because she thought it was Harry.
- ☐ Because she wasn't sure who it was and the person said "Your end is near".
- ☐ Because there was a horror film on Channel 5.

INFORMATION

Liebe Schülerin, lieber Schüler,

Wir sind überzeugt davon, dass du den Englischunterricht mit MORE! cool findest. Wichtig ist aber auch, dass du bei allem Spaß am Englischlernen nicht aufs Üben vergisst, damit du in der Fremdsprache mit Sicherheit immer fit bist!

Wer Englisch zu Hause intensiv üben möchte, kann dies am besten mit der **MORE! DVD-ROM (Lernsoftware)** oder dem ansprechenden Grammatiktraining **MORE! Grammar Practice** tun. Für das Wiederholen des Lernstoffes in den Ferien ist ab sofort das **MORE! Holiday Book** erhältlich. Darüber hinaus bieten wir jede Menge **Readers** zu den unterschiedlichsten Themen und Interessen an. Da ist sicher auch für dich die passende Lektüre dabei!

Auf der **MORE! Homepage www.helbling-ezone.com** findest du zusätzliche kostenlose Angebote:

- Gratis MP3-Downloads aller Stories, Songs, Chants und Poems. So kannst du sie dir zu Hause nochmals in Ruhe anhören!
- Interaktive Lernspiele
- Online Progress Checks

Schau doch mal (am besten mit deinen Eltern) rein!

Viel Spaß beim Lernen – mit MORE!
wünscht dir das MORE!-Team

MORE! ④: Die DVD-ROM

Englischlernen am Computer macht Spaß! Mit der MORE! DVD-ROM* kann aber auch der Lernstoff zu Hause effizient gefestigt werden. Das Zusatz-Tool „Test-Training-Software" bietet dir außerdem die ideale Vorbereitung auf Tests und Schularbeiten.

Die MORE! DVD-ROM bietet:

- Animated cartoon stories
- Vocabulary games
- Dialogue karaoke
- Karaoke – so kann die ganze Familie Spaß mit den Liedern haben
- zahlreiche wertvolle Grammatikübungen
- intensives Wortschatztraining
- interaktive Ausspracheübungen
- tolle Hörverstehensübungen
- interessante Lesetexte
- Dialogübungen
- Kurzvideos zu den *Time for Action*-Stories im Buch
- Training zum Schreiben von Texten
- Diktate
- Das MORE! Trivia Quiz!
- Test-Training-Software – so trainierst du zu Hause für deine Schularbeiten

* Systemvoraussetzungen:
Windows: mind. x86-kompatibler Prozessor mit mind. 2 GHz oder Intel® Atom™ mit mind. 1,6 GHz für Netbooks; Microsoft® Windows® XP Home, Professional oder Tablet PC Edition mit Service Pack 3, Windows Vista® Home Premium, Business, Ultimate oder Enterprise (auch 64 Bit) mit Service Pack 2, Win 7, Win. 8
Mac: mind. Intel Core™ Duo 1.83 Ghz; MacOSX 10.4.11, MacOSX 10.5.4, 10.5.5, 10.6, 10.7 und 10.8
Linux: mind. Linux Pentium 4, 1 GB RAM; Fedora ab 8, Ubuntu ab 7.10, OpenSuse ab 10.3; xterm sollte auf dem System installiert sein.

MORE! INFORMATION

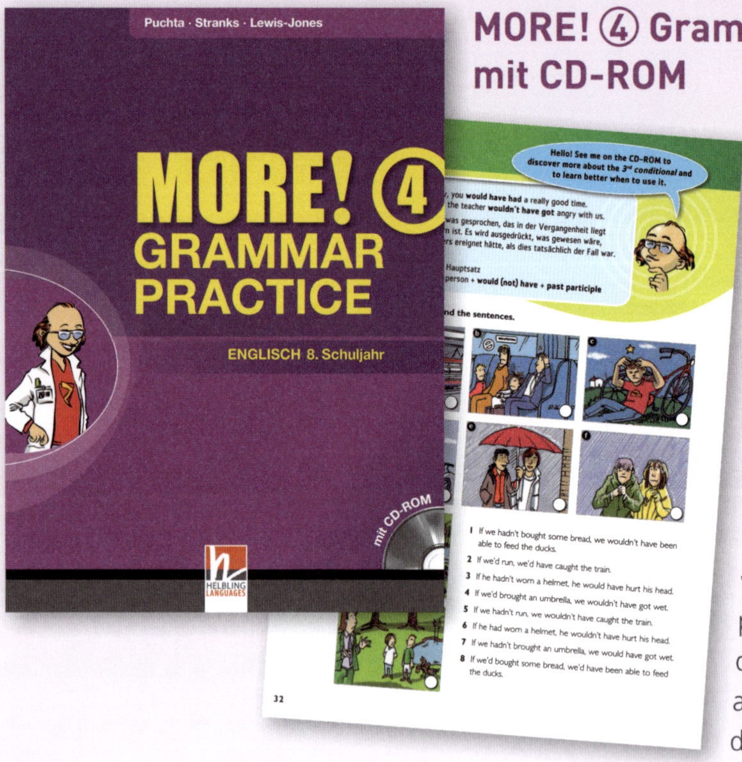

MORE! ④ Grammar Practice mit CD-ROM

Dieses Übungsheft mit CD-ROM bietet auf 92 Seiten zusätzliche Übungen zu allen wesentlichen Grammatikinhalten von MORE! ④. An den Themen und damit an der Wortschatzprogression von MORE! orientiert, kannst du dich speziell auf die grammatikalischen Aufgabenstellungen konzentrieren, ohne vorher neue Inhalte erarbeiten zu müssen. Die dem Buch beiliegende CD-ROM bietet zusätzliche Übungen mit innovativen Features. Diese helfen dir komplexe grammatikalische Strukturen, deren alltägliche Verwendung und vor allem den Unterschied zur Grammatik der Muttersprache besser zu verstehen.

HELBLING READERS – RED SERIES

Wer viel liest, kann bald besser Englisch!
Hast du Lust darauf, englischen Lesestoff zu Hause zu genießen?
Die HELBLING READERS bieten dir Gelegenheit dazu!

Princess on the Run by Paul Davenport
König Alexander möchte seine Tochter, Prinzessin Priscilla, mit seinem besten Freund, Lord Huntington, verheiraten. Doch die Prinzessin hat andere Pläne. Sie liebt Toby, einen jungen, schönen Diener des Königs. Priscilla und Toby beschließen zu fliehen. Doch das Leben auf der Flucht stellt die Liebe auf eine harte Probe.

The Adventures of Tom Sawyer by Mark Twain
Tom Sawyer lebt gemeinsam mit seinen Freunden Huck Finn und Joe Harper in einem verträumten Städtchen am Mississippi. Die drei haben es faustdick hinter den Ohren. Sie laufen weg, um Piraten zu werden, kommen gerade rechtzeitig zur eigenen Beerdigung zurück, werden Zeugen eines Mordes und finden einen Schatz.

Mr Football by Janet Olearski
Gary ist 15 und möchte Fußballprofi werden, genau wie sein Vater. Schließlich sollen drei Schüler aus Gary's Schule die Chance erhalten, in die Crossbridge Fußball Akademie aufgenommen zu werden. Gary geht selbstverständlich davon aus, dass er einer von ihnen sein wird. Aber oft liegen die Dinge nicht so einfach, wie es scheint …

Weitere Helbling Readers findest du unter:

➜ www.helblinglanguages.at

MORE! INFORMATION

MORE! ④ Holiday Book mit Audio-CD

Das MORE! Holiday Book ist zur Wiederholung des Jahresstoffes in den Sommerferien gedacht. Es ist in *10 Days* unterteilt, die die Themen der *20 Units* aus dem *MORE! Student's Book* aufgreifen und Grammatik- bzw. Sprachschwerpunkte üben.

Die kniffligen Rätsel und Übungen sowie die Höraufgaben, spannenden *Urban Legends* und lustigen *Jokes of the Day*, welche alle Teil der beiliegenden Audio-CD sind, sorgen dafür, dass der Spaß nicht zu kurz kommt.

Die Lösungen zur Selbstkontrolle befinden sich am Ende des Heftes.

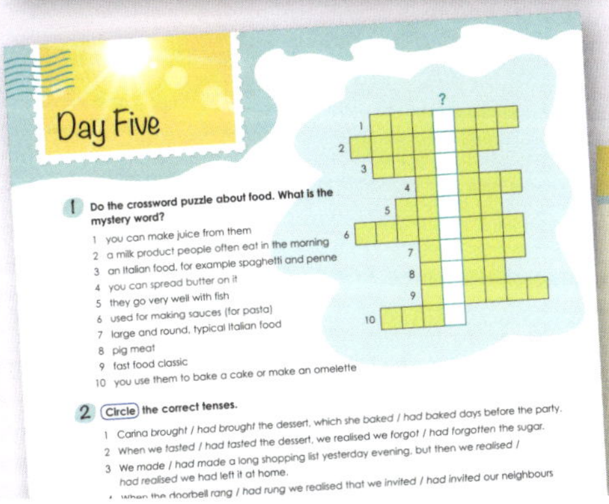

BESTELLKARTE

Infos und Prospekte bei

HELBLING
Kaplanstraße 9
A-6063 Rum
Tel. 0512 / 26 23 33-0
Fax 0512 / 26 23 33-111

E-Mail:
office@helbling.co.at

www.helblinglanguages.at

Stück	Titel	Preis
	MORE!④-DVD-ROM mit Schularbeitentraining ISBN 978-3-85272-221-4	€ 39,90
	MORE!④ Grammar Practice mit CD-ROM ISBN 978-3-85272-326-6	€ 15,50
	MORE!④ Holiday Book mit Audio-CD ISBN 978-3-85272-748-6	€ 11,90
	Princess on the Run, Paul Davenport Buch mit CD, 94 Seiten, ISBN 978-3-85272-160-6	€ 9,90
	The Adventures of Tom Sawyer, Mark Twain, adapted by David A. Hill Buch mit CD, 98 Seiten, ISBN 978-3-85272-154-5	€ 9,90
	Mr Football, Janet Olearski Buch mit CD, 94 Seiten, ISBN 978-3-85272-159-0	€ 9,90

Preisänderungen sowie Irrtum und Liefermöglichkeiten vorbehalten. Die Lieferung erfolgt zzgl. Versandkosten. Ab einem Bestellwert von € 50,00 liefern wir an Privatkunden portofrei.

Datum　　　　Unterschrift (Bei Minderjährigen der Erziehungsberechtigte)

Preisänderungen sowie Irrtum und Liefermöglichkeiten vorbehalten. Die Lieferung erfolgt zzgl. Versandkosten. Ab einem Bestellwert von € 50,00 liefern wir an Privatkunden portofrei.

MORE! INFORMATION

Liebe Eltern!

Auch fürs Englischlernen gilt: Übung macht den Meister/die Meisterin! Wer zu Hause regelmäßig übt, erzielt mit Sicherheit die besseren Leistungen.

MORE! bietet mit der MORE! DVD-ROM, MORE! Grammar Practice und den MORE! Holiday Books attraktive Materialien für das Üben zu Hause. Die Helbling Readers runden das Angebot mit interessantem Lesestoff ab.

Wie können Sie die MORE! DVD-ROM, das Grammatikheft oder die Readers bestellen?
Ganz einfach – Bestellkarte ausfüllen und an Helbling Languages schicken. Sie können die ausgefüllte Bestellkarte auch in einer Buchhandlung abgeben, um die gewünschten Produkte dort zu kaufen.

Ihrem Kind viel Spaß beim Lernen mit MORE!
wünscht das MORE!-Team

Einfach zu bestellen!

Die beiliegende Bestellkarte zum Ausschneiden einfach in einer Buchhandlung abgeben oder an folgende Adresse senden:

HELBLING Verlagsgesellschaft m.b.H. · Kaplanstraße 9 · 6063 Rum
Tel. 0512 / 26 23 33 - 0 · Fax 0512 / 26 23 33 - 111

Sie können auch via Internet bestellen.
Unsere E-Mail Adresse lautet: office@helbling.co.at

Oder besuchen Sie unsere Homepage. Hier finden Sie, neben unserem Bestellservice auch umfangreiche Poduktinformationen: www.helblinglanguages.at

Absender:
(Bitte in Blockschrift)

Vorname Familienname

Straße

Postleitzahl Ort

Schule (Name und Ort)

Bitte freimachen!

HELBLING LANGUAGES
Vertrieb f. Österreich
Helbling VerlagsGmbH

Kaplanstraße 9
6063 Rum/Innsbruck

How did Tony react when his phone rang at midnight?

- [ ] He thought it was a trick.
- [ ] He just laughed about it.
- [ ] He was really frightened.
- [ ] He answered it and heard "Your end is near".

What does "That film's rubbish" mean?

- [ ] It's fantastic.
- [ ] It's interesting.
- [ ] It's nonsense.
- [ ] It's the best film I've ever seen.

Get talking Talking about a film/events

22 CD 2

3 Listen and repeat.

A What did you do last night?
B I watched a film.
A What film was it?
B It's called *Kung Fu Panda*.
A Was it good?
B It was really funny. I loved it.
A What is it all about?
B It's about a Panda who wants to be a Kung Fu master.
A Does he become a Kung Fu master?
B Well, not really, but he saves his village.
A Sounds interesting. Maybe I can get the DVD.

4 a Ask and answer questions about films. For each answer, choose two sentences from the box.

What was the film like yesterday?

It was quite funny. I laughed a lot.

Tell me the story.

There is …

1 It was quite funny.	I laughed a lot.
2 It wasn't very good.	I turned it off.
3 It was rubbish.	I hated it.
4 It was okay.	My mum and dad watched it, too.
5 It wasn't very exciting.	I don't want the DVD.
6 It was super.	I really loved it.

b Ask and answer questions about other events in your lives. Use the phrases above.

What was your weekend / Maths lesson like?

It was awful / great!

WB p. 60
CYBER HOMEWORK 16

Progress Check Units 5–8

Listening

23 CD 2 **Listen to a scene from *The Black Heart*. Complete the sentences.**

1 Kidevil .... that Superkid has got the Black Heart.

2 The Black Heart belongs to the Masters from the .... Deco.

3 Kidevil wants to have .... over the world.

4 Superkid says Kidevil has no ....

5 Kidevil doesn't let Janet go, because he still .... her.

☐ 5

Reading

BiSt **Read the text. Then choose the correct answers to the questions.**

On his first day in the USA, George Oman lost all his money. George had left his country, Syria, because there was fighting there. When the 19 year-old landed in New York, he got in a taxi. Suddenly, the driver took out a gun and pointed it at him. "He took all my money," George said.

George called the New York police. Two nice police officers helped him. They gave him some money and put him on a train to Washington.

When he got to Washington, George looked for a job. He washed cars, sold ice cream, and worked as a taxi driver at night. He worked very hard. In 1993, he got a job doing the washing up at a small restaurant. The manager liked George. He told him to study the menu carefully so he could become a waiter. "All the food on the menu was new to me," George said. But George became a waiter. Sometimes George worked 20 hours a day! When he was tired, he slept in his car.

That was 11 years ago. George is 33 now. He's married and has two children. Today he is the manager of a big restaurant. There are six people working for him. George has made it – thanks to his hard work!

1 On George's first day in the USA,
- **a** ☐ fighting started.
- **b** ☐ he became a taxi driver.
- **c** ☐ he bought a gun.
- **d** ☐ someone took all his money.

2 In Washington, George
- **a** ☐ drove a taxi day and night.
- **b** ☐ couldn't get a job.
- **c** ☐ had more than one job.
- **d** ☐ opened his own café.

3 Then George got a job in a
- **a** ☐ dentist's office.
- **b** ☐ restaurant.
- **c** ☐ supermarket.
- **d** ☐ bank.

4 What is the best title for the text?
- **a** ☐ A day in the USA
- **b** ☐ Helpful police
- **c** ☐ A new menu
- **d** ☐ Hard work pays

☐ 4

Grammar **Circle the correct option.**

1 It's half past four. At six the bus *comes in* / *would come in* and we have to be there.
2 Hurry up. The train *leaves* / *left* in an hour.
3 I wanted to know what she *thought* / *will think* of the story.
4 He asked us where *we lived* / *did we live*.
5 After I *had been* / *was* for a run, I had a large breakfast.
6 Your garden looks really *beautifully* / *beautiful*.
7 I can *hard* / *hardly* wait for the lesson to end.
8 I want you to be very *careful* / *carefully*, Superboy.
9 You haven't met Celia, *have you* / *did you*?
10 Please tell me. I said something wrong, *haven't I* / *didn't I*?

☐ 10

Vocabulary

Match the sentences with the pictures.

a 
b 
c 
d 
e 
f 
g 
h 
i 
j 

1 I want to be a dancer when I leave school.
2 My father works outdoors.
3 Burgers aren't healthy, so I don't eat them.
4 She is overweight.
5 I like to eat fresh fruit.
6 Scientists work in labs.
7 I had a nightmare about an evil superhero.
8 We saw alligators in Florida.
9 Our flight leaves in ten minutes.
10 I got a great tan at the beach.

☐ 10

Dialogue

Match the sentences and the answers.

1 Do you want some meat with your vegetables?
2 What do you want to do when you leave school?
3 Did you get to school on time today?
4 When do you have to be at the airport?
5 Is the Czech Republic in the European Union?

☐ Yes, but I had to walk quickly.
☐ Yes, I think it is.
☐ No thanks. I'm a vegetarian.
☐ I want to work in an office.
☐ Our plane leaves at 10 a.m.

☐ 5

How did you do?

Listening		
☺ 4-5	😐 2-3	☹ 0-1

Reading		
☺ 3-4	😐 2	☹ 0-1

Grammar		
☺ 8-10	😐 5-7	☹ 0-4

Vocabulary		
☺ 7-10	😐 4-6	☹ 0-3

Dialogue		
☺ 4-5	😐 2-3	☹ 0-1

Total		
☺ 25-34	😐 14-24	☹ 0-13

▶ MORE! ONLINE PROGRESS CHECK - www.helbling-ezone.com

UNIT 9 Body talk

MP3
SbX

1 **a** **Look at the picture and the text for a minute. Cover it up and write down the names of the countries you remember.**

b **Read the text and check your answer to 1 a.**

Did you know ... ?

Body piercing and tattooing can be a serious health risk. Every year a large number of people get infections and other illnesses (even hepatitis) when needles that are not sterile are used for piercing.

The trendy ice man

What does Ötzi (the mummy found a few years ago near the Austrian-Italian border) have in common with people who want to be trendy? Body piercing! The "ice man" from about 4,000 years ago had pierced ears!

Piercing in the ancient world

In the ancient world, body piercing was often a symbol of courage and class. That's why it was popular with the Pharaohs in Egypt and with important people in ancient Rome. Tongue piercing was part of a religious ritual of the high priests of the Aztecs. They believed that if their tongues were pierced, they could communicate better with the gods.

Piercing in Africa and Central America

In these areas, people believed that demons could enter the body through the ears. So they pierced their ears and put ornaments in. They thought that the metal would stop demons from getting into the body.

Piercing in the time of Queen Elizabeth I

In Elizabethan England, a lot of famous men like Shakespeare, Sir Walter Raleigh and Sir Francis Drake wore gold rings in their ears. In those days, sailors also wore earrings, for two reasons: firstly, they thought they could see better if their ears were pierced; and secondly, they thought, "If our ship sinks and we die, and our bodies are found on the beach, the gold earrings will pay for our funeral."

Piercing today

In the United States in the 1960s, body piercing became a form of rebellion for young people. Later, it lost its rebellious meaning and just became fashionable: because more and more film stars and sports stars were getting pierced, young people wanted to imitate them.

2 What is the best title for the text?

a Piercing means protesting
b A short history of piercing
c Piercing in the old days
d The future of piercing

3 CHOICES

a Read the text again. Tick the sentences T (*True*) or F (*False*).

		T	F
1	Piercing was used a long time ago.	☐	☐
2	In Egypt and in ancient Rome, poor people often had their bodies pierced.	☐	☐
3	People in North America had their ears pierced to stop demons from entering their bodies.	☐	☐
4	English sailors thought they could hear better if their ears were pierced.	☐	☐
5	In the US, young people first had their body pierced as a sign of protest.	☐	☐
6	Body piercing can be very dangerous.	☐	☐

★ **b Read the text again. Find words in the text that mean:**

1 very fashionable
2 very old / from a long time ago
3 devils
4 a ceremony when a dead body is buried or burned
5 to do the same as someone else / copy

Get talking

BiSt **4 Work in pairs. One of you will play the role of a teenager (A), the other one the role of a parent (B). You have one minute to prepare your discussion. Use the prompt cards to help you. Talk for four minutes.**

Prompt Card A:

You are 14. You want to have your nose pierced. Your parents are very strict. You don't want a fight, but you want to discuss the situation with your parents and hope they will give you their permission.

You start the discussion – you can use the following arguments if you want to:

- Body piercing isn't new. (Give examples.)
- You think it looks good. (Some stars have it, too.)
- You are 14 – you want to decide for yourself.
- Lots of your friends have done it.
- You will pay for it with your pocket money.

Prompt Card B:

You are a strict parent. You are absolutely against body piercing. Your son/daughter wants to talk with you about getting their nose pierced. You are very worried about this, but you want to talk about the situation.

Your daughter/son starts the discussion. You can use the following arguments if you want to:

- You aren't interested in hearing how old body piercing is.
- You think body piercing looks awful.
- 14-year-olds can't decide for themselves – their parents have to.
- You don't care what your son's / daughter's friends do.
- Piercing can be a health risk.

▶ WB p. 63

5 CHOICES

MP3
BiSt

a READ THE TEXTS

1 **Match them with the photos. (One text doesn't have a photo!)**

2 **Put the missing expressions in the texts.**

are "dirty"	"No"	It's a rude sign
is unclean	feel good	not polite

Middle and Far East:
Do not point with your index finger. It is [1]..................... . Only point with an open hand, never with your index finger.

Thailand:
Do not show the soles of your feet or shoes! People think the soles [2]..................... .

Austria/Japan:
We smile when we [3]..................... . In Japan, people may smile also when they are confused or angry.

The "V" sign means victory in many countries. But don't turn the palm of your hand towards your face. [4]..................... in some countries.

Middle/Far East:
Don't give something to another person with your left hand. People could be hurt. They think the left hand [5]..................... .

Greece/Bulgaria:
Do you think nodding your head up and down means "Yes"? You might be surprised if you go to Greece or Bulgaria. In those countries, nodding means [6].......... !

WB p. 64

★ b A STORY: GOTH

Vocabulary Weddings

24 CD 2

1 Listen to the words. Look at the picture. Where can you see:

a a bride?
b a wedding dress?
c a bridegroom?
d a wedding suit?
e a bridesmaid?

The bride is number …

2 Look at the girl in the picture. Would you like to be her friend? Why / Why not?

MP3 SbX BiSt

3 Read the story and choose the best title for it.

☐ They both giggled ☐ Unfunny Uncle Jack ☐ The spider's web ☐ It must be her age

When mum and I came into the sitting room, Aunt Nancy sighed and Uncle Jack looked at me and shouted, "Look, it's Dracula's daughter!" And then he laughed like mad. I ignored them and walked across their horrible orange carpet to the sofa. From there I could see myself in the mirror.

I looked cool.

I looked goth.

Black clothes, fishnet stockings, heavy boots. White face, black eyeliner, black lipstick. Totally, totally goth.

They all looked at me. Mum said, "It's her age, you know. It's a phase." Aunt Nancy smiled sadly and Uncle Jack said, "Does it speak?" "Ha-ha!" I said. "Yes, I can hear and speak." "Good," he said, "because with all that black stuff round your eyes, you probably can't see." He looked at mum and his wife for some applause and they both giggled.

"I hope she doesn't look like that on the wedding day," Aunt Nancy said. "Joy wouldn't want her to look like that." "Oh no," Mum said quickly. "She'll wear the dress Joy bought for her. Won't you, Felicity?" "Mum, please!" I said. "Sorry, Flicka – as she likes to be called now," Mum said to Aunt Nancy. "And what's that on its neck?" Uncle Jack shouted. "A tattoo," I said. "A tattoo of a spider's web." "Not a real one!" Mum said, hastily again. "It's a wash-off one." "Wash-off, eh?" my uncle said.I ignored him. I was embarrassed. I would have liked a real tattoo and not my wash-off one. I didn't say anything for the rest of the evening.

The dress Joy gave me was terrible. All violet and white and cute. But I've always liked my cousin Joy. "I know I'm asking a lot, but I really want you to wear it for the wedding," Joy said. "You're my bridesmaid and I want everything to be just right."

On the day of the wedding, I felt terrible. But Joy looked really happy, so I tried to smile, too. Everyone was wearing suits and flowery dresses – yuck. And then I saw a decent-looking boy. He had a suit and short hair, but he didn't look bad. Not bad at all.

A few minutes later he walked over to me. "Cousin of the bride?" he said. "Yes," I said. "And who are you?" "I'm Lawrence. Cousin of the bridegroom."

BiSt

4 Read the story again. Write letters for the people's names next to the sentences.

Which of the people in the story

1 was a goth? ....F....
2 called Felicity "Dracula's daughter"? ....
3 didn't find Uncle Jack's jokes funny at all? ....
4 had a wedding? ....
5 was the bridesmaid? ....
6 bought a dress for Felicity? ....
7 was the cousin of Joy's future husband? ....
8 thought Lawrence was good-looking? ....

Felicity = **F**
Uncle Jack = **U**
Joy = **J**
Lawrence = **L**

25 CD 2

5 Listen to the ending of the story. Then put the pictures into the correct order.

26 CD 2

6 Underline the correct words to get a summary of the story. Then listen and check. Write the text into your exercise book.

Felicity hated normal *clothes* / *people*. She liked black clothes and heavy boots. She liked having a *white* / *black* face, black eyeliner and black lipstick. Felicity was a goth. Uncle Jack made lots of jokes about her.

But then Joy, Felicity's *cousin* / *mother*, had her *wedding* / *birthday*. Felicity was her bridesmaid. Joy bought her a *dress* / *skirt*. It was violet and white. Felicity didn't like it. But she liked Joy, so she put the dress on. On the day of the wedding Felicity met a boy, Lawrence. Lawrence was wearing a normal suit. But Felicity *liked* / *hated* him.

Later at the wedding party, Felicity put on her goth clothes again. Suddenly she saw that Lawrence had changed his *money* / *clothes* too.
He was also a goth. Felicity was very *sad* /*surprised*. Uncle Jack was surprised, too.

NOTE:
Writing a summary
- Use present tense
- Use important information only
- Type the text, so that you can easily shorten it if it is too long.

Free flow

BiSt **6 Read the questions. You have one minute to prepare them. Now you are going to talk for two minutes.**

1 Which countries have you been to?
2 How many people from different cultures have you met?
3 What things are the same in other cultures as in your own? (Food, family life, school life, sports, …).
4 What things are different?

I've been to …
A few years ago I went to…
My mum / dad / sister / brother / friend went on trip to…
He / She told me that there … / people don't …

I know a family who moved to Austria from … They …
One of our neighbours is from … .
He / She …

Sounds right /p/ at the beginning of words

27 CD 2 **7 Listen and say the sentences as quickly as possible.**

Young people use pocket money to pay for piercings.
Parents aren't prepared to pay the price or give permission!

8 CHOICES

Writing *for your Portfolio*

BiSt **a Look at prompt card A in 4 again. Write a note (40 – 70 words) to your parents telling them you want a piercing.**

★ **b Imagine you are Felicity ("Flicka") or Lawrence. You write about the wedding in your diary.**

Write about:

- the clothes you had to wear for the wedding ceremony and what you thought of them
- the boy/girl you met at the wedding
- the evening you spent with him/her at the party
- your feelings for him/her.

DVD The Mag 6 A visitor abroad

1 Watch the story. Circle the correct answer.

1 Katia is *Jessica's / Lucy's* penfriend.
2 Katia's *mum / dad* is from Hungary.
3 The headmaster didn't like Katia's *shoes / boots*.
4 Lucy *wants / doesn't want* to do a story on school uniforms.
5 Most people at the school *are / aren't* in favour of school uniforms.
6 *Nick / Liam* wants to take photos of Katia.

2 Complete the sentences.

1 Nick speaks slowly to Katia because …
2 Katia speaks perfect English because …
3 The headmaster objects to Katia's shoes because …
4 Lucy doesn't want to do an article on school uniforms because …
5 Nick wants to take photos of Katia because …

Everyday English

3 Say the missing words. Practise the dialogues.

Don't mention it. That's settled. Pleased to meet you I'll see what I can do.

▶ WB p. 63

Free flow

BiSt ★ **9** **a In pairs, do the following: Choose one question and tell your partner all you can think of. Talk as long as you can. Your partner times you.**

1 Would you ever consider getting your nose pierced? Why / Why not?
2 Would you ever consider getting a tattoo? Why / Why not?
3 Would you like to wear a school uniform? Why / Why not?
4 How much do you care about what you look like?

b Tell your partner which of his / her ideas you found most interesting and why. Tell your partner how long he / she was talking.

SbX

Grammar

might / may / could (possibility)

Circle the correct words:

Wenn du über [1] *Möglichkeiten / Wahrscheinlichkeiten* sprechen willst, kannst du die Modalverben **might** / **may** / **could** verwenden.

If you go to Greece or Bulgaria, you **might be** surprised.
It is a rude sign in some cultures and **might insult** people.

Japanese people **may smile** if they're confused or angry.
These questions **may help** you.

It **could get** you into trouble in Brazil.

Nach einem Modalverb kommt immer die [2] *Nennform / -ing Form.*

MORE fun with Fido!

WB p. 65

28 CD 2 BiSt

1 Listen to the dialogue and fill in the missing words and phrases.

Nadia What are you [1]... ?
Harry Today is Friday.
Nadia I know. So what?
Harry It's my dad's birthday in two days. I want to get him a special [2]... .
Nadia Why special?
Harry Dad helped me a lot with my Maths homework.
Nadia You're lucky. Nobody helped me. What would your dad like?
Harry I'm [3]... .
Nadia What are his hobbies?
Harry He likes going fishing.
Nadia That's easy then. There's a shop over there that sells fishing stuff.
Harry He's got [4]... for fishing.
Nadia What about giving him chocolates?
Harry He doesn't like [5].................................. . What did you give your dad for his last birthday?
Nadia My dad reads a lot. So I got him a book.
Harry Yes, that's it. Let's go over to the book store.
Nadia Yeah, let's [6]... books about fishing.

28 CD 2 BiSt

2 Now cover up the dialogue. Listen again and tick the correct answer. Then look at the dialogue and check.

What is the dialogue about?

- ☐ finding the right present for Harry's father
- ☐ buying birthday presents for parents
- ☐ the present that Nadia bought for her dad's last birthday
- ☐ trying to find a present for Nadia's father

Harry …

- ☐ likes Nadia's ideas about what to buy.
- ☐ isn't interested in what Nadia wants to buy.
- ☐ tries to help Nadia to decide what to buy.
- ☐ is in a hurry and has no time to listen to Nadia.

Vocabulary Presents

3 **Write the words below the pictures.**

MP3-player snowboard necklace bracelet earrings
clothes diary mobile phone globe microscope

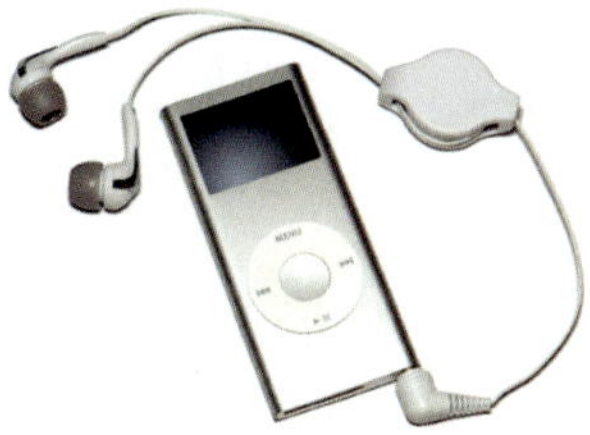
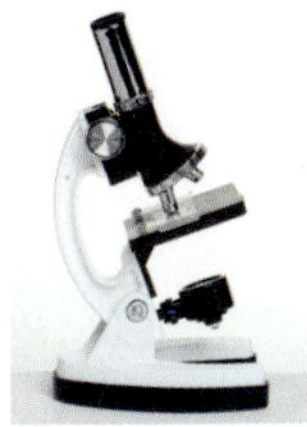

1 .... 2 .... 3 .... 4 .... 5 ....

6 .... 7 .... 8 .... 9 .... 10 ....

4 **Read and act out the dialogues.**

Adam What would you like for your birthday?
Daisy A microscope.
Adam Do you think you'll get it?
Daisy I don't know. It's pretty expensive.

Adam What would you like for your birthday?
Mia A bracelet.
Adam Do you think you'll get it?
Mia Yes, I'm sure. I heard mum telling my aunt on the phone.

5 **Act out similar dialogues.**

6 **Play the game with your partner. A thinks of a gift for B. B has got twenty questions to guess it. A can only answer with "Yes" or "No".**

Is it for indoors / outdoors?
Is it cheap / expensive?
Is it for school / free time?
Is it small / big / round / useful / heavy?
Can I play with it? Can I watch it? Can I listen to it? Can I read it?
Do I use it every day?
Is it made of plastic / metal / paper / wood?
Do I use it when I …

WB p. 66 CYBER HOMEWORK 18

UNIT 10 Crazy collectors

NOTE:
- *sand is normally only used in singular.*
- *sands is rare and means "types of sand".*

MP3 SbX BiSt

1 Look at the photo and the text for thirty seconds. What does the man collect? When did he start? Then read the magazine article carefully and check your answers.

From left to right:
Nick D'Errico, director of the International Sand Collector's Society
(1) Star Sand, Tonga, South Pacific
(2) Sacoma, Majorca
(3) Coromandel, New Zealand
(4) Papakolea, Hawaii

Mr Sandman

Sun, sea and surf are the last things on Nick D'Errico's mind during a trip to the beach. An interview with a sand collector.

How did your fascination with sand begin?

It all started on my honeymoon. My wife and I went to Jamaica. When I was walking along the beach one day, I decided to collect some sand to take home with me. I did it to have some memories of our wonderful holiday. I wasn't thinking of starting a new hobby then.

Why did you change your mind?

My wife worked for a travel agent and her colleagues started bringing sand for me from lots of exotic places. When I looked at the sands through a microscope, I discovered that they were all different. ☐ I was fascinated. That's how it all started.

How many kinds of sand do you have and where do you keep them?

I've collected between 18,000 and 19,000 different kinds of sand since I started my hobby. Last year I got a wonderful collection from a geology professor in North Carolina. It took four days for the two of us to pack them all up. The total weight was 2,722 kilos. ☐ They're still in the packages they arrived in and they have taken over the whole house.

What is the most expensive sand?

Probably moon sand. ☐ It hasn't turned up on the black market yet, but when it does, it will go for a lot of money.

If I wanted to become a sand collector, how would I go about it?

Just go to the beach and stand there. Take your time and look closely. ☐ Start comparing the sands. When you see how different they all are, your fascination will begin.

How many members are there in the Sand Society?

The Sand Society started about 40 years ago. It had only six members, but since then 240 people in 14 countries have joined. We also have a magazine called *The Sand Paper* with news for our members.

Check out www.sandcollectors.org for more!

BiSt

2 Four sentences are missing from the text above. Find them in the list below and write the correct numbers in the boxes in the text. Careful – one sentence is not from the text!

1 I have not unpacked most of them.
2 It costs thousands and thousands of dollars to make a few tons.
3 The sands were different in colour, size and shape.
4 Not long ago some very rare moon sand was stolen.
5 Take sand from different places on the beach.

Vocabulary

29 CD 2

3 Listen and write the words under the pictures.

monastery
library
librarian
monk
robber
bookshop
an expensive old book

1 

....

2 
....

3 

....

4 
....

5 
....

6 
....

7 
....

4 CHOICES

30 CD 2

Listen to this true story. It is about a man called Don Vicente. He loved books, but in an abnormal way.

a Which picture is about the true ending of the story: A, B or C?

Ending A

Ending B

Ending C

★ **b Complete the sentences with the words from 3. Use one word twice.**

1 Don Vicente was a .... in a monastery in Tarragona, Spain.
2 He worked as a ....
3 One day .... broke into the .... They stole gold, silver and old books.
4 Don Vicente moved to Barcelona where he opened a special ....
5 One day Don Vicente saw a .... He wanted to buy it, but he couldn't.
6 A bookseller named Augustino Patxot bought the book. Don Vicente was very angry. Three days later there was a fire in Augustino's .... Augustino was dead.

WB p. 69

MP3 BiSt

5 **Read through the text quickly to answer the questions.**

1 How old was Colin Watson when he died?
2 How many eggs did he have in his collection?

guardian.co.uk News

The egg collection with the RSPB.

Above: The golden eagle – one of the rarest birds in England
Right: Eggs in the nest

The day Britain's biggest egg collector climbed his last tree

Man falls to his death from tree while checking out unusual nest

Martin Wainwright • Saturday May 27 • The Guardian

Colin Watson's hobby was illegal, because since 1954 it has been against the law to take the eggs of wild birds. On a windy afternoon this week, Colin Watson risked too much. While a friend watched in horror, Watson, 63, fell out of a 12-metre tree he had climbed to check out yet another unusual bird's nest. The ambulance arrived soon afterwards, but the father of three died at the scene from his injuries.

Watson had started his hobby as a schoolboy. In those days, egg collecting was not illegal. He grew up in a town called Selby and some of his older neighbours were experienced egg collectors. They showed the boy how to blow eggs – to remove their contents through tiny holes. They also showed him how to start a collection.

Later, Watson became the biggest collector of wild birds' eggs in Britain. He was arrested many times for breaking the law and the police fined him thousands of pounds. Some years ago, officers of the RSPB (The Royal Society for the Protection of Birds) went to Watson's house to search for his collection. They were shocked to find more than 2,000 eggs, among them eggs of the very rare golden eagle.

"This is a very tragic incident," said Graham Madge of the RSPB yesterday. "It is very sad Mr Watson's life ended like this, but what he did to the birds was also a tragedy!"

6 **CHOICES**

BiSt

a **Read the newspaper article in 5 carefully.**
Tick the right answers to complete the sentences.

1 Colin Watson died when
- a ☐ the police wanted to arrest him.
- b ☐ he was playing hide-and-seek with his son.
- c ☐ he was looking into the nest of a rare bird.
- d ☐ he was bird watching.

2 When Colin Watson died,
- a ☐ his three children were there.
- b ☐ the ambulance was not there.
- c ☐ he was completely alone.
- d ☐ he was with a friend.

3 When Colin was a schoolboy, egg collecting was
- a ☐ a hobby for children only.
- b ☐ done by most children.
- c ☐ forbidden for boys.
- d ☐ not forbidden at all.

4 In the UK, egg collecting has been forbidden for
- a ☐ more than 10 years.
- b ☐ more than 50 years.
- c ☐ more than 80 years.
- d ☐ more than 90 years.

▶ WB pp. 70, 71

★ **b Read the newspaper article in (5) carefully.**

1 Underline the words or phrases in the newspaper article in (5) that mean:

1. not allowed by the law (*paragraph 1*)
2. to look at something carefully in order to find out what it is like (*paragraph 1*)
3. be good at something because you have done it often (*paragraph 2*)
4. very small (*paragraph 2*)
5. to make someone pay money because they have done something wrong (*paragraph 3*)
6. to look for something (*paragraph 3*)

2 Answer the questions.

1. When did Mr Watson start his dangerous hobby?
2. How did he learn to become a collector?
3. In what way did his hobby change over the years?
4. Why is egg collecting forbidden these days?

(7) CHOICES

Get talking

BiSt **a Talk to a partner for 3 – 4 minutes. The prompts will help you to think about the topic and ask questions. You have one minute to prepare.**

COLLECTING THINGS

- Have you ever …?
- Have you still got …?
- What do … think about …?
- What?
- Why?
- How many?
- good / bad things about collecting things
- Who from? / Where from?
- How long?
- Where do you keep …?

Report to the class.

I interviewed three classmates. One collected … when he/she was … He/She still has got … One collects … He/She has collected … since/for … He's/She's got … One has never collected anything, but knows someone who …

Free flow

BiSt ★ **b Talk about collectors for 1 – 2 minutes. The questions will help you to think about the topic. Take one minute to prepare.**

- What have you heard / read about collectors?
- Why are people called "crazy collectors"?
- What do you think about them?
- What do you think about people who collect birds' eggs, butterflies …?
- Do you know anybody who collects unusual things?
- What do they collect?
- Would you like to be a collector? Why / Why not?

▶ WB pp. 70, 71 ▶ CYBER HOMEWORK 19

Writing *for your Portfolio*

BiSt **8** **Write a short text (40 – 70 words) about collecting things for a game in class. Take about 10 minutes and write about:**

- what you collect
- when you first got the idea
- how many of the things you have collected
- what you can use the things for
- what other people think about you.

BiSt SbX **9** **a Read the following texts quickly and answer the questions.**

1 When did each of these people start collecting?
2 How many things have they collected so far?

Marcela T. is 30 and works as a photographer in Buenos Aires, Argentina. She has a rather unusual hobby: she collects tea bags. She started her hobby five years ago when she was in England for a holiday with her husband. They were sitting in a tea house and had ordered some tea. The waiter brought a pot of hot water and a wooden box with lots of different tea bags. Marcela, who had never really looked at tea bags before, began to study them carefully. She saw how colourful and attractive they were. So she asked friends to bring tea bags back from their holidays. So far, she has collected over 5,000 tea bags from 49 different countries.

John M. is 26 and he has a rather unusual hobby. He collects toilet seats. He started collecting them after his 20th birthday, when he was working as a plumber. He saw the bathrooms in many different houses and found it interesting how many different kinds of toilet seats people had. So one day he started collecting them and he has collected over 600 so far. At first, he kept them all in his house, but then there wasn't enough space any more. He rented an old factory near his hometown, Portsmouth, in the south of England, and that's where he keeps them all – 600 toilet seats from quite a few countries! John's friends think he is crazy. He thinks he has an interesting hobby!

b Now read the texts again more carefully. Find out what motivated them to start their collections.

SbX

Grammar

Present perfect versus past simple (Revision)

Read the sentences. Then answer the questions.

1) **I've collected** between 18,000 and 19,000 different kinds of sand since I began my hobby.
2) Last year I **got** a wonderful collection from a geology professor in North Carolina.
3) Some of his neighbours **showed** the boy how to start an egg collection.
4) In the UK, egg collecting **has been forbidden** for more than 50 years.

1 Which of these sentences talk about actions that:

a began in the past and are still going on? ....

b began in the past and are finished? ....

2 Which of the sentences are in the *past simple* and which are in the *present perfect*?

....

3 "... has been forbidden for more than 50 years" in the last sentence above means in German:

a ist verboten ☐

b war verboten ☐

c ist verboten worden ☐

Time expressions

Look at the sentences. Then complete the rule with the correct tense.

1) You often use the following time expressions with the .... : *yesterday / last year (month, weekend, Friday, ...) / in 2003 / 2 months ago*
2) You often use the following time expressions with the .... : *just / already / never / (not) yet* [= noch nicht]

MORE fun with Fido!

WB pp. 71, 72

31 CD 2 BiSt

1 **Listen to the dialogue and fill in the missing words and phrases.**

Sally Harry? Were you in my [1].. yesterday?
Harry No, I wasn't. Why?
Sally I can't find my [2].. .
Harry Well, I wasn't in there. I was in the living room. There was a football game [3].. .
Sally When was that?
Harry From 8 to 10.
Sally [4]..! I was there at half past 9. You weren't there.
Harry I was. Dad and I were there all the time.
Sally Mum!
Mum What is it?
Sally I can't find my diary. I think Harry was in my room.
Harry No, I wasn't.
Mum Your diary? It's in the kitchen. On the [5].. . You were there yesterday evening. With your diary.
Sally Was I? Ah, I [6]... . Sorry, Harry. Mum, is my MP3-player there too?
Harry Your MP3-player? Err, um …
Sally What?
Harry The game [7]...................................... so …
Sally Harry!!

31 CD 2

2 **Now cover up the dialogue. Listen again and tick the sentences T (*True*) or F (*False*). Then look at the dialogue and check.**

		T	F
1	Sally can't find her diary.	☐	☐
2	Harry was in the living room from 8 to half past nine.	☐	☐
3	Sally was there at 10 o'clock, too.	☐	☐
4	Mum has got the diary.	☐	☐
5	It was in the hall.	☐	☐
6	Sally is sorry.	☐	☐
7	Harry wasn't in her room.	☐	☐

BiSt **3** **Read the text and tick the correct answers.**

Yesterday I was late for karate training. When Mum came home from work I said, "Can you take me to karate practice, please? It's raining."
"Sure," said Mum. I just want to eat an orange." So she ate the orange and we put on our coats. But at the door she said, "Where are my car keys?" "I'm sure you put them on the kitchen table," I answered. We looked there and everywhere else in the kitchen, but we couldn't find the keys. We looked in the hall. We checked the car. Nothing. "Let's think," said Mum. "When did I last have the keys?" Then I had an idea. "The keys were on the table when you ate your orange. Maybe you threw them into the rubbish bin with the orange peel." And sure enough, there they were.

1 Where is the text taken from?

a ☐ a book of jokes
b ☐ a collection of teenage stories
c ☐ an advertisement for a karate school
d ☐ a report about how much people forget

2 What is the best title for this text?

a ☐ The stolen car keys
b ☐ Karate training on a rainy day
c ☐ Don't peel your oranges!
d ☐ A surprise in the rubbish bin

3 Where did they NOT look for the keys?

a ☐ in the kitchen
b ☐ in the coats
c ☐ in the car
d ☐ in the hall

4 What does "orange peel" mean?

a ☐ the part of the orange that you do not eat
b ☐ an orange that is so sour you cannot eat it
c ☐ the paper bag in which you buy oranges
d ☐ vitamin C

BiSt **4** **Work in pairs. You are on the way home from school. One of you has just discovered that he or she has lost something important. The other tries to be helpful. Take two minutes to prepare your discussion. Use the prompt cards to help you. Talk for four minutes.**

Prompt Card A

You are on your way home from school. Suddenly you notice that you have lost something important. You are with a friend. He/She is trying to be helpful.

- Decide what it is that you have lost.
- What does it look like?
- Why is it so important for you? What can you not do without it?
- When did you last have it?
- What could you do to find it?

Prompt Card B

You are with a friend, and you are on your way home from school. Suddenly your friend notices that he/she has lost something important. You are trying to be helpful.

- Find out what your friend has lost.
- Find out what it looks like.
- Ask why it is so important for your friend. What could he/she not do without it?
- As your friend when he/she last had it?
- Make suggestions about what your friend could do.

▶ WB p. 73 ▶ CYBER HOMEWORK 20

UNIT 11 A fair world?

Coffee beans are ...

Did you know ... ?

Coffee is the most popular drink in the world.

52% of Americans drink coffee.

Australians drink 60% more coffee than tea.

A coffee tree can produce up to 6 kilos of coffee a year.

Brazil produces a third of the world's coffee.

Oil is the number 1 thing that is bought and sold in the world. Coffee is number 2.

MP3 SbX

1 **a** **Look at the pictures and guess the answers to these questions:**

1. Who are the people?
2. Where do they live?
3. What are they doing?

b **Read the text and check your answers.**

2 **Complete the fact sheet about Juanita and Ramon.**

Juanita has a small ... in ...
She works very ... , but ...
She hasn't got a car, a ... , a ... or a ... .
Every morning she listens to ...
because she ...
She would have sold the farm if ...

Ramon is not as worried about ... as ...
Ramon doesn't listen ...
Ramon gets a fixed ...
Ramon is part of a ...

Hard work for little money

Juanita Carlos has a small coffee farm in the hills of Honduras. She works very hard, getting up at daybreak and getting to bed very late, but she can never save any money. She has just enough to buy food and clothes for herself and for her two children and her mother. She hasn't got a car, she hasn't got a TV, she only has an old fridge and a small radio. She listens to the radio every morning. She wants to hear what they say about the price of coffee in faraway New York. The news she hears is usually bad. Coffee prices are low and Juanita is very worried.

"If I had known that coffee prices would go down so much, I would have sold the farm a long time ago," Juanita says. Where Juanita lives, all the small farmers and their families are as poor as she is.

... dried ...

... & roasted.

Ramon Machado's farm is only three hours away from Juanita's. Ramon is not as worried as Juanita and he doesn't listen to the radio every morning to find out about coffee prices. Ramon and twenty other farmers are part of a Fair Trade project. They get a fixed price for their coffee. They don't use pesticides. On their small farms there are lots of trees that give shade to the coffee plants and there are also banana trees and avocado trees. This is good for the environment.

Ramon joined the project a year ago. If he had known that Fair Trade pays a fixed price, he would have joined earlier. Now he is happy because he doesn't have to worry about feeding his children or buying them clothes or books for school.

3 CHOICES

1 CD 3 BiSt

Listen to a journalist talking about coffee.

a Tick the correct information.

1 What percent of the world's coffee is grown on small farms?

- **a** ☐ 40%
- **b** ☐ 60%
- **c** ☐ 70%
- **d** ☐ 90%

2 When was the International Coffee Agreement stopped?

- **a** ☐ in 1969
- **b** ☐ in 1989
- **c** ☐ in 1999
- **d** ☐ in 1889

3 What was the minimum price for half a kilo of coffee?

- **a** ☐ 50 cents
- **b** ☐ $1.00
- **c** ☐ $1.20
- **d** ☐ $3.20

4 What is the price now?

- **a** ☐ 50 cents
- **b** ☐ $1.00
- **c** ☐ $1.20
- **d** ☐ $2.80

5 How much do the big buyers get when they sell it?

- **a** ☐ less than $2.00
- **b** ☐ around $3.00
- **c** ☐ more than $12.00
- **d** ☐ more than $7.00

Free flow

★ **b Discuss these questions.**

1 Are there any shops that sell Fair Trade products where you live?
2 Why are Fair Trade products more expensive than "normal" products?
3 Do you buy Fair Trade products? Why / Why not?

▶ WB pp. 76, 77

SbX BiSt

4 a **Who is the man in the picture? What do you know about him?**

b **Read the blog entries and find out who:**

- believes the colour of your skin is not important.
- believes her father makes racist comments.
- has a friend who has been a victim of racism.
- believes that black people are ignored by history.

★ c **Look at the underlined words in the text. What does each one refer to?**

E.g. they're refers to *"whites"/ white people*

Diary Project | **Living together in harmony**

Racism

The man in the picture is Martin Luther King. He was the winner of the Nobel Peace Prize. He had a dream – black and white people living together in harmony.

Racism comes from fear of other cultures. But we're all the same – we're just human beings. Write us an email in the form of a diary entry.

Why are blacks always put down? (by Martin J, 15, male)

Whites often believe they're better than black people. But what about the positive things blacks are doing? It's painful that even in history books blacks are not respected enough for their work. Blacks have done great things in history that many people don't know about.
If black slaves hadn't built America, it wouldn't have become the country we know. Our grandfathers overcame slavery. Let's all work together now – we can overcome racism!

wHo I aM (by Hannah, 16, female)

I'm sick of white people saying "I'm white" and black people saying "I'm black." And please don't ask me "Who are you?" I'll tell you who I am: I AM A HUMAN BEING, JUST LIKE YOU!!! Some people say I look Spanish – but so what???? Does it really matter? Does it really make a difference?

Hurtful comments (by Amy, 14, female)

Whenever my dad sees me watching TV shows or listening to music with a black actor or singer/rapper, he makes a comment like "Look at my little black girl." I'm white. He also says he's going to have a son-in-law who's black. I don't understand why he makes the comments. I hang out with a lot of black people. I'm not trying to be them, I just love hanging out with my black friends. I have white friends, too and I wish my dad would think before he makes comments that hurt my feelings.

Why???? (by Jason, 15, male)

I can't BELIEVE what happened today! Some idiots threw EGGS at K's house because she's Middle Eastern!!!! It was awful: the stink of half-rotten eggs and the foot-high letters in red spray paint on the garage door TERRORISTS GO HOME. Why would people attack my best friend just because of her religion and where she's from????? I helped her clean it up ... she was crying. I'd never seen her cry before. I can't see why people would do this when she's just trying to be a normal 16-year-old!

Vocabulary

5 **Use a dictionary to find the meaning of the words below.**

angry	helpless	proud
annoyed	hurt	shocked
frustrated	misunderstood	surprised

6 CHOICES

Get talking

a **Work with a partner. For each blog entry, say how the writers feel and what they believe and want to achieve.**

Martin Hannah Amy Jason	feels	annoyed because hurt by … because … shocked because … helpless because … angry because … frustrated because … surprised because … proud of … misunderstood by …

Martin Hannah …	believes thinks	it is wrong that … most people … whites / blacks … everybody / nobody should …
	wants	people / … father /… / to …
	claims	that people don't …

★ **b** **Say what you think about racism.**

In my opinion, …
I feel very strongly that …

I see what you mean.
I can / can't understand that / why …
I think people should …

A song 4 U *Ebony and Ivory (Paul McCartney and Stevie Wonder)*

2/3 CD 3

7 **a** **Use a dictionary to check the meaning of words you do not understand.**

b **Listen and say what the message of the song is.**

Ebony and ivory
live together
in perfect harmony,
side by side
on my piano keyboard.
Oh lord, why don't we?

We all know
that people are the same
wherever you go.
There is good and bad
in everyone.
We learn to live,
we learn to give
each other
what we need to survive
– together alive.

WB p. 78 CYBER HOMEWORK 21

Writing *for your Portfolio*

BiSt

a Write about an unfair situation you remember (120 – 180 words). Write about:

• what happened • how you felt • what you did • what you think you should have done.

★ **b Work in groups and design a website.**

www.A FAIR WORLD.com

Fair food | Fair to planet earth | Fair to animals | Racial fairness

On the road to hell!

There are over 600 million cars in the world today. Experts say that the number of cars on Earth will double in the next 30 years. This creates a lot of problems.

Firstly, lots of cars mean a lot of pollution. The air in some of the big cities has become so bad that many people suffer from the smog. But it's not only people who suffer – pollution is bad for trees, rivers and lakes.

Secondly, there are lots of accidents every year because there are so many cars. It is terrible that one million people every year die from road accidents.

So what can we do? I think there should be more buses and trains in big cities and people should use them more often. But there should also be more bicycle tracks so people can ride their bikes safely.

Prepare your website

a Work in groups of three or four. Create a website for a fair world.

b Go through the unit again. Which of the texts in the unit go with *Fair food*, and which ones go with *Racial fairness*?

c Check on the Internet for ideas you want to write about, e.g. fair trade, fair food, racial fairness, fairness to animals, fairness to the planet Earth, …

d Brainstorm ideas for your website in groups.

e Each student in the group chooses one of the topics.

Make your website

a Write your texts. Look at the model above:
Paragraph 1 is an introduction. It says that cars create lots of problems.
Paragraph 2 gives an example of a problem. (Firstly, …)
Paragraph 3 gives another example of a problem. (Secondly, …)
Paragraph 4 makes suggestions about what could be done to improve the situation. (So what can we do to …? I think there should be … People should … But there should also be …)
Don't forget to give your text an interesting title!

b Read the texts out in your group. Try to make them better.

c Find pictures in magazines or from the internet. Put the texts and the pictures on a big sheet of paper. Find a catchy title for your website.

d Hang your "web pages" up on the wall.

SbX

Grammar

Revision of 1st and 2nd Conditional

1 If I get a good price, I will sell the farm.
2 If I got a good price, I would sell the farm.

If you had read the invitation, you would have known what to wear.

Write 1 or 2.

.... : Der/Die Sprecher/in würde die Farm verkaufen, wenn er/sie ein gutes Angebot erhielte.

.... : Der/Die Sprecher/in wird die Farm verkaufen, wenn er/sie ein gutes Angebot erhält.

3rd Conditional

If I **had known** that coffee prices would go down, I **would have sold** the farm long ago.
If black slaves **hadn't built** America, it **wouldn't have become** the country we know.

Tick the correct statement.

☐ Der/Die Sprecher/in redet über etwas, das in der Vergangenheit liegt. Es ist nicht mehr zu ändern.
☐ Er/Sie redet über etwas, das in der Zukunft liegt. Er/Sie kann es vielleicht ändern.

Form:

If-Satz	Hauptsatz
If + Person + ***past perfect***	Person + **would (not) have + *past participle***

MORE fun with Fido!

WB pp. 78, 79

4 CD 3 BiSt

1 Listen to the dialogue and fill in the missing words and phrases.

Asher Hey, Nadia. We're going to South America in the summer.
Nadia Wow! Where are you going?
Asher Texas.
Nadia That's not South America. Didn't you [1].. in Geography?
Asher Not really. The subject is pretty boring. It's hot in Texas that's why I [2].. it's in South America.
Nadia It is hot [3].., but Texas isn't in South America. It's in the south of the USA. The USA is North America.
Asher Sorry. South America is Mexico, isn't it?
Nadia No. Mexico is in [4].. .
Asher Hang on. What's South America then?
Nadia Well, for example Brazil, Argentina, Chile, …
Asher Alright. Sorry. I need to go.
Nadia Where are you going?
Asher I need to look at a good [5].. . I want to see where Texas is.
Nadia Hey. Shall I also teach you some History?
Asher No, please don't.

4 CD 3

2 Now cover up the dialogue. Listen again and underline the correct word in each sentence. Then look at the dialogue and check.

1 Asher is going to *Mexico* / *Texas* in the summer.
2 He thinks Texas is in *South* / *North* America.
3 Texas is in *the USA* / *Central America*.
4 Mexico is in *the USA* / *Central America*.
5 Brazil and Argentina are in *South* / *Central* America.
6 Asher thinks he needs to look at his *atlas* / *Geography book*.

Vocabulary Subjects

3 Write the words under the pictures.

Geography History English French P.E. Design and Technology
Maths Information Technology Art Music Science

1 
....

2 
....

3 
....

4 
....

5 
....

6 
....

7 
....

8 
....

9 
....

10 
....

11 
....

5 CD 3

4 Listen to the dialogue and act it out.

Brian You look happy, Jenna.
Jenna Yeah, I got an A in Maths.
Brian Really? I never get As in Maths.
Jenna It's my favourite subject. What's yours?
Brian P.E. and Information Technology.
Jenna Are you good at them?
Brian Sure. Are there any subjects you don't like?
Jenna Yes, English and French. I think they are really difficult.
Brian I think so, too. And we get so much homework.
Jenna How about doing our homework together?
Brian Brilliant idea.

5 Talk about the following with a partner.

- Your favourite subjects.
- Subjects you dislike.
- Subjects you are good at.
- Subjects where you get a lot of homework.

WB p. 80 CYBER HOMEWORK 22

Progress Check Units 9–11

Listening

6 CD 3 BiSt

Listen to the conversation and choose the correct answers to the questions.

1 When and where did Monica's hobby start?

- **a** ☐ Five years ago on holiday.
- **b** ☐ Almost five years ago in Spain.
- **c** ☐ Around six years ago in Spain.
- **d** ☐ Seven years ago on a family holiday.

2 How many pens did Monica have when she returned from Spain?

- **a** ☐ less than 6
- **b** ☐ about 7
- **c** ☐ 67
- **d** ☐ 550

3 It's easier for Monica to collect hotel pens because

- **a** ☐ she gets them from other people.
- **b** ☐ she swaps them for postcards.
- **c** ☐ her friend works in a hotel.
- **d** ☐ her parents travel a lot.

4 Monica's favourite pen …

- **a** ☐ was very expensive.
- **b** ☐ belongs to her friend.
- **c** ☐ is from San Francisco.
- **d** ☐ is from an expensive hotel.

5 Monica has another pen that she got …

- **a** ☐ from the Ritz hotel in San Francisco.
- **b** ☐ when she was in San Francisco two years before.
- **c** ☐ in San Francisco, but she doesn't like it.
- **d** ☐ from a friend's father in San Francisco.

☐ 5

Reading

Read the text and tick (✓) T (*True*) or F (*False*).

Fairness at our school

Like all students at our school you are all different. You come from different families, and you have different interests and abilities. Some of you come from different countries and speak different languages. You are all important to us.

Please keep to these rules:

- Please make sure you respect all the other students, too, no matter how different they are.
- If there are problems, talk to your teachers. They will help you to solve problems. Don't forget that you have a right to learn.
- Use friendly language when you talk to teachers and other students.
- Everyone has the right to be in a school that looks nice. Keep your classrooms tidy. Do not throw things in the corridors and do not damage anything.
- Ask yourself: If I were at an ideal school, what would it be like? Then help us to create that ideal school together!

A message to your parents:

- Parents should make sure their child comes to school regularly and on time.
- Parents should make sure their child is well dressed and wears the school uniform.

		T	F
1	The school is only for British children.	☐	☐
2	You should talk to a teacher if you're not happy.	☐	☐
3	The leaflet asks students to look after their school.	☐	☐
4	The leaflet asks parents to make sure their children aren't late for school.	☐	☐
5	The leaflet asks students to take care how they are dressed.	☐	☐

☐ 5

Grammar

Circle the correct option.

1 If she *hadn't studied / didn't study* all last night, she would have got bad marks in the test.
2 It *might / must* be a good idea to let people know they want to close the park.
3 If they play badly, they *can / could* lose the game.
4 I *haven't seen / didn't* see the guy with the tattoos since last week.
5 I *wouldn't have met / would meet* her if it hadn't been for you.
6 I would *have phoned / phone* you if I'd had my phone with me.
7 If I *had seen / saw* him last night, I would have told him.
8 He *has collected / collected* 25 pens yesterday.
9 We *could / must* always say that the piercing was our idea.
10 It *has been / was* five years ago that I started collecting garden gnomes.

☐ 10

Vocabulary

Choose words in the box to complete the sentences. There are two you won't use.

proud
go
furious
story
done
bridegroom
say
bride
telling
library
helpless
saying

1 There wasn't anything I could do. I felt really ....
2 The police let him .... free after four hours.
3 I read a great .... about Nelson Mandela.
4 The .... looked really beautiful in her white dress.
5 When he didn't get all the books he wanted, he was really ....
6 I want you to .... "sorry" to him. Now!
7 I got top marks in the test. I felt so ....
8 In his .... there were some books that were very important to him.
9 I hadn't .... anything wrong but the teacher didn't believe me.
10 I could see in his eyes that he wasn't .... the truth.

☐ 10

How did you do?

Listening		
☺ 4-5	😐 2-3	☹ 0-1

Reading		
☺ 4-5	😐 2-3	☹ 0-1

Grammar		
☺ 8-10	😐 4-7	☹ 0-3

Vocabulary		
☺ 8-10	😐 4-7	☹ 0-3

Total		
☺ 22-30	😐 10-21	☹ 0-9

UNIT 12 Ready for reading

Get talking

1 Which of these books looks interesting to you? If you had to pick one, which one would it be and why?

I'd pick	…	because	it looks interesting / funny / thrilling / exciting … I like thrillers, love / horror / sci-fi (etc.) stories … I've already read … by the same author.

MP3 **2 Read Brenda's book review. Does she recommend the book?**

Brenda's Books

Hi, this is *Brenda's Books* online, and this week I'm recommending a book that really, really grabbed me. It's *The Boy in the Striped Pyjamas* by John Boyne. It came out in 2006. My history teacher told me about it, so I got myself a copy and I finished the book in one go. I passed it on to some of my friends and they all were really moved by the book.

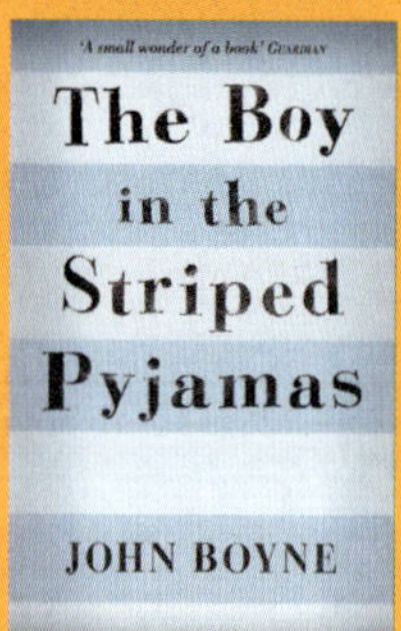

The Boy in the Striped Pyjamas

by John Boyne

Bruno is nine and he lives in Berlin with his parents. His father is a soldier. One day his father and the family are sent to a place called Out-With. The place is terrible. There is nobody to play with and Bruno is bored. So he starts exploring and finds out that there are people living in a large camp on the other side of a high fence. Bruno notices that they all wear striped pyjamas. Then he sees a boy on the other side of the fence. The boy is called Shmuel. They get talking, but they can't play together because of the fence between them.

Bruno visits Shmuel as often as he can. One day Shmuel tells Bruno that his father has gone missing somewhere in the camp. Bruno crawls through a small hole in the fence, puts on striped pyjamas and helps Shmuel explore the camp.

The fascinating thing about the book is that we see everything through Bruno's eyes. Bruno has no idea that Out-With is the concentration camp of Auschwitz. He's mostly interested in his world of games and dreams and he only finds out the truth about the concentration camp very slowly. Through the eyes of this innocent little boy, the reader sees and feels the horrors of that time. A great read, not only for people who are interested in history, but for everyone.

WB p. 83

3 **Read the review again and put the events in the order they happen in the book.**

- ☐ Bruno makes a new friend.
- ☐ Bruno's friend tells him about a problem.
- ☐ Bruno sees many people wearing striped pyjamas.
- ☐ Bruno and his family move to another place.
- ☐ Bruno goes to help his friend.
- ☐ Bruno starts looking around his new home.

7 CD 3 SbX ★

4 **Listen to kids talking about "The Boy in the Striped Pyjamas". What do they say about the film? What do they say about the ending? Which other books do they recommend? Discuss in groups of four.**

Vocabulary Types of books

5 **Match the books with the definitions.**

1 poetry anthology	☐ a collection of short pieces of fiction
2 novel	☐ a book about someone's life
3 anthology of short stories	☐ a work of fiction to be performed on stage
4 biography	☐ a collection of poems
5 play	☐ a work of fiction to be filmed
6 dictionary	☐ a reference book used when you want to find the meaning of a word
7 screenplay	☐ a fictional story in pictures
8 comic	☐ a long piece of fiction

Free flow

BiSt ★

6 **Give a short talk about your reading habits. You have one minute to prepare, then you will talk for 1 – 2 minutes. You can talk about:**

- how often you read
- when and where you read
- why you read
- how many books you read a year
- where you get the books from
- what types of books you can think of
- which of them you read most
- what books you would choose if you could only have three books for the rest of your life
- why you would choose them
- why you like / don't like reading.

▶ WB p. 84

Study tip Reading

So you want to read a thrilling book written for young people like you? You can go to a library or a bookshop. Or you can check in the Internet.

Here are some more tips:

- Browse the Internet for young adult novels or talk to your teacher.
- See what interests you. You should enjoy your reading.
- Find a good place to read.
- Have a dictionary with you but don't open it too often. Many words can be understood from their context.
- Let your classmates know if you liked a book. (And let your teacher know, too.)

SbX BiSt

7 **Louise Rennison has written a series of books about a girl called Georgia. In the extract above from one of the books, Georgia is very bored because her boyfriend is away in New Zealand. Read the text.**

12:05 p.m.

Phoned my bestest* pally, Jas.

"Jas. It's me."

"What?"

"Jas, you don't sound very pleased to hear from me."

"Well … I would be but it's only five minutes since you last phoned …"

***bestest** – very informal spoken English for 'best'

1:30 p.m.

This is boring. I've been cooped up for about a million years. What time is it?

Phoned Jas.

"Jas?"

"Oh God."

"What time is it?"

"What?"

"Why are you saying 'what' for? I merely asked you a civil question."

"Why don't you look at your own clock?"

"Jas, have you noticed I am very, very upset and that my life is over? Have you noticed that?"

"Yes, I have, because you have been on the phone telling me every five minutes for a month."

"Well, I am soo sorry if it is too much trouble to tell your bestest pal the time. Perhaps my eyes are too swollen from tears to see the clock."

"Well, are they?"

"Yes."

"Well, how come you could see to dial my number?"

8 CHOICES

a Tick T (*True*) or F (*False*).

	T	F
1 Jas is pleased to hear from Georgia.	☐	☐
2 Jas says "What?" because she didn't hear Georgia's question well.	☐	☐
3 Georgia hasn't got a clock.	☐	☐
4 Jas thinks that Georgia has phoned her a lot in the last month.	☐	☐

BiSt ★

b Choose the text which best sums up the extract above.

a Georgia phones her best friend pal to find out what time it is. Her friend tells her that it is 1:30 p.m.

b Jas is happy with Georgia.

c Jas is angry because Georgia has been phoning her a lot during the last month.

d Jas is upset because Georgia tells her that her life is over.

Writing *for your Portfolio*

★ **9 Write the next paragraph for the text in 7.**

BiSt ★ **10 Write a book report. Use the text in 2 or the text below as a model. Write 120 – 180 words. Do not forget to use paragraphs and take about 20 minutes.**

Mention the title of the book and the author.
Summarise the content of the book.
Say
- what you like and what you don't like about the book
- why you like / dislike that
- if you would recommend the book to your best friend and why / why not.

Book: *Dead Girls Don't Write Letters*
Author: *Gail Giles*

What's it about?
Sunny's sister Jazz (who is NOT a nice girl) dies in a fire. Her parents are really sad, but one day Sunny gets a letter from Jazz. "I'll be coming home soon," it says. And in fact, one day Jazz turns up. She has turned into a nice, friendly girl, and she knows everything about the family's past. But Sunny asks herself a big question: Who is this stranger who says she's Jazz? She knows that dead girls can't write letters!

What do I think of it?
Wow! This is really a good read. Really exciting and full of twists. I liked the idea that the sisters are so different (aren't they often in real life?) and that suddenly the bad one is good, too. What do you do if you've always been the good one? I won't tell you the ending, but I can tell you that there are a couple of surprises. And have a look at Giles' next book Playing in Traffic, it's an awesome thriller, too.

(Review by Anahita)

DVD The Mag 7 Sales figures

1 Watch the story. Complete with the words in the box. There are four you don't need.

120 | music column | horoscope | 150 | Jessica | down | Lucy | up | librarian | doctor

1 Sales of *The Mag* are going ……………………………… .
2 The last issue of the magazine sold ……………………………… copies.
3 Miss Elliot is the school ……………………………… .
4 Liam suggests putting a ……………………………… in the magazine.
5 Nick wants to do a ……………………………… in the magazine.
6 In the end, ……………………………… gets a really good idea.

2 Answer the questions.

1 Why is Lucy worried?
2 Why don't they want to do another raffle?
3 What does Miss Elliot think?
4 Why doesn't Jessica think Stern would be a good agony uncle?
5 Why doesn't Stern think Nick would be a good music critic?

Everyday English

3 Say the missing words. Practise the dialogues.

Leave it out | The penny's dropped. | I doubt it. | Get out of here!

▶ WB p. 83

SbX

Grammar Reflexive pronouns

1) Wenn das Subjekt und das Objekt eines Verbs die gleiche Person sind, verwendest du ein Reflexivpronomen als Objekt.

2) Mit Hilfe des Reflexivpronomens kannst du betonen, dass die jeweilige Person etwas selbst getan hat/tun wird oder der Person selbst etwas zugestoßen ist.

Which kind of reflexive is it?

Write 1 or 2 after each example sentence:

He decides to **enjoy himself** by travelling with his friends. ....1....
I wrote the book **myself**. (= only me, no one helped me) ....2....
I'll look after myself. ....
She asks herself a big question. ....
They're free to have parties and **enjoy themselves**. ....
We bought the book **ourselves**. ....
We're going to **enjoy ourselves** a lot. ....
Would **you call yourself** a reader? ....
You'll have to read the book **yourself**. ....

WB pp. 86, 87

8 CD 3 BiSt

1 **Listen to the dialogue and fill in the missing words and phrases.**

Asher Hey, Sally, I'm really bored. Let's go and [1].. at the youth club.

Sally Can't you see I'm reading a book?

Asher Come on. You can [2].. it later.

Sally I'm sorry. It's such a good book I can't put it down.

Asher What are you reading anyway?

Sally It's a book by Scott Westerfield. It's called *Uglies*.

Asher *Uglies?* What's that [3].. then?

Sally Do you really want to know? Or are you just bored?

Asher How can you say such a thing. Of course, [4].. . Honestly.

Sally Well, OK. So it all takes place in the future. All kids are Uglies until they're 16. Then they have an operation and [5].. Pretties. Pretties are good-looking and have parties all the time.

Asher It sounds like fun.

Sally Yeah, but it's not what it seems. There's this group of kids who run away to escape the operation. It's called The Smoke. The [6].. are after them before they find out the truth. It's all very exciting.

Asher It all seems very strange to me.

Sally Yeah, but if you start reading it you'll really get into it, I promise.

Asher You know, I'm so bored I might just do that. Give me the book.

Sally No way. You'll have to wait until I've finished!

2 **Now cover up the dialogue. Listen again and tick the correct answer. Then look at the dialogue and check.**

CD 3 8 BiSt

What is the dialogue about?

a Sally's boyfriend Asher and his friends
b a book that Sally is reading
c young people's strange lives in the past
d teenagers at school

What is the main reason why Sally doesn't want to give Asher the book?

a It's not her book.
b She thinks she won't get it back.
c She hasn't finished reading it yet.
d She thinks he won't understand it.

Get talking Giving reasons

CD 3 9

3 **Write the answers under the questions. Listen and check.**

1 It was so great I didn't want it to end.
2 It was so exciting I couldn't put it down.
3 It was so noisy I couldn't talk to anyone.
4 It was so long I slept most of the way.

A How was the book?

....

B How was the journey?

....

C How was your holiday?

....

D How was the party?

....

4 **Work with a partner. Student A chooses a picture to ask about. Student B chooses prompts from the A and B boxes to reply.**

A How was the film?

film

rollercoaster

pizza

test

beach

hotel bed

B It was so boring that I walked out of the cinema.

A		B	
boring	hot	walk out of cinema	not want to get out of it
comfortable	good	get a headache	have another go straightaway
exciting	difficult	want another piece	spend all the time in the water

CYBER HOMEWORK 24

UNIT 13 Space

Vocabulary Space

10 CD 3

1 Listen. Write the numbers next to the words. Then match the pictures and the words.

- ☐ a space shuttle
- ☐ an orbit
- ☐ an astronaut
- ☐ a plaque
- ☐ an explosion
- ☐ sunset

11 CD 3 MP3 SbX

2 a Read and listen to the text.

Space travel

☐ A space shuttle takes 90 minutes to orbit the earth. In these 90 minutes, daylight and night time constantly change for the astronauts. They see 16 sunsets and 16 sunrises!

☐ Astronauts on the space shuttle can choose from about 100 different food items and 50 drinks. The taste of food often changes in space. Your favourite food might taste awful 200 kilometres above the earth.

☐ Neil Armstrong was the first man to walk on the moon. His Apollo 11 mission left a plaque on the Moon. It says: *Here men from the planet Earth first set foot upon the Moon July 1969, A.D. We came in peace for all mankind.*

☐ Space travel has always been dangerous. There were two terrible accidents in the last 30 years. The Challenger space shuttle exploded 1 minute after its start in 1986. In 2003 the Columbia broke up when it re-entered the earth's atmosphere. On both flights all seven members of the crew died.

BiSt

b Match the titles with the paragraphs. There is one title you won't use.

1 A message on the moon
2 A day in space
3 16 days and 16 nights in an hour and a half
4 When things go wrong
5 Eating in space

Get talking

3 Work with a partner. Take notes of five facts from the text. Then test each other.

How long does it take to …? /
What do astronauts …?
Who was the first …? /
When did he set foot …?

12 CD 3

4 **Listen. Write the numbers into the pictures. Then match the pictures and the words.**

- ☐ injury
- ☐ damage
- ☐ prize
- ☐ a child and an adult
- ☐ government money
- ☐ height

13 CD 3

5 **Listen to the radio advert and complete the text.**

The race for space

Human history is full of stories of explorers who have risked their lives to go places no one has ever been before – from the top of the highest mountain to the bottom of the deepest sea. Would you like to join them? You can win $[1]............................ million at the same time!

We offer the Ansari X prize to the first people to build a spaceship that can be used more than once. Interested? These are the rules.

- The spaceship must be able to carry [2]............................ adults.
- The spaceship must reach a height of [3]............................ . This height is where a space orbit begins.
- The spaceship must return with no [4]............................ and no injury to any of the crew.
- A second flight must be made within [5]............................ weeks, using the same spacecraft.
- No government [6]............................ can be used in the project.

Does that sound easy? What are you waiting for?

6 **Match the pictures to the five rules above. Write 1 – 5.**

▶ WB p. 89

Vocabulary

14 CD 3

7 **Listen and match. Listen again and check.**

1 win	☐ higher than a hundred kilometres
2 fly	☐ history
3 take	☐ the crew
4 make	☐ a lot of money
5 welcome	☐ to start commercial flights
6 plan	☐ a trip

15 CD 3 SbX BiSt

8 **Listen to the radio news and tick the correct options.**

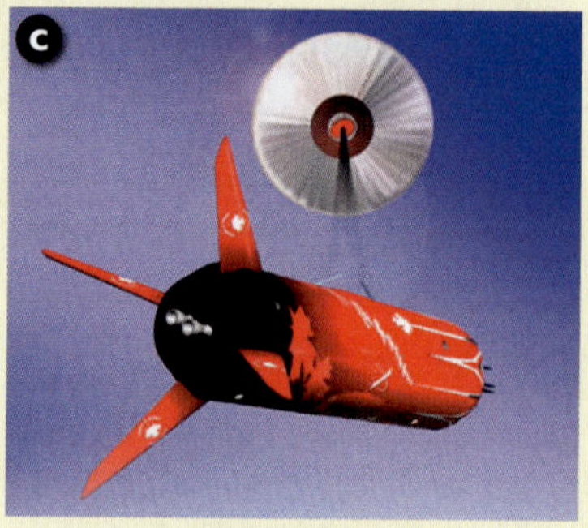

1 Which spacecraft won the Ansari X prize? Look at the pictures.

a ☐ Canadian Arrow
b ☐ SpaceShipOne
c ☐ da Vinci Wild Fire
d ☐ Superflight

2 How high did the spaceship fly?

a ☐ 100 km **c** ☐ 115 km
b ☐ 110 km **d** ☐ 125 km

3 When did the flight take place?

a ☐ 4/10/2004
b ☐ 4/11/2004
c ☐ 14/10/2004
d ☐ 10/4/2004

4 Who flew the plane?

a ☐ Peter Diamandis
b ☐ Paul Allen
c ☐ Brian Binnie
d ☐ Paul Binnie

5 Who wants to use SpaceShipOne for big bussiness flights?

a ☐ Peter Diamandis
b ☐ Paul Allen
c ☐ Richard Branson
d ☐ Paul Binnie

6 How much will a flight into space cost?

a ☐ $20,000
b ☐ $200,000
c ☐ $2,000,000
d ☐ $2,000,000,000

7 How many people does Richard Branson want to put into space in the next five years?

a ☐ 3,000
b ☐ 13,000
c ☐ 30,000
d ☐ 3,300

A song 4 U *Ticket to the Moon (Electric Light Orchestra)*

16/17 CD 3

9 Listen to the song and decide if the statements are T (*True*) or F (*False*).

Remember the good old 1980s?
When things were so uncomplicated?
I wish I could go back there again
And everything could be the same.

I've got a ticket to the moon.
I'll be leaving here any day soon.
Yeah, I've got a ticket to the moon.
But I'd rather see the sunrise in your eyes.

Got a ticket to the moon.
I'll be rising high above the earth so soon.
And the tears I cry might turn into the rain
That gently falls upon your window.
You'll never know.

Ticket to the moon (ticket to the moon).

Fly, fly through a troubled sky,
Up to a new world shining bright, oh, oh.
Flying high above.
Soaring madly through the mysteries that come.
Wondering sadly if the ways that led me here
Could turn around and I would see you there,
Standing there (and I would see you there, waiting …)

Ticket to the moon.
Flight leaves here today from Satellite Two.
As the minutes go by, what should I do?
I paid the fare, what more can I say?
It's just one way (only one way) …

Ticket to the moon (ticket to the moon).

	T	F
1 The man is happy because he is going to the moon.	☐	☐
2 The rocket leaves in a few minutes.	☐	☐
3 He plans to come back soon.	☐	☐

Free flow

★ **10 Think of the story behind the song. Think about these questions.**

Who is the man?
Who is he singing to?
Why is he leaving Earth?
Why can he never come back?

Tell your stories in groups. Use the past tense.

SbX 11 a *The Price* is a story about a girl called Emily who loves to paint. Look at the pictures. What kind of things does she paint? Read the first part of the story quickly to check.

b Read the story and answer the questions at the end of each section.

THE PRICE

Emily was a quiet kid. She didn't say much, even to her mother. Her father was always too busy to listen anyway. She never caused any problems. Her grades at school were good. She got on well with everyone. So her mother never worried. Until the space paintings.

Emily had always loved to paint and she was good at it, too – very good. She spent all her pocket money on paint and paper. She'd started painting when she was seven. At first it had always been animals, flowers and other things that she saw out of her bedroom window. As she got older, her subjects changed: cars, then people and then sports events. Nothing strange there.

But then one day Emily found something new to paint – scenes of outer space. But these weren't pictures of Mars or Saturn and its rings. These were paintings of weird and wonderful worlds. They showed alien cities on a planet that had three suns. And there were strange forests where strange animals lived. Emily's mother sometimes looked at the paintings and although she didn't know why, she felt a little bit scared. There was something a bit too real about the scenes. She asked her daughter where her ideas came from.

"They're places I go at night," she explained.

"What, in your dreams?" she asked.

"Yeah, sort of," Emily replied.

1 Why was Emily's mother not worried at first about her daughter?
2 What things had Emily liked to paint at different times in her life?
3 What did Emily say about her ideas for her space paintings?

Emily's mother wanted to talk to her husband about the pictures, but she didn't. Emily's father was a writer. A few years before, he had written a very successful science fiction series for TV. He was famous and got lots of work. But now people were starting to forget about him, because he hadn't come up with anything good for a long time. So he had become depressed. He didn't want to talk to anyone and he often got angry very quickly if someone disturbed him.

Emily was in her room. She had run out of paint, but she had no pocket money left. She couldn't disturb her dad. He was in his office and no-one was allowed to go in there – not even Emily's mother. Emily didn't want to wait, so she picked up some of her paintings and set off for the art shop. She explained to the owner that she needed some paint, but she hadn't got any money. She asked the man if he wanted to buy some of her space scenes.

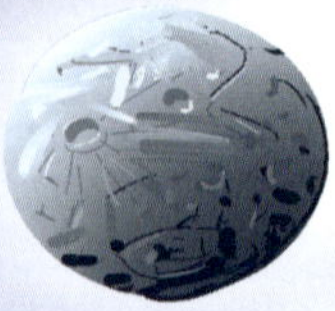

"OK," said the man, "I'll give you £20 for all four of them." Emily didn't think twice. She took the money, bought some paint and ran home.

A few days later, Emily's dad was walking past the art shop when he stopped and looked in the window. He saw the four paintings that Emily had done. He was fascinated by them. He walked into the shop and bought them.

4 Why was Emily's dad unhappy?
5 Why did Emily go to the art shop?
6 What happened when Emily's dad saw the paintings?

Emily's dad took the paintings home and put them on the wall in his office. He sat down in his chair, looked at the paintings and started to write. For the next week, neither Emily nor her mother saw her dad. Day after day, night after night, he locked himself in his office. All they heard was the sound of him working at his computer.

Then one day he came out of the office. They had never seen him so happy.
"It's finished," he told them. "My masterpiece."

A week later they were celebrating. The TV studio had loved his ideas for his new series and they were going to start filming it as soon as possible. A famous Hollywood actor was going to be in it. The series was simply called *Alien Worlds.*

The next morning, Emily's mum went into her daughter's bedroom. There was no sign of Emily. Her mum knew that something was wrong. She shouted for her husband. He came quickly. The window was open. They looked into the garden, but there was no sign of Emily. Then they walked over to the table where Emily usually did her painting. There was a picture lying there. For some reason they didn't want to look, but they had to.

It was Emily's most perfect picture ever – an alien spaceship taking off from earth. Emily's father looked at the picture more closely. There at the door was a teenage girl. It was Emily. Emily's father and mother looked at each other. They knew she was never coming back.

7 What effect did the paintings have on Emily's dad?
8 Why do you think her parents knew their daughter would never come back?

Writing *for your Portfolio*

★ **12** **How could the story continue? Choose one of these two texts to start. Discuss with a partner how it could go on. Write your story.**

A It was exactly ten years after Emily had left. Her mum and dad were in her room. They hadn't changed anything and they came here every day to think of their daughter. Suddenly Emily's mum saw something strange.

B The flight had been long and tiring for Emily, but she was glad to be back in her real world. She landed her spaceship close to the city. The commander was waiting for her at headquarters. "I have an important message for you," he said.

DVD The Mag 8 UFOs

1 Watch the story. Cross out the incorrect word(s) and make the correction.

1 Liam shows ~~Jessica~~ the photos on his camera. Lucy
2 The photos on the camera are of ghosts. ....
3 Liam's school bag goes missing from the computer lab. ....
4 Lucy has the key to the library. ....
5 They tell the headmaster the photos are of a tennis match. ....
6 They find the camera in the school café. ....

2 Complete the sentences with the names in the box. You can use the names more than once.

Lucy
Stern
Liam

1 .... believes they've got a really big story.
2 .... leaves the camera in the lab.
3 .... doesn't believe the photos are of UFOs.
4 .... suggests that aliens have taken the camera.
5 .... tells the headmaster that the photos are of a sports match.
6 .... is embarrassed by their visit to the headmaster.

Everyday English

3 Say the missing words. Practise the dialogues.

Cross my heart. a matter of life and death. don't just stand there. I might have known.

 WB p. 92

18 CD 3

13 **Fill in the numbers 1 – 6 to get the text. Then write the text and add your own ending.**

1 switched on
2 help
3 thing
4 room
5 saw
6 light

Claire was in her … . It was late. She looked out into the garden and saw a funny … . "I'll do my emails first and then I'll check," she thought. She … her computer. Suddenly a window popped up on the screen. 'Click here if you want to … a friend,' it said. At first, Claire didn't want to open it, but then she clicked on the window. She … a photo. In the photo she saw her garden and a strange round … in it. It was as big as a car. Below the photo she read: Please get me out of this thing.

SbX

Grammar / Vocabulary   Phrasal verbs

Im Englischen stehen Präpositionen, die zu einem Verb gehören, häufig nach dem Verb:
What are you **waiting for**?
She **spent** all her pocket money **on** paint and paper.

Gelegentlich gibt die Präposition dem Verb eine spezielle Bedeutung:
Astronauts can **choose from** 100 different food items.
The Challenger **broke up** when it re-entered the earth's atmosphere.
Have you ever **blown up** a balloon and let it go?
The balloon goes **flying off** about the room.
When Emily's mother **looked at** the paintings, she felt a little bit uncomfortable.
She **picked up** some of her paintings.

When Mr Green set off to hunt for bears, his neighbours couldn't believe their eyes.

Manchmal erhält das Verb durch die Verwendung einer oder mehrerer Präposition(en) eine völlig andere Bedeutung:

Rockets have several hundred tons of fuel on board when they **take off**.
She **got on** well **with** everyone.
She **set off** for the art shop.

She'd **run out of** paint, but she had no pocket money left.
He hadn't **come up with** anything good for a long time.

WB p. 93

19 CD 3

1 Read the facts and tick T (*True*) or F (*False*). Listen and check your answers.

		T	F
1	From 1836 to 1926, a man had to walk in front of all cars to warn people that they were coming.	☐	☐
2	In 1962, John Glenn became the first American to circle the Earth in the Friendship 7.	☐	☐
3	There is a building where they build airships which is so tall that clouds form and it rains inside.	☐	☐
4	The woman pilot, Amelia Earhart, set three world records for flying in 1932.	☐	☐
5	In 1939, the Graf Zeppelin airship flew non-stop around the world.	☐	☐

2 Read and complete the text.

cities
traffic
noise
in front
travel
wheels

UNUSUAL SOLUTIONS to TRANSPORT PROBLEMS

From tuk-tuks to sky trains in Thailand.

Tuk-tuks have three [1]................................ . The driver sits [2]................................ and the people sit behind him. Lots of people use tuk-tuks for short trips in big [3]................................ in Thailand. Tuk-tuks make a funny [4]................................ . That's why they are called tuk-tuks.

The best way to [5]................................ around Bangkok is by SkyTrain. They built the SkyTrain some years ago because [6]................................ was so bad.

Vocabulary Travel

3 Match the sentences and the pictures.

Lauren is a pilot. Every day she flies from London Gatwick to Munich and back.

1 Lauren sets off for work at about 5.30 a.m.
2 She gets into her car.
3 She gets to the airport at about 6.10 a.m.
4 She gets on the plane at 6.50 a.m., half an hour before the passengers.
5 The plane takes off at 7.30 a.m.
6 The journey takes about an hour and a half. The plane lands at about 9 a.m.
7 After a rest in Munich she flies back. She gets off the plane at about 4 p.m.
8 She drives home. She gets out of the car at about 5 p.m.

Get talking Talking about your journey to school

20 CD 3

4 Write the phrases on the right under the questions. Then listen and check.

I leave the house at twenty past eight.

I arrive at about ten to nine.

Half an hour.

On foot usually, but my mum takes me by car if I'm late.

A How do you get to school?
B 1 ....
A What time do you set off?
B 2 ....
A What time do you get to school?
B 3 ....
A So how long does the journey take?
B 4 ....

5 Practise the dialogues with a partner. Then find out how your partner gets to school.

Best friends

Vocabulary

SbX **1 Match the words / phrases that have similar meaning.**

1	He's not my type.	☐	**a**	Don't get too close to Jamie.
2	Keep away from Jamie.	☐	**b**	Have you got a problem?
3	Leave him alone.	☐	**c**	I'm not interested in him.
4	What's wrong with you?	☐	**d**	Don't show an interest in him.
5	Sheri wasn't invited to the party.	☐	**e**	They told her to go.
6	They threw her out.	☐	**f**	She wasn't a guest at the party.

21 CD 3 MP3 **2 Read and listen to part 1 of the play.**

3 Tick the sentences T (*True*) or F (*False*).

		T	F
1	Dylan's not Sheri's type, but she thinks he's OK.	☐	☐
2	Lisa thinks Jamie is cool.	☐	☐
3	Jamie's got a girlfriend.	☐	☐
4	Her name's Sandra.	☐	☐
5	Jamie's girlfriend is 17.	☐	☐

22 CD 3 MP3

4 Read and listen to part 2.

5 Put the sentences in the correct order. Write 1 – 5.

- ☐ Jamie and Sheri kissed.
- ☐ Jenny finds out about Sheri and Jamie and is angry.
- ☐ Jenny wasn't at the party.
- ☐ Sheri thinks Jenny won't find out.
- 1 Sheri went to Jamie's party.

23 CD 3 MP3

6 **Read and listen to part 3.**

7 **Underline the correct words.**

1 Sheri wasn't at the *rap show* / *cinema* on Saturday.
2 She went to Jamie's *house* / *school* with him.
3 Jenny's not in town *at the moment* / *next weekend*.
4 Lisa thinks it's *OK* / *wrong* that Sheri is seeing Jamie.
5 Sheri tells Lisa to stop telling her what to *eat* / *do*.

24 CD 3 MP3

8 **Read and listen to part 4.**

25 CD 3

9 **Complete the sentences to get a summary of the play. Then listen and check.**

Lisa and Sheri are best [1]................................ . Sheri thinks Jamie is [2]................................ . She goes to his [3]................................ . They [4]................................ . Jamie's girlfriend Jenny finds out about this. Jenny gets very [5]................................ . She warns Sheri to leave Jamie alone. Sheri does not listen. The next [6]................................ there is Jenny's party. Sheri has not got an invitation, but she goes there. Jenny and Sheri have a [7]................................ and Sheri starts shouting. Jamie tells Sheri to leave. His friends take her and throw her out. Sheri throws stones at the [8]................................ . The police arrive and take Sheri [9]................................ .

Dylan tells Lisa what happened to Sheri. Lisa is very [10]................................ for Sheri.

▶ WB p. 98 ▶ CYBER HOMEWORK 27

The Mag 9 Here's to us!

1 Watch the story. Write one word to complete the sentences.

1 Liam's going to work on his uncle's .... in the summer.
2 Last year, Nick did a .... round.
3 Lucy's .... job is with *The Daily Herald*.
4 Her first story will be about the ....
5 Now, Lucy works for a .... magazine.
6 Now, Nick and .... work together.

2 Answer the questions.

1 What are they going to do in the holidays?
a Liam: ....
b Nick: ....
c Lucy: ....

2 Where are they in this episode?
a Liam: ....
b Nick: ....
c Lucy: ....

Everyday English

3 Say the missing words. Practise the dialogues.

Lucky you! | Better late than never! | Let me guess | Here's to us!

▶ WB p. 98

Free flow

BiSt ★ **10** **Give a short talk about friendship. You will talk for 1 – 2 minutes. Take one minute to prepare. You can talk about:**

- why friendship is important to you
- what is important for you in a friend
- what a good friend should / shouldn't do
- who your best friend is
- where he / she lives
- what he / she looks like
- what his / her hobbies are
- how often you meet
- what you do together
- what you like best in him / her.

Writing *for your Portfolio*

11 **Think of an episode you went through with your best friend and make a picture story / photo story.**

SbX

Grammar
Questions in the past (Revision)

So bildest du Fragen im *past simple*:
did + Person + *base form* des Verbs.

Did she **like** it?
Did you **read** the newspaper?

Oder du bildest die Fragen im *past simple* mit:
question word + *did* + Person + *base form* des Verbs.

What did Armstrong **leave** on the moon?
When did the flight **take place**?
How high did the spaceship **fly**?

Kein *did* kommt bei Fragen nach dem Subjekt!
Which spacecraft **won** the Ansari X prize?
Who **flew** the plane?

MORE fun with Fido!

WB p. 99

26 CD 3 BiSt

1 Listen to the dialogue and fill in the missing words and phrases.

Asher Sally I think I'm lost.
Sally Where are you?
Asher I don't really know. I'm walking along a river at the moment and there's a farm on the other side. I can see horses.
Sally Horses? Or can you see horses [1]........................? They're called cows.
Asher Sally, please. There're lots of horses in the field on the other side of the river.
Sally Can you see a [2]........................?
Asher No, it's very flat here.
Sally Asher! You've got your GPS with you, haven't you? You didn't forget it at home?
Asher No, I didn't. When I [3]........................ the bus I put your address in.
Sally The one I sent you by email, right?
Asher Yeah, I think so. I didn't print it out.
Sally So you put in an address you remembered.
Asher That's what I did.
Sally And what's the address you put in?
Asher 45, Rosebush Lane.
Sally Ah, a GPS unit is a great thing, but you [4].. the correct address.
Asher Isn't it right?
Sally No, it isn't. It's 45 Rosewood Lane. See you in an hour. Have a [5].. .
Asher Oh no!

26 CD 3

2 Now cover up the dialogue. Listen again and circle the correct word. Then look at the dialogue and check.

1 Asher phones Sally because he has lost his *way / GPS unit.*
2 Asher can see *horses / cows* on the other side of the river.
3 Asher put Sally's address in his GPS when he got off the *train / bus.*
4 Sally sent her address by *post / email.*
5 Asher put in the *correct / wrong* address.
6 Asher will be *at the bus stop / at Sally's place* in about an hour.

Vocabulary Geographical features

27 CD 3

3 **Listen. Write the correct number next to the words in the box. Then match with the picture.**

- ☐ hill
- ☐ fence
- ☐ valley
- ☐ meadow
- ☐ rock
- ☐ forest
- ☐ signpost
- ☐ fields
- ☐ mountain
- ☐ road
- ☐ village
- ☐ lake
- ☐ waterfall
- ☐ stream

4 **Test your partner.**

28 CD 3

5 **Complete the dialogues with words on the left. Listen and check.**

road
cache
coordinates
forest
lake
hill

Matthew So, where should we go now? Into the [1]..?
Jill No, I'd rather go up the hill. I think the cache is up there.
Matthew Are you sure? Read your [2].. again.
Jill Yes, I'm pretty sure. I don't want to go into the forest. I want to walk up the [3].. .

Helen Let's take the [4].. down into the valley.
Archie No, let's walk through the field. Then we can go down to the [5].. .
Helen No, not the field! I want to walk on a real road.
Archie But a [6].. is never so close to the road!

6 **Interview your partner.**

Do you like to go for walks or hikes?
How often do you do that?
Where do you like to walk?
How long does your walk usually last?
Do you know people who like walking?
Do you know why they walk?

WB p. 100
CYBER HOMEWORK 28

Progress Check Units 12–14

Listening

29 CD 3

Listen to Laura and Martin talking about *Plan 9 From Outer Space*. Tick the statements T (*True*) or F (*False*).

	T	F
1 *Plan 9 From Outer Space* is a new movie.	☐	☐
2 It is one of the worst movies ever.	☐	☐
3 The story is about aliens who are zombies.	☐	☐
4 Laura didn't think it was funny.	☐	☐
5 Martin might watch the film.	☐	☐

☐ 5

Reading

BiSt **Read the book review. Then choose the correct answers to the questions after it.**

The Boy in the Dress
by David Walliams

This is a lovely book!

Walliams is an actor and a writer for TV (*Little Britain*), and this is his first children's book. The story is about 12-year-old Dennis, who lives with big brother John and their dad. Mum has gone and Dennis misses her terribly.

Dennis really likes two things: playing football with his friend Darvesh – and looking at fashion* magazines. Everybody knows that Dennis is a great footballer, but not everybody knows that Dennis has bought the famous fashion magazine *Vogue*. Raj, who runs the shop, knows, but Dennis said to him it was for a friend. Dad knows and is shocked, because boys don't buy fashion magazines. And Lisa, the most beautiful girl in the school knows. Lisa is two years older, but they become friends because both are really interested in fashion.

Then Lisa has an idea. Dennis should dress up* as a girl and come to school with her as a French girl who came to visit. At first Dennis doesn't want to, but then he dresses up as a girl – and everybody, even his friend Darvesh, thinks he is a girl. A pity there's a double French lesson that day! Everything becomes very difficult, and I don't want to tell you what happens when the headmaster finds out, what happens when Dennis is not allowed to play football, what happens, when Lisa and Dennis meet the headmaster at Raj's shop. Let me just tell you: it's all very funny (and a bit sad).

Walliams invented some very fine and funny characters and he wrote a great book. With the great story come great drawings. Quentin Blake, who did the drawings for Roald Dahl, makes the book great to look at, too. Let's hope there will be more from Walliams and Blake!

1 What family problems does Dennis have?
- **a** ☐ His mother has left them.
- **b** ☐ His father is often away at work.
- **c** ☐ He doesn't get on well with his brother.
- **d** ☐ He is lonely* because he's an only child.

2 Why do Lisa and Dennis become friends?
- **a** ☐ Because they are in the same class at school.
- **b** ☐ Because Lisa is secretly in love with Dennis.
- **c** ☐ Because they share the same interest.
- **d** ☐ Because they are both good-looking.

3 What does Dennis think of Lisa's idea to dress him up as a girl?
- **a** ☐ He can't wait to do it.
- **b** ☐ He refused to do it.
- **c** ☐ He is not very keen on it to start with.
- **d** ☐ He doesn't think she's serious.

4 What happens to their plan?
- **a** ☐ Nobody knows that the "French girl" is really Dennis.
- **b** ☐ It goes wrong.
- **c** ☐ Everyone thinks it's really funny.
- **d** ☐ Dennis decides not to do it at the last minute.

5 Who illustrated the book?
- **a** ☐ David Walliams.
- **b** ☐ Roald Dahl.
- **c** ☐ Quentin Blake.
- **d** ☐ None of the above.

VOCABULARY: fashion – Mode
dress up – sich verkleiden
lonely – einsam

☐ 5

Grammar Circle the right word.

1 I fell over and hurt *himself / myself.*

2 Who *flew / did fly* the plane?

3 Helen always buys her school things *herself / myself.*

4 *What did / What do* you have for dinner yesterday?

5 I made this cake *me / myself.*

☐ 5

Vocabulary Write the words under the pictures.

prize sunrise race fly orbit spaceship win astronaut adult invitation

1 
....

2 
....

3 
....

4 
....

5 
....

6 
....

7 

....

8 
....

9 

....

10 
....

☐ 10

Dialogue

Complete these mini-dialogues with the sentences in the box.

Then it serves him right!

I think you know that!

You're kidding. Why did it happen?

No, you can't. Not now and not ever!

1 **Boy** Did you hear about Connie having a fight with Fred?
Girl 1 ....
Boy She caught him kissing Natalie.
Girl 2 ....

2 **Boy** Can I talk to you?
Girl 3 ....
Boy Why not? What did I do?
Girl 4 ....

☐ 4

How did you do?

Listening		
☺ 4-5	😐 2-3	☹ 0-1

Reading		
☺ 4-5	😐 2-3	☹ 0-1

Grammar		
☺ 4-5	😐 2-3	☹ 0-1

Vocabulary		
☺ 7-10	😐 4-6	☹ 0-3

Dialogue		
☺ 3-4	😐 2	☹ 0-1

Total		
☺ 25-29	😐 12-24	☹ 0-11

▶ MORE! ONLINE PROGRESS CHECK - www.helbling-ezone.com

Get talking

SbX 1 a **Talk in groups. Use the prompts in the speech bubbles to answer the question in blue.**

It's the time when … / What makes July great is …
I love it when … / There's nothing better than …

Actually, I don't really like it because …

b **Read the letter from the editor. What summer activities does she mention?**

FLY HIGH

Five Oaks Middle School Magazine

What's so great about July?

The next issue of the school magazine is all about our favourite month – July! And we want to know what makes it so great. Send us your ideas.

July around the World

A letter from the editor

Hi,

Welcome to the new edition of FLY HIGH, the school magazine of Five Oaks Middle School. The last two weeks have been terribly busy for the magazine team, thanks to you. You sent us so many great ideas, photos and texts – a clear sign that making *July around the world* the topic for this issue was a good choice.

Whenever you decide to read this edition – right now before the end of the school year, or later during the holidays when you're lying on the beach, climbing in the Himalayas, scuba-diving (sorry, there isn't a water-proof edition of FLY HIGH), or whatever – enjoy your holidays!

With best wishes from me and the team,

Claire, 4a

2 **Imagine your perfect festival. Which five artists / bands would play? Read the text below quickly and find the names of five artists / bands who played at the Guilfest.**

★ **3** **Read the text below again and answer the following questions.**

1 How many days does the festival last?
2 Who did Olivia go with?
3 Which band did Olivia get autographs from?
4 Where did they stay?
5 What can you do if you get tired of listening to the bands?
6 Where in Guildford is the festival?

Chill out at the Guilfest

Want some ideas for things to do in July? Here's my highlight from last July. My elder brother Daniel and I went to the Guilfest in Guildford for three days.

What is it? A three-day festival with six stages. It started on Friday and went on for three days. Great bands! I liked *Morning Runner*, *Nizlopi*, *Gary Numan*, *Big Wednesday* and *Billy Idol* best. As far as autographs go, I was really successful. I got autographs from John and Luke of *Nizlopi* and one from *Gary Numan*. Daniel's been going to the Guilfest for a couple of years. And know what he told me? The first time *Nizlopi* came to the Guilfest, they played in a tent with about a thousand people in it. When they'd been playing for some time, they got off the stage and went down in the middle of the crowd. Suddenly two or three people sat down and then everyone else did the same. Daniel says that it was a really special moment. Everyone kept really quiet, and Daniel says he had the feeling that the band were playing just for him.

We camped at the Guilfest and if you have the money, you can rent a camper. And if you get tired of listening to the bands, you can walk over to the Guildford outdoor swimming pool and spend some time there.

Olivia, 5c

Four more things I liked:

1 There's a big leisure centre nearby. So having a shower's not a problem.

2 Stoke Park, where the festival's held, is really beautiful.

3 There was a theatre tent, too. We went to the Guilfest for the music, of course, but it's nice to have something else to do occasionally.

4 Last but not least, the toilets were clean.

SbX **4** **Read the text. What do these numbers refer to?**

a 400
b 160
c 1,500
d 14

Wimbledon for free

1 Thousands of people would love to get a ticket for the world's most important tennis tournament at the end of June / beginning of July every year. But only a few of them actually get a chance to see the matches live, for a price of about £1,500 per match!

2 But you can get in for free – honestly! If you're keen on tennis, know the rules and are in year 10 (so at least 14 years old!) Why? Because then you can apply to become a ball boy or girl (a BBG, as they are called) in next year's tournament. But don't think it's easy!

3 About 400 boys and girls apply to become a BBG every year, but only 200 are chosen, after they've been for training (four times a week, from mid February to mid July). BBGs don't get paid. But if you've been a BBG, it can help later when you're looking for a job. "If you were a BBG as a teenager, it tells the interviewer that you've probably got a lot of discipline," says Kay Williams, a BBG some years ago herself and now a student at Oxford university.

4 "What's so difficult about picking up a tennis ball?" you might ask. Sorry, but you have no idea! Being a BBG can be tough. When you apply, for example, you have to show that you can run for twelve minutes and stand still for four minutes!

5 And it can be dangerous! One year, a ball boy broke his leg running into the net during a match. He finished the match and then he was taken to hospital! And don't forget that in some of the serves, the ball can reach speeds of more than 160 kph. A few years ago, a BBG called Abdalla was hit by a 200 kph serve from champion Pete Sampras. "The crowd let out an 'Ooooh', and it hurt, but I had to smile and keep going," he said. And in 1995, Tim Henman was disqualified from Wimbledon for hitting a ball at a ball girl's head!

6 As you can see, there are easier things than being a BBG at Wimbledon. But not many are as interesting!

James, 4b

BiSt **5** **In which paragraphs does James talk about these things? Write numbers in the boxes.**

- ☐ Accidents that can happen to BBGs.
- ☐ How difficult it is to get a ticket.
- ☐ How to get into Wimbledon without paying.
- ☐ How popular Wimbledon is.
- ☐ Minimum age for BBGs.
- ☐ How BBGs need to be fit.
- ☐ How BBGs are chosen.
- ☐ How being a BBG can help you in later life.

BiSt **6** **Which of these does Nayana not talk about?**

- ☐ How long the Mangani festival lasts.
- ☐ What people wear in the Mangani festival.
- ☐ The story behind the Mangani festival.
- ☐ Where the Mangani festival takes place.

A festival in southern India

Hurray! In July I'm going to visit my grandmother in Pondicherry in southern India. There's an interesting event there, the Mangani Festival. It lasts for a month. A picture of the god Shiva is carried through the streets and people go to the roof of their houses and throw ripe mangoes. Imagine a ripe mango hitting your head! Wham! Ouch! I asked my mum about the legend behind the festival. Here's what she told me.

Karaikal Ammaiyar was the wife of a rich man. One day, her husband got two very good mangoes as a present. He gave them to his wife to keep for him. Then he went to work. A little later, a beggar arrived at the house. (In fact, it was the god Shiva.) Karaikal wanted to give the poor beggar some food, so she gave him some rice and one of the mangoes. When her husband came back from work, he ate the other mango with his lunch. The mango tasted so good that he wanted the second one. His wife was scared of her husband's reaction and didn't know what to do. So she prayed to Shiva and suddenly, there was a mango in her hand. She gave it to her husband and told him that it was a present from Shiva. Her husband didn't believe her. So she went away and prayed again.

And suddenly another mango was in her hands. From that day on, her husband believed whatever his wife said.

Mum said that there's another festival in July, too. In the other one, people dressed in yellow clothes who haven't eaten for 40 days walk over red hot coals. I must really see that, but I don't think I'll try it.

See you in September.

Best,
Nayana

7 **Match the sentence halves.**

1	Nayana's grandmother	☐	a picture of Shiva.
2	In the Mangani Festival, people carry	☐	the people who walk over red hot coals.
3	They also throw	☐	two mangoes.
4	Nayana's mum	☐	the second mango was a present from Shiva.
5	Karaikal's husband gave his wife	☐	lives in Southern India.
6	Karaikal was scared because	☐	told her the story behind the legend.
7	Karaikal told her husband that	☐	she had given the second mango away.
8	Nayana wants to see	☐	ripe mangoes.

Writing *for your Portfolio*

★ **8** **Work in groups. Choose a month that you want to write about. Look at the texts from FLY HIGH in this unit again. Brainstorm possible topics, e.g.:**

- Important sports events that take place in that month
- International festivals that take place in that month
- Music events that take place in that month
- Countries where the weather is very different from Austria in that month
- Famous people whose birthday is in that month
- …

Use the Internet, your school library, magazines and books to find information. Then write an article for your magazine (200 words). Make sure you download attractive pictures from the Internet.

In your text, include the following:

- What is the article about? Make sure it contains all the necessary facts.
- What is the history of the event? Write when the event was first organised and how it developed over the years.
- What do you like about it? Why would you like to go there?

Remember, each time you change the focus of your text, you should start a new paragraph.

Free flow

9 **Work with a partner. Look at the picture and think of a story that goes with it.**

30 CD 3 ★

10 **Listen to the story. Then write a summary of the story in no more than 150 words.**

★ **11** **What emotions do you think Emma felt at these different points in the story? Explain your reasons.**

I think she was excited when she got her driving licence in the post because she was free to drive …

1 She got her driving licence.
2 Her father asked her to drive her little sister to a friend's house.
3 Buddy refused to get out of the car.
4 She decided to leave her sister in the car while she got an ice cream.
5 She was waiting in the queue to pay.
6 She saw the man in the car.
7 She saw the man run away.
8 She found out her sister was fine.

31 CD 3 BiSt

1 **Listen to the dialogue and fill in the missing words and phrases.**

Harry I haven't [1]...................................... for a long time.

Nadia I was training for Wimbledon.

Harry You are kidding, aren't you?

Nadia No, this year they asked my school for a [2]...................................... . And my school sent me.

Harry Wow! How long did you train?

Nadia We started training in early February. The matches started in June.

Harry Five months training. I don't get it. It isn't difficult to pick up tennis balls.

Nadia You have no idea. You have to run very fast. Then you sometimes stand very still [3]...................................... .

Harry Could you talk to the players?

Nadia No. Only after the match.

Harry Did they pay you?

Nadia No, they didn't.

Harry Too bad. Did you get some [4]...................................... ?

Nadia Yes, six. And a few [5]................................ photos too.

Harry Could I have one of the photos?

Nadia If you [6]..................... me an ice cream, I might give you one.

Harry It's a deal!

31 CD 3 BiSt

2 **Now read the dialogue and answer the questions. Then listen to the dialogue again and check.**

Which statement about Harry is NOT true?

- ☐ At first, Harry doesn't believe that Nadia trained for Wimbledon.
- ☐ Harry thinks it's difficult to work as a ball girl.
- ☐ Harry asks Nadia if she got any money for being a ball girl.
- ☐ Harry would like one of Nadia's photos.

Nadia ...

- ☐ doesn't want to talk about being a ball girl at Wimbledon.
- ☐ thinks it wasn't fair that she didn't get paid.
- ☐ says she spoke to some of the players during the matches.
- ☐ likes the photos she got at Wimbledon.

Vocabulary Special events

3 Match the words and pictures.

- ☐ book fair
- ☐ tennis tournament
- ☐ rock festival
- ☐ opening night
- ☐ fashion show
- ☐ cycling race
- ☐ car show
- ☐ school fête

4 Where would you expect to find these people?

actors and actresses	fans	teachers	models
sportsmen and women	authors	pop stars	journalists

Get talking Talking about events

32 CD 3

5 Complete the dialogues with the replies. Listen and check.

I loved it. I saw Nadal play.
Yes, I went to Glastonbury last year.
Yes, I went on a school trip to Wimbledon two years ago.
It was fantastic. All my favourite bands were there.

Dialogue 1

A Have you ever been to a rock festival?
B 1 Yes, I went to Glastonbury last year.
A What was it like?
B 2 ……………………………………

Dialogue 2

A Have you ever been to a tennis tournament?
B 3 ……………………………………
A What was it like?
B 4 ……………………………………

6 Work with a partner. Ask each other questions about the events in 3. Use the dialogues from 5 to help you.

Early US history

KEY WORDS

belief	harvest	turkey	tax
successful	native	colony	merchants
fight	corn	independent	harbour

1 Look at the text for a minute. Find the answers to the questions below.

a Where did the Pilgrims come from?
b What was their biggest problem when they arrived in America?
c When do Americans celebrate Thanksgiving?
d What sort of bird did they find in America?

2 Read the article about the Pilgrims. Match the questions and the paragraphs.

a What happened when they got to America?
b How do Americans remember them?
c Who were they?
d Why did they go to America?
e How and when did they go to America?

The Pilgrims

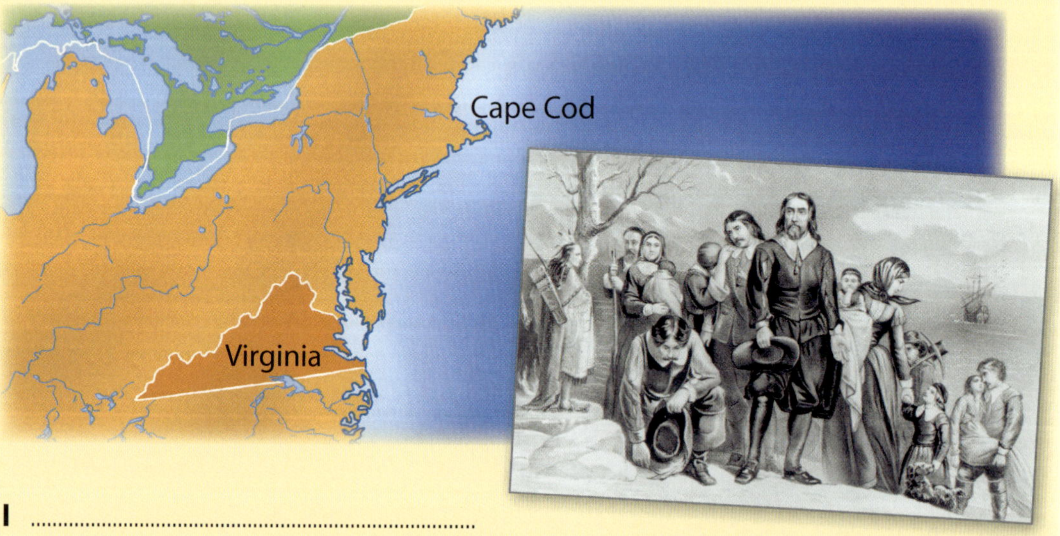

1 ....

The Pilgrims were Puritans. The Puritans were people who lived in England in the 16th and 17th centuries. They had problems with the church in England and the king because they only wanted to follow what was written in the bible.

2 ....

The Pilgrims thought that America (the "New World") was a place where they could be rich and happy – a place where they could live as they wanted. So some Puritans made plans to go America.

3 ....

On the 5th of August, 1620, 101 Pilgrims went to America in a ship called *The Mayflower*. They left Southampton in England and began a six-week journey to the New World. Many people died on the journey.

4 ....

The Pilgrims did not have enough food. But they were lucky because friendly native Americans showed them how to hunt animals, how to make sugar and how to grow corn. The Pilgrims also found a strange bird that they could eat – the turkey.

5 ....

In the autumn of 1621, the Pilgrims had their first successful harvest. To say "Thank You", they gave themselves a holiday and had a special meal with turkey. This was the first *Thanksgiving*. In 1863, *Thanksgiving* became a national holiday in the USA. Americans celebrate *Thanksgiving* on the fourth Tuesday in November every year. *Thanksgiving* dinner usually has roast turkey.

3 **Work in pairs. Write five questions about the text. Give them to another pair to answer. Answer the questions they have written for you.**

Mini-project A moment in time

4 **Write a project about an important event in your country's history.**

Look for information on the Internet or in a library. Write a text.

- Describe what happened.
- Say why it is still important.

Use pictures to illustrate the text and present the information as a poster to your class.

Glaciers

KEY WORDS

glacier	carved out valleys	plant	melts
masses of snow	flow	mummy	level of water

33 CD 3

1 Do the quiz about glaciers. Underline the correct solution. Then listen and check.

1 Glaciers today are getting *smaller / bigger.*
2 We can call glaciers *lakes / rivers* of ice.
3 Very big glaciers can be *40 / 80* km long.
4 Glaciers cover about *2% / 10%* of the Earth's land area.
5 Glaciers have *75% / 25%* of the Earth's fresh water.
6 The Antarctic ice is about *4,000 / 400* metres thick in some places.
7 Most of the glaciers in the USA are in *California / Alaska.*
8 There are glaciers in *half of / all* the continents.

2 Read the text about glaciers.

What are glaciers? Glaciers are masses of snow that have become ice. Snow falls, stays on the ground for a long, long time. Over many years it turns into ice and that is a glacier.

Glaciers are great rivers of ice. The glaciers flow like very slow rivers. For millions of years, moving glaciers have formed mountains and carved out valleys. They continue to flow and form the landscape in many places.

But today there is a big problem. Glaciers are becoming smaller because the world is getting warmer. This is true everywhere in the world. An American professor found some plants near a glacier in Peru. The plants were about 5,000 years old. The ice of the glacier covered them 5,000 years ago, but when the glacier got smaller, the plants appeared again.

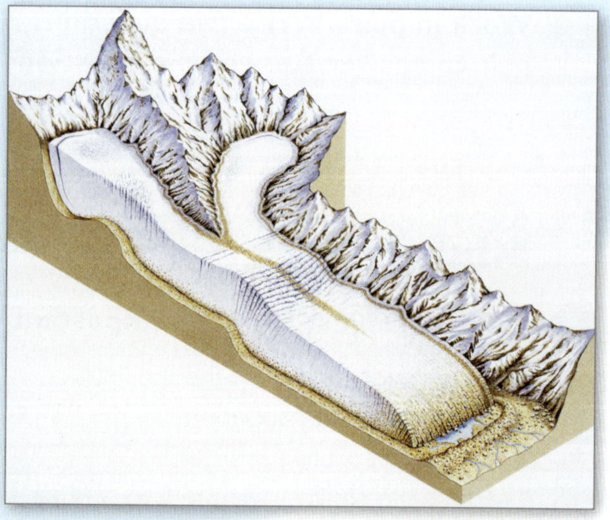

In 1991, hikers found a mummy in the Alps at 3,210 metres. It was a sensation because the man crossed the glacier about 5,300 years ago. Then snow and ice covered him for thousands of years. But as the weather got warmer and the ice melted, the famous *Iceman* appeared.

3 **Compare the photos below.**

The water of glaciers is very important. People need it for drinking and for watering their fields. But now, as the ice melts, glaciers all over the world will get smaller.

Perhaps the biggest problem is this: what is going to happen to all the ice in Greenland and the Antarctic when it gets warmer? When the huge masses of ice melt and flow into the ocean, then the level of the water of the ocean will go up. Cities near the sea will be in trouble. And people on islands that are only one or two metres above sea level are very worried today.

The leaders of Tuvalu – a tiny island country in the Pacific Ocean between Hawaii and Australia – want to leave their islands. During the twentieth century, the sea level rose by 20–30 centimetres. As the sea level has risen, the fields on Tuvalu have been flooded by salt water. This means that people do not have fresh water to drink any more and that they cannot water their vegetables in the fields.

Mini-project Rising sea levels

4 **Check the Internet or in your library for facts and ideas about rising sea levels. Write an article for your school magazine about what might happen as a result.**

CLiL

That nasty flu!

KEY WORDS

cause	infected
temperature	sneeze
pain	cough
fall ill	spikes
illness	cell
virus	immune system
breathe in	multiply

1 Answer the following questions before you read the text.

a What causes flu?
b What time of the year do people mostly get flu?
c Who is in danger?
d What happens when you get the flu?

2 Headache, high body temperature and pain all over the body – when you have influenza, or "flu" as it is usually called, you feel really miserable. Find out why this illness can be quite dangerous – and what you can do about it.

It was November 1918 in Alaska. A ship had just arrived and the 80 people in the village of Teller were happy. They didn't often get visitors. They loved to meet people from outside. The people of Teller heard that the people on the ship had brought an illness with them. But they did not care. They organised a big party for the people on the ship.

The people from Teller didn't know that their visitors had a deadly virus. Only a week later, most of the people from Teller fell ill and another week later 72 of the 80 were dead!

Teller is only one example. In the winter of 1918/19, the illness – called "Spanish" Flu – killed more than 50 million people all over the world. The flu comes every year and most people have had it once. Usually flu is not dangerous, but sometimes it is. In 1957, the "Asian influenza", and in 1968, the "Hong Kong influenza" killed lots of people. In recent years, people have been afraid of "bird flu". People were infected by a virus carried by birds in Hong Kong in 1997 and 2003. And then "swine flu" arrived …

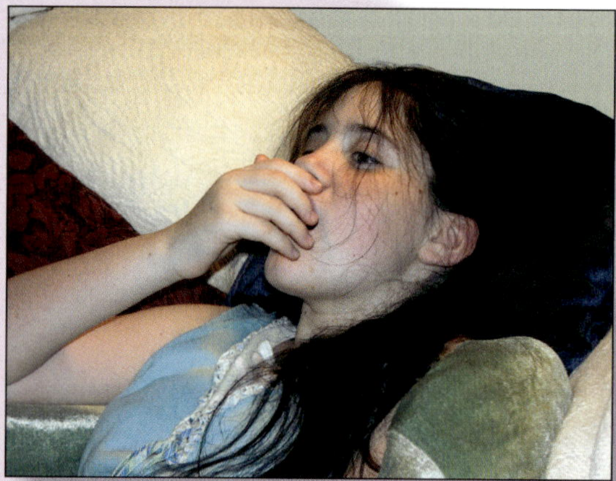

INFLUENZA

In many countries doctors recommend getting a flu shot before the flu season starts. This is what you can do when you already have the flu:

- Stay in bed
- Drink lots of liquid like water and fruit juice
- Take medicine for fever, aches and pains
- Cover each cough and sneeze with a handkerchief
- Keep warm

We hope you're flu-free this year, but if you do get flu, now you know what to do!

Learn MORE through English

3 Read the text. How Does the Flu Spread?

Influenza spreads through viruses. You can get them when you breathe in little drops that come from an infected person's mouth and nose when they sneeze, cough, or even laugh. You can also catch the flu if the drops get on your hands and you touch your mouth or nose.

Influenza viruses can easily get into your body. They have lots of spikes and with these they stick to cells and travel through the body.

Influenza viruses

When the body's immune system notices the viruses, it raises body temperature. When the body temperature is higher, the virus cannot multiply so easily. Normally, and with the help of medicines, the immune system wins the fight against the flu in a week. So why is influenza sometimes so dangerous? Because small children and old people do not have a very strong immune system. But also because the influenza virus often changes. And then we need new medicines because the old medicines do not help any more.

> **What can you do when you get flu?**
>
> Stay in bed for about a week. Drink a lot and take your medicine.

Mini-project Illnesses

4 Use a dictionary. Find the names of these illnesses in your language.

chicken pox   mumps   pneumonia   measles

Choose one of the illnesses. Search the Internet or check in the library to answer the following questions:

1 What causes the illness? A virus? Something else?
2 Who normally gets the illness?
3 Is it a dangerous illness?
4 What can you do when you get it?
5 Have you ever had this illness yourself?

Flu is an illness that often occurs during the cold months. It spreads through viruses, and it is especially dangerous for older people and small children. If you have flu, you have to stay in bed for about a week. You should drink a lot, and take medication. I always get a flu shot before the cold months start. I think it helps.

The city of Vancouver

KEY WORDS
capital
scenery
climate
moderate
current
rainfall
minority
population
community

1 Work in pairs. Can you answer the following questions?

a Is Canada larger than the United States?
b What is the capital of Canada?
c Which is the biggest city?
d What leaf is shown in the flag of Canada?

2 Read the text. Would you like to go to Vancouver or not? Why?

Vancouver is a city in the south west of British Columbia, very close to the border with the USA, and it is the third largest in Canada (after Toronto and Montreal) with a population in Greater Vancouver of just over 2 million people. It is named after a British explorer, Captain George Vancouver.

It is a popular place for tourists. The city is famous for its beautiful scenery and it has one of the largest city parks in North America, called Stanley Park. The mountains near the coast can be seen from many places within the city.

Vancouver also has beaches that are popular with the people who live there and tourists during the summer. Lots of people in Vancouver have sailing boats and you can see lots of white sails on beautiful days.

In the winter, people go skiing in the mountains. It's not very cold in the winter because there is a warm ocean current that flows past the city. The summer months are sunny with moderate temperatures (the daily maximum averages 22°C in July and August) and are often quite dry as well. In the winter months, there is quite a lot of rain. Snow falls on only eleven days per year, with only three days getting six centimetres or more.

3 **Read the quiz questions. What do you think the answers are? Tick a, b or c.**

1 Which are the two official languages of Canada?
- a ☐ English and French
- b ☐ English and Spanish
- c ☐ English and Mandarin Chinese

2 Which two languages are mainly spoken in Vancouver?
- a ☐ English and French
- b ☐ English and Spanish
- c ☐ English and Mandarin Chinese

3 What percentage of Vancouver's population is white?
- a ☐ 51%
- b ☐ 71%
- c ☐ 75%

4 What are the two largest minority groups in Vancouver?
- a ☐ Chinese and French
- b ☐ Chinese and Indian
- c ☐ Indian and Vietnamese

4 **Read the text and check your ideas.**

Hongcouver

Many people know that Canada has two official languages, which are English and French. This is why the information on anything you buy in Canada is written in both languages. But there one thing that not so many people know. The two main languages in Vancouver you'll hear in the streets are English and Mandarin Chinese.

The Chinese community in Vancouver is very big – Mandarin Chinese is spoken as the first language in about 30% of the homes. There has been a Chinese community in British Columbia for a very long time, but it grew a great deal in the 1980s. Then many people left Hong Kong before it became part of China. The Chinese community is now so large that many people call the city "Hongcouver".

But the Chinese are not the only non-white community in Vancouver. Indeed, the white population makes up only 51%. The largest group after the Chinese are Indians, but there are also lots of people from Vietnam and Korea.

Mini-project City guide

5 **Choose a city that you know something about and/or are interested in. It could be a city in your own country, or somewhere else in the world. Research on the internet and find information about things like:**

- its location
- its geographical features (e.g. is it on a river? is it near the sea or mountains?)
- its climate
- its population (ethnic mix)
- the language(s) that people speak

6 **Write a text about the city you have chosen. Find/Download some photographs that can illustrate the main points of your text.**

Geography

U6/10 = Unit 6 Exercise 10; D = DVD; ME = More Essential English; G = Grammar; F = Fido; EU = Extra Unit;
MORE I = Wörter, die schon in MORE I vorgekommen sind; MORE II = Wörter, die schon in MORE II vorgekommen sind;
MORE III = Wörter, die schon in MORE III vorgekommen sind

A

a matter of life and death U13/D3	[ə'mætə əv 'laɪf n 'deθ]	Es geht um Leben und Tod.
(be) able to do MORE III	[bi: 'eɪbl tə 'du:]	tun können
abnormal U10/4	[æb'nɔ:məl]	anormal
Aboriginal U8/8	[æbə'rɪdʒɪnəl]	der Ureinwohner
Aborigine U8/1	[æbə'rɪdʒənɪ]	Ureinwohner/in
(be) about MORE III	[bi ə'baʊt]	handeln von
about (5.30 a.m.) U8/4	[ə'baʊt]	so gegen (halb sechs Uhr morgens)
above MORE I	[ə'bʌv]	über
abroad U9/D	[ə'brɔ:d]	Ausland
absolutely MORE III	[æbsə'lu:tli]	absolut
accept U6/11	[ək'sept]	hinnehmen, akzeptieren
accident MORE I	['æksɪdənt]	Unfall
accountant U5/1	[ə'kaʊntənt]	Buchhalter/in, Wirtschaftsprüfer/in
ache MORE II	[eɪk]	Schmerz(en)
achieve U11/6a	[ə'tʃi:v]	erreichen
across MORE III	[ə'krɒs]	über
act MORE III	[ækt]	handeln; hier: auftreten
act out MORE III	['ækt 'aʊt]	nachspielen
actor/actress MORE III	['æktə, 'æktrəs]	Schauspieler/in
add MORE III	[æd]	hinzufügen
admire U7/8b	[əd'maɪə]	bewundern
advert U13/5	['ædvɜ:t]	Reklame, Anzeige
advertisement U10/ME3	[əd'vɜ:.tɪs.mənt]	Reklame, Anzeige
advice MORE III	[əd'vaɪs]	Rat
aerobics U5/ME3	[eə'rəʊbɪks]	Aerobic
affected U6/10	[ə'fektɪd]	beeinflusst
(be) afraid (of) MORE III	['bɪ ə'freɪd]	Angst haben/sich fürchten (vor)
I'm afraid (so) MORE II	[aɪm ə'freɪd]	leider
African MORE III	['æfrɪkən]	Afrikaner/in; afrikanisch
African-American MORE III	['æfrɪkən ə'merɪkən]	Afroamerikaner/in; afroamerikanisch
after MORE III	['ɑ:ftə]	nachdem
afterwards U6/11	['ɑ:ftəwədz]	nachher
against MORE II	[ə'genst]	gegen
age MORE II	[eɪdʒ]	Alter
aged (11) MORE II	[eɪdʒd]	(11) Jahre alt
agree MORE III	[ə'gri:]	zustimmen
agreement U11/3a	[ə'gri:mənt]	Vereinbarung
aircraft U8/8	['eəkrɑ:ft]	Flugzeug
airport MORE II	['eə'pɔ:t]	Flughafen
airship U13/ME1	['eəʃɪp]	Luftschiff
alive MORE II	[ə'laɪv]	lebendig, am Leben
all over MORE III	['ɔ:l 'əʊvə]	überall in/auf
(be not) allowed to do sth MORE III	[bi: ə'laʊd tə 'du:]	etwas (nicht) tun dürfen
allow sth MORE III	[ə'laʊ]	etwas erlauben, ermöglichen, gestatten
almost MORE II	['ɔ:lməʊst]	fast, beinahe
already MORE II	[ɔ:l'redi]	schon
alternative U7/ME3	[ɒl'tɜ:nətɪv]	Alternative
although MORE III	[ɔ:l'ðəʊ]	obwohl
ambition U5/9	[æm'bɪʃən]	Ehrgeiz
American MORE III	[ə'merɪkən]	Amerikaner/in; amerikanisch
among U1/5	[ə'mʌŋ]	unter
amongst U4/1	[ə'mʌŋst]	unter, zwischen
annoy U11/5	[ə'nɔɪ]	(ver)ärgern
anthology U12/5	[æn'θɒlədʒɪ]	Anthologie, Sammlung
(not) any more MORE III	['nɒt eni 'mɔ:]	nicht mehr
anybody MORE II	['eni'bɒdi]	irgendjemand
anyone MORE III	['eniwʌn]	irgendjemand
Anything else? MORE III	['ænɪθɪŋ 'els]	Sonst noch was?
anyway MORE III	['eni'weɪ]	sowieso; jedenfalls
appear MORE II	[ə'pɪə]	erscheinen
appearance MORE III	[ə'pɪərəns]	Erscheinen; Auftritt
apply for EU/4	[ə'plaɪ]	sich bewerben
aquarium (pl -s or -ria) MORE III	[ə'kweəriəm]	Aquarium
arch enemy U7/3	['ɑ:tʃ 'enəmɪ]	Erzfeind/in
are we still on for U4/D3	['ɑ: wi: stɪl'ɒn fə]	Gilt das noch ...?
area MORE II	['eəriə]	Gebiet, Region
Argentina MORE III	[ɑ:dʒən'ti:nə]	Argentinien
army MORE III	['ɑ:mi]	Armee
arrest MORE III	[ə'rest]	Verhaftung
arrow MORE III	['ærəʊ]	Pfeil
artificial U6/6b	[ɑ:tɪ'fɪʃəl]	künstlich
artist EU/2	['ɑ:tɪst]	Künstler/in
as MORE III	[æz]	wie
Asia U6/10	['eɪʒə]	Asien
ask sb for sth MORE III	['ɑ:sk fə]	jdn um etwas bitten
ask sb out U12/4	['ɑ:sk aʊt]	jdn einladen
asylum U3/1b	[ə'saɪləm]	Asyl
at least MORE III	[ət 'li:st]	mindestens, wenigstens
at the same time MORE III	[æt ðə 'seɪm 'taɪm]	gleichzeitig
atmosphere U13/2	['ætməsfɪə]	Atmosphäre
attack MORE III	[ə'tæk]	Angriff
attention U7/3	[ə'tenʃn]	Aufmerksamkeit
attractive U2/2	[ə'træktɪv]	attraktiv
Austrian U9/1	['ɒstriən]	Österreicher/in, Österreichisch
author U12/1	['ɔ:θə]	Autor/in
autograph EU/3	['ɔ:təgrɑ:f]	Autogramm
automatically U2/15	[ɔ:tə'mætɪklɪ]	automatisch
avenue U1/ME1	['ævənju:]	Allee; Boulevard
average MORE II	['ævərɪdʒ]	durchschnittlich
award MORE III	[ə'wɔ:d]	Preis, Auszeichnung

(be) aware (of) U1/2	[ə'weə]	(etwas) bewusst sein
awesome MORE II	['ɔ:səm]	beeindruckend
awful MORE III	['ɔ:fl]	furchtbar, schrecklich, scheußlich
Aztec U9/1	['æztek]	Azteke/Aztekin

B

back MORE III	[bæk]	Hinter-
back seat MORE III	['bæk 'si:t]	Rücksitz
background U4/5	['bæk'graʊnd]	Hintergrund
backup U2/ME3	['bækʌp]	hier: Sicherheitskopie
badly U1/3b	['bædli]	hier: dringend
balcony MORE III	['bælkəni]	Balkon
bandage MORE II	['bændɪdʒ]	Verband
bark U8/4	[bɑ:k]	(Baum)rinde, Borke
basically U3/1b	['beɪsɪklɪ]	im Grunde genommen
be (not) sure MORE III	[bi: 'ʃɔ:]	sich (nicht) sicher sein
be against sb/sth MORE III	[bi: ə'genst]	gegen jdn/ etwas sein
be up late MORE III	[bi: 'ʌp 'leɪt]	lange aufbleiben
beam U7/7	[bi:m]	(Licht-) Strahl
beat MORE III	[bi:t]	schlagen, klopfen
beat sb up U3/1b	[bi:t 'ʌp]	jdn zusammenschlagen
Beats me. U6/D3	['bi:ts mi:]	Ist mir ein Rätsel.
because of MORE III	[bɪ'kɒz əv]	wegen
become MORE I	[bɪ'kʌm]	werden
beggar EU/6	['begə]	Bettler/in
begin MORE III	[bɪ'gɪn]	anfangen, beginnen
behave MORE II	[bɪ'heɪv]	sich benehmen
believe MORE I	[bɪ'li:v]	glauben
belong MORE II	[bɪ'lɒŋ]	gehören
below MORE II	[bɪ'ləʊ]	unten; unterhalb
best wishes EU/1	[best 'wɪʃɪz]	mit den besten Wünschen
Better late than never. U14/D3	['betə 'leɪt ðən 'nevə]	Besser spät als nie.
between MORE II	[bɪ'twi:n]	zwischen
between me and you U6/D3	[bɪ'twi:n mi: n 'ju:]	unter uns beiden
bewitched U4/3b	[bɪ'wɪtʃt]	verhext
bicycle U11/8b	['baɪsɪkl]	Fahrrad
bill MORE III	[bɪl]	Rechnung
bin MORE III	[bɪn]	Mülleimer
biography MORE III	[baɪ'ɒgrəfi]	Biografie
bit U4/5	[bɪt]	Stück, Teil
black and white U1/D3	['blæk n 'waɪt]	schwarzweiß
black market U10/1	[blæk 'mɑ:kɪt]	Schwarzmarkt
blackmail U2/3	['blækmeɪl]	Erpressung
blanket MORE III	['blæŋkɪt]	(Bett)decke
bleeding MORE III	['bli:dɪŋ]	Blutung
block sth MORE III	['blɒk]	etwas blockieren
blond MORE III	[blɒnd]	blond
blow MORE III	[bləʊ]	wehen, blasen
(on) board MORE III	[ɒn 'bɔ:d]	an Bord
body U2/1	['bɒdi]	Leiche
book MORE III	[bʊk]	reservieren, buchen
boot MORE II	[bu:t]	Stiefel
booth U7/3	[bu:ð]	Zelle
border MORE III	['bɔ:də]	Grenze
(be) born MORE II	[bɔ:n]	geboren (sein/ werden)
borrow (from) MORE II	['bɒrəʊ]	ausleihen (von)
bowl MORE II	[bəʊl]	Schüssel
bracelet U9/ME3	['breɪslət]	Armreif
brave MORE III	[breɪv]	mutig, unerschrocken
break sth MORE III	['breɪk]	etwas zerbrechen
break up U13/2	[breɪk 'ʌp]	auseinanderbrechen
breakthrough U7/7	['breɪkθru:]	Durchbruch
brick U1/3a	[brɪk]	Backstein
bride U9/5b	[braɪd]	Braut
bridegroom U9/5b	['braɪdgrʊm]	Bräutigam
bridesmaid U9/5b	['braɪdzmeɪd]	Brautjungfer
bright MORE II	[braɪt]	hell, leuchtend
(the) British MORE III	[ðə 'brɪtɪʃ]	die Briten
burn MORE III	[bɜ:n]	(ver)brennen
bury U9/3b	['berɪ]	begraben
business MORE III	['bɪznəs]	Geschäft
businessman (pl -men) MORE III	['bɪznəsmən, 'bɪznəsmen]	Geschäftsmann
by U1/9	[baɪ]	bis (spätestens)
by MORE III	[baɪ]	durch
by MORE III	[baɪ]	von
by the way U4/D3	['baɪ ðə 'weɪ]	übrigens

C

cab U3/10	[kæb]	Taxi
cabbage MORE II	['kæbɪdʒ]	Kohl, Kraut
call MORE III	[kɔ:l]	Anruf
call MORE III	[kɔ:l]	hier: nennen
caller MORE III	['kɔ:lə]	Anrufer/in
calm MORE III	[kɑ:m]	ruhig, friedlich; windstill
calm down MORE II	[kɑ:m 'daʊn]	sich beruhigen
calorie U6/10	['kælərɪ]	Kalorie
can't stand sth U6/14	[kænt 'stænd]	etwas nicht leiden können
care for MORE II	['keə fə]	sich kümmern um
career U5/9	[kə'rɪə]	Karriere, Berufslaufbahn
carpet MORE II	['kɑ:pɪt]	Teppich
case MORE I	[keɪs]	Fall; Hülle
cash U3/ME2	[kæʃ]	Bargeld
cash desk EU/10	['kæʃ desk]	Kasse
catchy U7/6	['kætʃɪ]	eingängig
Catholic U1/2	['kæθəlɪk]	katholisch, Katholik/in
cause U7/4	[kɔ:z]	weil
celebrate U13/11	['selɪbreɪt]	feiern
celery U6/6a	['selərɪ]	Sellerie
central MORE III	['sentrəl]	zentral, Mittel-
century MORE III	['sentʃəri]	Jahrhundert
ceremony U9/3b	['serɪməni]	Zeremonie
certainly MORE I	['sɜ:tnli]	sicher(lich); bestimmt
champagne U1/5	[ʃæm'peɪn]	Champagner; Sekt
champion EU/4	['tʃæmpjən]	Meister/in
championship U4/3a	['tʃæmpjənʃɪp]	Meisterschaft
chance MORE III	[tʃɑ:ns]	Möglichkeit; Chance
change MORE I	[tʃeɪndʒ]	(sich) (ver)ändern
change U6/6b	[tʃeɪndʒ]	Veränderung, Wechsel
cheap MORE III	[tʃi:p]	billig, preiswert
cheer MORE III	[tʃɪə]	Hurraruf, Beifallsruf; Jubel

cheque U8/2	[tʃek]	Scheck
chest U2/1	[tʃest]	Brust
chew gum U5/8b	[tʃu: gʌm]	Kaugummi kauen
chill out EU/2	[tʃɪl 'aʊt]	relaxen
Chinese U6/ME4	[tʃaɪ'ni:z]	chinesisch
choice MORE III	[tʃɔɪs]	Wahl
choose MORE II	[tʃu:z]	auswählen
chorus U2/12	['kɔ:rəs]	Refrain
church MORE II	[tʃɜ:tʃ]	Kirche
civil U12/7	['sɪvəl]	höflich, beherrscht
claim U11/6a	[kleɪm]	behaupten
classmate MORE II	['klɑ:smeɪt]	Klassenkamerad/in, Mitschüler/in
clerk U2/2	[klɑ:k]	Sachbearbeiter/in
climb U8/4	[klaɪm]	Klettertour
climbing U7/ME1	['klaɪmɪŋ]	Bergsteigen, Klettern
close MORE III	[kləʊs]	nahe
clothes MORE I	['kləʊðz]	Kleider, Kleidung
clothing U3/ME3	['kləʊðɪŋ]	Kleidung
coach MORE III	[kəʊtʃ]	Trainer
coal EU/6	[kəʊl]	Kohle
cold MORE III	[kəʊld]	Erkältung
cold MORE III	[kəʊld]	Kälte
collapse MORE III	[kə'læps]	zusammenbrechen, einstürzen
colleague U10/1	['kɒli:g]	Kollege/Kollegin
collection MORE III	[kə'lekʃn]	Sammlung
collector U10	[kə'lektə]	Sammler/in
college MORE III	['kɒlɪdʒ]	Gymnasium, College
colony U4/5	['kɒlənɪ]	Kolonie
colourful U10/9	['kʌləfl]	bunt
column MORE III	['kɒləm]	Säule; hier: Spalte
comedy MORE III	['kɒmədi]	Komödie
commander U13/12	[kə'mɑ:ndə]	Kommandant/in
commercial U13/7	[kə'mɜ:ʃəl]	kommerziell
commit U2/15	[kə'mɪt]	begehen
communicate U9/1	[kə'mju:nɪkeɪt]	kommunizieren
communication U4/G	[kəmju:nɪ'keɪʃən]	Kommunikation
community U3/1b	[kə'mju:nəti]	Gemeinschaft
company MORE III	['kʌmp(ə)ni]	Gesellschaft, Firma
compare U1/4	[kəm'peə]	vergleichen
comparison U6/10	[kəm'pærɪsən]	Vergleich
completely MORE III	[kəm'pli:tli]	völlig
comprehensive (school) U3/1b	[kɒmprɪ'hentsɪv sku:l]	Gesamtschule
computer programmer U2/2	[kəm'pju:tə 'prəʊgræmə]	Programmierer/in
computing U5/3	[kəm'pju:tɪŋ]	Computerbranche
concentration camp U12/2	[kɒnsən'treɪʃən 'kæmp]	Konzentrationslager
conflict U14/2	['kɒnflɪkt]	Konflikt; Streit
confused U9/5a	[kə'fju:zd]	verwirrt
consequence MORE III	['kɒnsɪkwəns]	Folge, Konsequenz
consider U9/9	[kən'sɪdə]	erwägen
constantly U13/2	['kɒnstəntlɪ]	ständig
contact MORE III	['kɒntækt]	Kontakt
contact sb MORE III	['kɒntækt]	sich mit jdm in Verbindung setzen
contain EU/8	[kən'teɪn]	enthalten
contents U10/5	['kɒntents]	Inhalt
contestant U8/2	[kən'testənt]	Teilnehmer/in
context U12/7	['kɒntekst]	Zusammenhang
continue MORE III	[kən'tɪnju:]	fortsetzen
control sth MORE III	[kən'trəʊl]	etwas regulieren/ kontrollieren
cookery U6/6b	['kʊkərɪ]	Kochen
cooped up U12/7	[ku:pt 'ʌp]	eingesperrt
coordinate MORE II	[kəʊ'ɔ:dɪnət]	Koordinate
copy MORE III	['kɒpi]	Kopie; hier: Exemplar
correct sth MORE III	[kə'rekt]	etwas korrigieren
correction U13/D1	[kə'rekʃn]	Korrektur
cost MORE III	[kɒst]	kosten
could MORE III	[kʊd]	könnte(n)/ könntest/könntet
countryside MORE III	['kʌntri'saɪd]	Land(schaft)
(a) couple of U12/10	[ə 'kʌpl əv]	einige, ein paar
courage MORE III	['kʌrɪdʒ]	Mut
course MORE III	[kɔ:s]	Kurs, Lehrgang
court U5/ME3	[kɔ:t]	Gericht
cover MORE II	['kʌvə]	bedecken
cover MORE III	['kʌvə]	Abdeckung; hier: Cover
crash into sth MORE III	['kræʃ 'ɪntə]	mit jdm / etwas zusammenstoßen
crawl U8/4	[krɔ:l]	kriechen
cream of potato soup U6/ME3	['kri:m əv pə'teɪtəʊ'su:p]	Kartoffelcreme-suppe
create MORE II	[kri'eɪt]	erschaffen, kreieren
credit card MORE III	['kredɪt 'kɑ:d]	Kreditkarte
crew U13/2	[kru:]	Mannschaft, Besatzung
crime scene U2/16	['kraɪm'si:n]	Tatort
criminal U2/9	['krɪmɪnl]	Verbrecher/in
crisps U6/1	[krɪsps]	Kartoffelchips
critic MORE III	['krɪtɪk]	Kritiker/in
crop U1/3b	[krɒp]	Ernte
cross MORE II	[krɒs]	durchqueren, überqueren; Kreuz
cross my heart U13/D3	['krɒs maɪ 'hɑ:t]	Ehrenwort
cross out U1/5	[krɒs 'aʊt]	ausstreichen, durchstreichen
crowd EU/2	[kraʊd]	(Menschen)menge; Zuschauermenge
culture U3/5	['kʌltʃə]	Kultur
cure U7/7	['kjʊə]	Heilmittel
curious U2	['kjʊərɪəs]	neugierig; hier: seltsam
cute MORE III	[kju:t]	süß, niedlich

D

dagger U2/15	['dægə]	Dolch
daily MORE III	['deɪli]	täglich
damage U13/4	['dæmɪdʒ]	Schaden
danger MORE II	['deindʒə]	Gefahr
dangerous MORE II	['deɪndʒərəs]	gefährlich
darling U7/8a	['dɑ:lɪŋ]	Schatz
daybreak U11/1	['deɪbreɪk]	Tageseinbruch
daydream U4/D3	['deɪdri:m]	tagträumen; Tagtraum
daylight U13/2	['deɪlaɪt]	Tageslicht
dead MORE II	[ded]	tot
deal MORE III	[di:l]	Deal
death MORE III	[deθ]	Tod
debit card U3/ME1	['debɪt kɑ:d]	Bankkarte; Kundenkarte
decent-looking U9/5b	['di:sənt'lʊkɪŋ]	einigermaßen gut aussehend
decide MORE III	[dɪ'saɪd]	(sich) entscheiden; beschließen

definitely MORE II	['defənətli]	eindeutig, definitiv; auf jeden Fall
definition MORE III	['defə'nɪʃn]	Definition, Erklärung
delicious MORE III	[dɪ'lɪʃəs]	köstlich, lecker
demonstrate U6/D2	['demənstreɪt]	demonstrieren
demonstrator U6/D2	['demənstreɪtə]	Demonstrant/in
dentist MORE III	['dentist]	Zahnarzt/ Zahnärztin
depend MORE II	[dɪ'pend]	abhängen von
depressed U13/11	[dɪ'prest]	deprimiert
describe MORE III	[dɪ'skraɪb]	beschreiben
desert sb MORE III	[dɪ'zɜ:t]	jdn verlassen; jdn im Stich lassen
deserve U5/6	[dɪ'zɜ:v]	verdienen
design U5/MEI	[dɪ'zaɪn]	gestalten
destroy MORE II	[dɪ'strɔɪ]	zerstören
detailed U8/8	['di:teɪld]	detailliert
developed U6/10	[di'veləpt]	entwickelt
devil U9/3b	['devl]	Teufel
dial U12/7	['daɪəl]	wählen (Telefon)
diary entry U1/3b	['daɪərɪ 'entrɪ]	Tagebucheintrag
die out MORE III	[daɪ 'aʊt]	aussterben
diet U6/14	['daɪət]	gesunde Ernährung
difference U3/5	['dɪfrəns]	Unterschied
directions MORE II	[dɪ'rekʃəns]	Anweisungen
director MORE III	[dɪ'rektə]	Direktor/in; hier: Regisseur/in
disability U7/8b	[dɪsə'bɪlɪtɪ]	Behinderung
disagree U5/8b	[dɪsə'gri:]	anderer Meinung sein
disappear MORE II	[dɪsə'pɪə]	verschwinden
disappointed MORE II	[dɪsə'pɔɪntɪd]	enttäuscht
disaster MORE III	[dɪ'zɑ:stə]	Katastrophe, Unglück
discipline EU/4	['dɪsəplɪn]	Disziplin
discount U7/MEI	['dɪskaʊnt]	Rabatt; Preisnachlass
discover MORE II	[dɪ'skʌvə]	herausfinden, entdecken
discuss MORE III	[dɪ'skʌs]	besprechen, diskutieren
dishwasher U2/7	['dɪʃwɒʃə]	Spülmaschine
dislike U6/9	[dɪ'slaɪk]	nicht mögen
disqualified EU/4	[dɪs'kwɒlɪ'faɪd]	disqualifiziert
distance MORE III	['dɪstəns]	Strecke; Entfernung
disturb U13/11	[dɪ'stɜ:b]	stören
diving EU/1	['daɪvɪŋ]	Tauchen
do the dishes MORE III	['du: ðə 'dɪʃɪz]	(ab)spülen, abwaschen
don't just stand there U13/D3	['dəʊnt dʒʌst 'stænd ðeə]	Steh nicht einfach da!
don't mention it U9/D3	[dəʊnt 'menʃn ɪt]	Keine Ursache!
don't you dare! U2/D3	['dəʊt jʊ 'deə]	Wage es nicht!
double MORE I	['dʌbl]	doppelt, Doppel-
down MORE I	[daʊn]	hinunter, hinab
down under U8	[daʊn'ʌndə]	da unten, Name für Australien/ Neuseeland
download EU/8	[daʊn'ləʊd]	herunterladen
downtown U4/1	[daʊn'taʊn]	Innenstadt
drag U8/4	[dræg]	schleppen
dramatic MORE III	[drə'mætɪk]	dramatisch
dress MORE I	[dres]	Kleid
driving licence EU/10	['draɪvɪŋ 'laɪsəns]	Führerschein
drugs U8/7	[drʌgz]	Drogen; hier: Medikamente
during MORE III	['djʊərɪŋ]	während

E

e.g. MORE III	['i:'dʒi:]	z. B.
each MORE I	[i:tʃ]	jede/r/s
each other MORE III	['i:tʃ 'ʌðə]	einander
earn U5/8a	[ɜ:n]	verdienen
earring MORE III	['ɪərɪŋ]	Ohrring
earth MORE II	[ɜ:θ]	Erde
Easter U1/3b	['i:stə]	Ostern
eat out U6/14	[i:t 'aʊt]	zum Essen ausgehen
eating disorder U6/11	['i:tɪŋ dɪ'sɔ:də]	Essstörung
ebony U11/7	['ebnɪ]	Ebenholz
edition EU/1	[ɪ'dɪʃn]	Ausgabe
editor MORE III	['edɪtə]	Herausgeber/in
effect MORE III	[ɪ'fekt]	Auswirkung, Folge
(not) either MORE III	[nɒt 'aɪðə]	auch nicht
elder EU/2	['eldə]	älter
electrician U5/1	[ɪlek'trɪʃn]	Elektriker/in
embarrassed U9/5b	[ɪm'bærəst]	verlegen, beschämt
emotion U3/1a	[ɪ'məʊʃn]	Emotion, Gefühl
employee U2/1	[ɪm'plɔɪi:]	Angestellte/r
enemy U7/2	['enəmɪ]	Feind/in
enjoy MORE I	[ɪn'dʒɔɪ]	genießen
enjoyable U7/7	[ɪn'dʒɔɪəbl]	nett, unterhaltsam
enormous U8/8	[ɪ'nɔ:məs]	riesengroß
enough MORE I	[ɪ'nʌf]	genügend, ausreichend, genug
enter U9/1	['entə]	eintreten
entertainment U5/8a	[entə'teɪnmənt]	Unterhaltung
enthusiastic U8/8	[ɪnθju:zɪ'æstɪk]	begeistert, enthusiastisch
entry MORE III	['entri]	Eintritt; Eintrag
envelope U8/2	['envələʊp]	Kuvert, Briefumschlag
environment MORE III	[ɪn'vaɪrənmənt]	Umgebung; hier: Umwelt
escape MORE II	[ɪ'skeɪp]	(ent)fliehen; entkommen
estate car EU/10	['ɪsteɪt 'kɑ:]	Kombiwagen
even MORE II	['i:vn]	selbst; sogar
even though U6/6b	['i:vn ðəʊ]	obwohl
event MORE III	[ɪ'vent]	Ereignis
event manager U5/8a	[ɪ'vent 'mænɪdʒə]	Veranstaltungs-organisator/in
ever MORE II	['evə]	je
every MORE I	['evri]	jede/r/s
everybody MORE I	['evribɒdi]	jede/r; alle
everyone MORE II	['evriwʌn]	jede/r; alle
everything MORE I	['evriθɪŋ]	alles
everywhere MORE II	['evriweə]	überall
evil U7/8a	['i:vl]	böse
except U6/F	[ɪk'sept]	außer
excited MORE I	[ɪk'saɪtɪd]	aufgeregt
exciting MORE I	[ɪk'saɪtɪŋ]	aufregend; spannend
exhausted U3/MEI	[ɪg'zɔ:stɪd]	erschöpft
expect U5/11	[ɪk'spekt]	erwarten
expensive MORE III	[ɪk'spensɪv]	teuer
experience U5/9	[ɪk'spɪərɪəns]	Erfahrung
experienced U10/5	[ɪk'spɪəriənst]	erfahren, geschult
expert U8/2	['ekspɜ:t]	Experte/Expertin
explain MORE II	[ɪk'spleɪn]	erklären
explore MORE III	[ɪk'splɔ:]	erforschen, erkunden
explorer MORE III	[ɪk'splɔ:rə]	Forscher/in
explosion U13/1	[ɪk'spləʊʒn]	Explosion
extract MORE III	['ekstrækt]	Auszug, Exzerpt

eye contact U5/8b	[aɪ'kɒntækt]	Augenkontakt
eyelashes U9/5b	['aɪlæʃɪz]	Wimpern
eyeliner U9/5b	['aɪlaɪnə]	Eyeliner

F

be full of MORE III	['fʊl əv]	voller… sein
face MORE I	[feɪs]	sich zuwenden, ins Auge sehen
fact file U7/2	['fækt faɪl]	Info-Akte
factory MORE III	['fæktri]	Fabrik; Werk
Fair Trade U11/1	['feə 'treɪd]	"Fair Trade", eine Organisation sie sich für fairen Handel einsetzt
fairness U11/8b	['feənəs]	Gerechtigkeit, Fairness
fall in love MORE III	['fɔ:l ɪn 'lʌv]	sich verlieben
fall off MORE III	['fɔ:l 'ɒf]	zurückgehen; hier: herausfallen aus, herunterfallen von
familiar U7/3	[fə'mɪliə]	bekannt
famine U1/3b	['fæmɪn]	Hungersnot
Far East U9/5a	[fɑ: 'ri:st]	Fernost
fare U13/9	['feə]	Fahrpreis
fascinate U10/1	['fæsɪneɪt]	faszinieren
fascination U10/1	[fæsɪ'neɪʃn]	Faszination
fashion EU/ME3	['fæʃn]	Mode
fashionable U9/1	['fæʃnəbl]	in Mode
fattening U6/6a	['fætnɪŋ]	dick machend
fault MORE II	[fɔ:lt]	Schuld
fear MORE III	[fɪə]	Angst; fürchten
feed MORE I	[fi:d]	zu essen geben, füttern
feeling U5/8a	['fi:lɪŋ]	Gefühl
fellow U7/2	['feləʊ]	-kollege/-kollegin
female U5/6	['fi:meɪl]	weiblich
fence MORE II	[fens]	Zaun
fête EU/ME3	[feɪt]	Fest
few MORE II	[fju:]	wenige
(for a) few (minutes) U2/4	['fju:]	einige (Minuten lang)
fight MORE III	[faɪt]	Kampf; hier: Streit
figure U6/10	['fɪgə]	Zahl
fine MORE III	[faɪn]	schön
finance U5/3	['faɪnæns]	Finanzwesen
first MORE III	[fɜ:st]	zuerst, als Erstes; zum ersten Mal
first aid U8/8	['fɜ:st eɪd]	Erste Hilfe
firstly U9/1	['fɜ:stlɪ]	erstens
fix MORE III	[fɪks]	reparieren
flight MORE II	[flaɪt]	Fliegen; Flug
flight attendant U5/1	['flaɪt ə'tendnt]	Flugbegleiter/in
fluent U1/1	['flu:ənt]	fließend (Sprache)
focus EU/8	['fəʊkəs]	Richtung, Betonung
following MORE III	['fɒləʊɪŋ]	folgende/r/s
footprint U2/15	['fʊtprɪnt]	Fußabdruck
for MORE III	[fɔ:]	hier: nach
for MORE III	[fɔ:]	seit
for the first time MORE III	[fə ðə 'fɜ:st 'taɪm]	zum ersten Mal
foreigner U1/6	['fɒrənə]	Ausländer/in
form U13/ME1	[fɔ:m]	(sich) bilden
fortunately U8/4	['fɔ:tʃnətlɪ]	glücklicherweise
found U1/3b	[faʊnd]	gründen
four-leaf clover U1/F	['fɔ: li:f 'kləʊvə]	vierblättriger Klee
free state U1/3b	['fri: 'steɪt]	Freistaat
fresh MORE III	[freʃ]	neu; frisch
frightening MORE III	['fraɪtnɪŋ]	Furcht erregend, beängstigend
from … to … MORE III	['frəm 'tə]	von … nach …
frustrated MORE III	[frʌ'streɪtɪd]	frustriert
fuel U13/G	['fjʊəl]	Treibstoff
funeral U9/1	['fju:nərəl]	Begräbnis
fungus U1/3b	['fʌŋgəs]	Pilz
further U4/1	['fɜ:ðə]	weiter

G

gain U6/14	[geɪn]	zunehmen
gap U4/1	[gæp]	Lücke
gay U3/1b	[geɪ]	schwul, homosexuell
gently U13/9	['dʒentlɪ]	sanft
get MORE III	[get]	gelangen, kommen
get hold of sth U2/7	[get 'həʊld əv]	etwas in die Hände bekommen
get off U11/ME1	[get 'ɒf]	aussteigen (aus)
get on U13/ME3	[get 'ɒn]	einsteigen (in)
get on well (with) MORE III	['get ɒn 'wel wɪð]	sich gut verstehen
get out of here U12/D3	[get 'aʊt əv 'hɪə]	hier: Hör doch auf!
get out of sb's way MORE III	[get 'aʊt əv'weɪ]	jdm aus dem Weg gehen
get to MORE III	['get tu:]	ankommen, gelangen
gift U9/ME6	[gɪft]	Geschenk
giggle U9/5b	['gɪgl]	kichern
give up MORE III	[gɪv 'ʌp]	aufgeben
globe U9/ME3	[gləʊb]	Globus
go (to) MORE III	[gəʊ]	fahren
go ahead MORE III	[gəʊ ə'hed]	fortfahren, weitermachen
go by (sth) MORE III	['gəʊ 'baɪ]	mit (etwas) fahren
go down MORE III	[gəʊ 'daʊn]	hinunterfahren
go for a walk MORE III	['gəʊ fɔ:r ə 'wɔ:k]	spazieren gehen
go in MORE III	['gəʊ 'ɪn]	hineingehen
go off (the road) MORE III	['gəʊ 'ɒf]	(die Straße) verlassen; (von der Straße) abkommen
go wrong U13/2	['gəʊ 'rɒŋ]	schief gehen
golden eagle U10/5	['gəʊldn 'i:gl]	Steinadler
goth U9/5b	[gɒθ]	Grufti
government MORE III	['gʌvnmənt]	Regierung
governor U4/3b	['gʌvnə]	Gouverneur
grade (AE) U13/11	[greɪd]	Note
grain U1/3b	[greɪn]	Getreide
grand procession U4/1	['grænd prə'seʃn]	großer Umzug
green MORE III	[gri:n]	grün, umweltfreundlich, ökologisch
grounds U1/9	[graʊndz]	Gelände, Anlagen
group MORE III	[gru:p]	hier: Konzern
grow MORE II	[grəʊ]	wachsen; werden
grow sth U11/3	['grəʊ]	etwas anbauen, etwas wachsen lassen
grub (informal) U1/4	[grʌb]	ugs: Fraß
guess MORE I	[ges]	(er)raten
guilty U4/3b	['gɪltɪ]	schuldig
gym U5/ME3	[dʒɪm]	Turnhalle
sth grabs sb U12/2	[græb]	etwas interessiert jdn, etwas begeistert jdn

H

(to be) honest MORE III	[tə bi: 'ɒnɪst]	um die Wahrheit zu sagen; ehrlich gesagt
habit U6/9	['hæbɪt]	Gewohnheit
hand out MORE III	[hænd 'aʊt]	austeilen, verteilen
handbag U6/D1	['hænd'bæg]	Handtasche
hang out MORE III	['hæŋ 'aʊt]	heraushängen; hier: rumhängen
harbour U4/5	['hɑ:bə]	Hafen
hard disk U2/ME1	['hɑ:d'dɪsk]	Festplatte
hardly (ever) U7/8a	['hɑ:dli]	kaum
harmful U6/6a	['hɑ:mfəl]	schädlich
harmony U11/4	['hɑ:mənɪ]	Harmonie
hastily U9/5b	['heɪstɪlɪ]	hastig
have a look MORE III	['hæv ə 'lʊk]	sich ansehen
have an interest in sth MORE III	[hæv ən 'ɪntrəst ɪn]	an etwas Interesse haben, sich für etwas interessieren
have lunch MORE III	['hæv 'lʌntʃ]	zu Mittag essen
have no (pocket money) left U13/11	[həv nəʊ 'left]	kein (Taschengeld) mehr übrig haben
Have you got a moment? U2/D3	['hæv jʊ 'gɒt ə 'məʊmənt]	Haben Sie einen Moment Zeit?
head of state U8/2	['hed əv 'steɪt]	Staatsoberhaupt
headlight U8/4	['hedlaɪt]	Scheinwerfer
headline U1/9	['hed'laɪn]	Schlagzeile
headquarters MORE III	['hed'kwɔ:tez]	Hauptquartier, Zentrale
health U6/6a	[helθ]	Gesundheit
health risk U9/1	['helθrɪsk]	Gesundheitsrisiko
health care U5/3	['helθkeə]	Gesundheitsfürsorge
healthy MORE II	['helθi]	gesund
heart MORE III	[hɑ:t]	Herz
heavy MORE II	['hevi]	schwer
hell U11/8b	[hel]	Hölle
helpful U10/ME4	['helpfəl]	hilfreich
helping MORE III	['helpɪŋ]	hilfreich
helpless U11/5	['helpləs]	hilflos
here's to us U14/D	['hɪəz tə 'ʌs]	Auf uns!
herself U5/8a	[hɜ:'self]	sich selbst (weibl.)
hide-and-seek U10/6a	[haɪd ən 'si:k]	Versteckspiel
high school MORE III	['haɪ sku:l]	Gymnasium
highlight EU/2	['haɪlaɪt]	Höhepunkt
hike U14/ME6	['haɪkɪŋ]	Wandern
hiking U1/4	['haɪkɪŋ]	Wandern
himself U12/G	[hɪm'self]	sich selbst (männl.)
historical U2/9	[hɪ'stɒrɪkl]	historisch
hit MORE III	[hɪt]	treffen
hole MORE I	[həʊl]	Loch
hometown U10/9	[həʊmtaʊn]	Heimatstadt
honest MORE III	['ɒnɪst]	ehrlich
honestly MORE III	['ɒnɪstli]	wirklich, ehrlich
honeymoon U10/1	['hʌnɪmu:n]	Flitterwochen
hope MORE III	[həʊp]	Hoffnung
horrible MORE III	['hɒrəbl]	schrecklich
how come U1/8	['haʊ kʌm]	Wieso?
How could you? U2/D3	['haʊ 'kʊd ju:]	Wie konntest du?
How does that grab you? U1/D3	['haʊ dəz 'ðæt græb ju:]	Was hältst du davon?
however MORE III	[haʊ'eva]	jedoch
human being U11/4	['hju:mən 'bi:ɪŋ]	Mensch
hurt MORE III	[hɜ:t]	verletzt, verwundet
hurtful U11/4	['hɜ:tfəl]	verletzend
husband MORE I	['hʌzbənd]	Ehemann

I

I doubt it. U12/D3	[aɪ 'daʊt ɪt]	Das bezweifle ich.
I guess. MORE III	['aɪ 'ges]	Vermutlich.
I might have known. U13/D3	['aɪ 'maɪt əv 'nəʊn]	Das hätte ich mir denken können.
I'd rather U1/7	[aɪd 'rɑ:ðə]	ich würde lieber
I'll see what I can do. U9/D3	['aɪl si: wɒt 'aɪ kən 'du:]	Ich schaue mal, was ich machen kann.
I'm sorry. MORE III	[aɪm 'sɒri]	Das tut mir leid.
if MORE III	[ɪf]	wenn, falls; ob
ignore U9/5b	[ɪg'nɔ:]	ignorieren
illegal MORE III	[ɪ'li:gl]	ungesetzlich, rechtswidrig, illegal
illness MORE III	['ɪlnəs]	Krankheit, Erkrankung
imagine MORE II	[ɪ'mædʒɪn]	sich vorstellen
imitate U9/1	['ɪmɪteɪt]	imitieren
immediately U2/16	[ɪ'mi:diətli]	sofort
impossible MORE III	[ɪm'pɒsəbl]	unmöglich
improve U1/6	[ɪm'pru:v]	verbessern
in case ... MORE III	[ɪn 'keɪs]	für den Fall, dass...; falls...
in common U9/1	[ɪn'kɒmən]	gemein
in fact MORE III	[ɪn 'fækt]	genau genommen
in order to U3/G	[ɪn 'ɔ:də tə]	um... zu
incident U3/1a	['ɪnsɪdnt]	Vorfall
include MORE III	[ɪn'klu:d]	beinhalten, einschließen; beifügen
including U6/10	[ɪn'klu:dɪŋ]	einschließlich
incredible MORE III	[ɪn'kredəbl]	unglaublich
independent U1/2	[ɪndɪ'pendnt]	unabhängig
index finger U9/5a	['ɪndeks 'fɪŋgə]	Zeigefinger
industry U5/3	['ɪndəstri]	Industrie
infection U9/1	[ɪn'fekʃn]	Infektion
information MORE III	[ɪnfə'meɪʃn]	Information
ingredient U2/15	[ɪn'gri:dɪənt]	Zutat
injury U10/5	['ɪndʒrɪ]	Verletzung
innocent U12/2	['ɪnəsnt]	unschuldig
insult U9/G	['ɪnsʌlt]	beleidigen
intake U6/9	['ɪnteɪk]	Aufnahme
interest MORE III	['ɪntrəst]	Interesse
interrupt U4/5	['ɪntə'rʌpt]	unterbrechen
introduce U3/3	['ɪntrə'dju:s]	vorstellen
introduction U11/8b	[ɪntrə'dʌkʃn]	Einleitung
invent MORE II	[ɪn'vent]	erfinden
investigate U2/1	[ɪn'vestɪgeɪt]	ermitteln, untersuchen
investigation U2/15	[ɪnvestɪ'geɪʃn]	Ermittlungen, Untersuchung
invitation U11/G	[ɪnvɪ'teɪʃn]	Einladung
Irish U1/2	['aɪrɪʃ]	irisch, Ire/Irin
issue MORE III	['ɪʃu:]	Ausgabe; Nummer
it takes ... MORE III	[ɪt 'teɪks]	man braucht ...
it's a deal EU/ME1	['ɪts ə 'diəl]	Abgemacht!
It's her fault. U14/8	['ɪts hɜ: fɒlt]	Sie ist (selbst) schuld.
It's not really my scene. U8/D3	['ɪts 'nɒt 'rɪəlɪ maɪ 's:n]	Da stehe ich eigentlich nicht drauf.
item MORE III	['aɪtəm]	Punkt; hier: Gegenstand
ivory U11/7	['aɪvrɪ]	Elfenbein

J

Japanese MORE III	['dʒæpə'ni:z]	Japaner/in; japanisch
jewel MORE II	['dʒu:əl]	Juwel
journalism U5/9	['dʒɜ:nəlɪzm]	Journalismus
journalist MORE III	['dʒɜ:nəlɪst]	Journalist/in
judge U5/ME3	[dʒʌdʒ]	Richter/in
jump-start U8/4	['dʒʌmp'stɑ:t]	Starthilfe geben
junior cadet U5/6	['dʒu:nɪə kə'det]	Juniorkadett
just MORE III	[dʒʌst]	direkt, gleich

K

kangaroo U8/1	['kæŋg'ru:]	Känguru
(be) keen on MORE II	[ki:n]	sich begeistern für
keep an eye on U2/3	['ki:p ən 'aɪ ɒn]	aufpassen auf
keep away from U14/1	[ki:p ə'weɪ frəm]	die Finger von etwas lassen
kind MORE III	[kaɪnd]	Art, Sorte
knife (pl knives) MORE II	[naɪf, naɪvz]	Messer
knock MORE I	[nɒk]	Klopfen; klopfen

L

any longer MORE III	['eni 'lɒŋə]	nicht mehr
at least MORE II	[ət 'li:st]	mindestens, wenigstens
lab (= laboratory) MORE III	[læb]	Labor
ladder MORE III	['lædə]	Leiter
ladies' room U2/4	['leɪdiz ru:m]	Damentoilette
landing U8/8	['lændɪŋ]	Landung
landlord U1/3b	['lændlɔ:d]	Grundbesitzer
lane U14/ME1	[leɪn]	Weg
lantern U1/3a	['læntən]	Laterne
last but not least EU/2	['lɑ:st bʌt nɒt li:st]	nicht zuletzt
laugh MORE I	[lɑ:f]	lachen
laugh MORE III	[lɑ:f]	Lachen, Gelächter
leader U1/3b	['li:də]	Leiter/in, Führer/in
leading U1/2	['li:dɪŋ]	führend
leaflet MORE III	['li:flət]	Prospekt; hier: Flugblatt
(at) least MORE II	[li:st]	am wenigsten
least U4/2	[li:st]	geringste/r/s wenigste/r/s
leave it out U12/D3	['li:v ɪt aʊt]	Vergiss es.
leave sb alone U3/9	['li:v ə'ləʊn]	jdn in Ruhe lassen
legend EU/6	['ledʒnd]	Legende
leisure centre EU/2	['leʒə 'sentə]	Freizeitzentrum
lemonade U6/ME4	[lemə'neɪd]	Zitronenlimonade
lend MORE III	[lend]	leihen; borgen
let me guess U14/D3	[let mɪ' ges]	Lass mich raten.
Let's get cracking! U4/D3	[lets get' krækɪŋ]	Los jetzt!
librarian U10/3	[laɪ'breərɪən]	Bibliothekar/in
lie MORE III	[laɪ]	lügen
life (pl lives) MORE I	[laɪf, laɪvz]	Leben
like sth best U1/4	[laɪk best]	etwas/jdn am liebsten mögen
line MORE III	[laɪn]	Linie; Zeile; hier: (Telefon)leitung
lips MORE III	[lɪps]	Lippen
lipstick U1/5	['lɪpstɪk]	Lippenstift
live MORE III	[laɪv]	live, lebend
load U8/9	[ləʊd]	laden
lobster U4/1	['lɒbstə]	Hummer
local MORE III	['ləʊkl]	hiesig, örtlich
(door) lock MORE II	['dɔ: lɒk]	(Tür)schloss
look after MORE I	[lʊk 'ɑ:ftə]	sich kümmern um
look for MORE I	['lʊk fə]	suchen nach
look forward to MORE III	['lʊk 'fɔ:wəd]	sich freuen auf
look up U7/7	['lʊk 'ʌp]	nachschlagen
looks like ... (informal) U7/8a	['lʊks laɪk]	sieht so aus, als...
(be in) love MORE III	[bi: ɪn 'lʌv]	verliebt sein
lover MORE III	['lʌvə]	Freund/in; Liebhaber/in
luck MORE III	[lʌk]	Glück; Erfolg
lunchtime MORE III	['lʌntʃ'taɪm]	Mittagszeit; Mittagspause
lyrics MORE III	['lɪrɪks]	(Lied)text

M

made of MORE III	['meɪd 'əv]	bestehend aus
main dish U6/ME4	['meɪn dɪʃ]	Hauptgericht
major U4/1	['meɪdʒə]	Haupt-, wichtig
majority U1/3b	[mə'dʒɒrətɪ]	Mehrheit
make friends MORE III	[meɪk 'frendz]	sich anfreunden
make sth MORE III	['meɪk]	etwas machen, etwas herstellen
make sure MORE III	[meɪk 'ʃɔ:]	sich versichern; darauf achten
make up MORE III	[meɪk 'ʌp]	hier: bestehen aus
male U5/6	[meɪl]	männlich
man-made U6/7	[mæn 'meɪd]	künstlich
mankind U13/2	[mæn'kaɪnd]	Menschheit
march MORE III	[mɑ:tʃ]	marschieren
mark MORE III	[mɑ:k]	Markierung
mark MORE III	[mɑ:k]	Note, Zensur
market MORE III	['mɑ:kɪt]	Markt
marketing U5/3	['mɑ:kɪtɪŋ]	Marketing, Vertrieb
married MORE II	['mærɪd]	verheiratet
marry MORE III	['mæri]	heiraten
masterpiece U13/11	['mɑ:stəpi:s]	Meisterwerk
mate U3/3	[meɪt]	Kumpel
material U8/8	[mə'tɪərɪəl]	Material
matter MORE III	['mætə]	Materie; Angelegenheit; Frage; Thema; Problem
maybe MORE III	['meɪbi]	vielleicht, möglicherweise
Me, too. MORE III	['mi 'tu:]	Ich auch.
meadow U14/ME3	['medəʊ]	Wiese
meal MORE III	[mi:l]	Mahlzeit, Essen
mean MORE II	[mi:n]	meinen; bedeuten
meaning MORE III	['mi:nɪŋ]	Bedeutung
meat MORE II	[mi:t]	Fleisch
mechanic U5/1	[mə'kænɪk]	Mechaniker/in
media U5/8a	['mi:dɪə]	Medien
medical U8/8	['medɪkl]	medizinisch
meeting MORE III	['mi:tɪŋ]	Versammlung; Treffen; Veranstaltung
member MORE III	['membə]	Mitglied
memorial MORE III	[mə'mɔ:riəl]	Denkmal
mention U12/10	['menʃn]	erwähnen
merely U12/7	['mɪəlɪ]	lediglich

mess MORE II	[mes]	Unordnung, Durcheinander
metal U9/1	['metl]	Metall
microscope U9/ME3	['maɪkrəskəʊp]	Mikroskop
middle school EU/1	['mɪdl 'sku:l]	Sekundarschule
might MORE II	[maɪt]	könnte; vielleicht (tun, sein)
mind MORE III	[maɪnd]	Geist, Verstand
I don't mind. MORE III	[aɪ dəʊnt 'maɪnd]	Ich habe nichts dagegen.
mind you U3/3	[maɪnd 'ju:]	obwohl
mine U5/ME3	[maɪn]	Mine (Ausgrabung)
miner U5/ME3	['maɪnə]	Bergarbeiter/in
mirror MORE III	['mɪrə]	Spiegel
mission U13/2	['mɪʃn]	Mission
mistake sth for sth MORE III	[mɪ'steɪk fə]	etwas mit etwas verwechseln
misunderstood U11/5	['mɪsʌndəstʊd]	missverstanden
model U6/11	['mɒdl]	Model
monastery U10/3	['mɒnəstrɪ]	Kloster
monk U1/4	[mʌŋk]	Mönch
mostly U3/3	['məʊstlɪ]	meistens
motivate U10/9	['məʊtɪveɪt]	motivieren
motive U2/3	['məʊtɪv]	Motiv
move to ... MORE III	['mu:v tə]	nach ... kommen; nach ... gehen
movement MORE III	['mu:vmənt]	Bewegung
movie MORE III	['mu:vi]	(Kino)film
(the) movies MORE III	[ðə 'mu:viz]	das Kino
moving MORE III	['mu:vɪŋ]	bewegend, ergreifend
multibillion U13/8	[mʌltɪ'bɪljən]	Multimilliarden-
murder U2/1	['mɜ:də]	Mord
murder mystery U2/1	['mɜ:də 'mɪstərɪ]	geheimnisvoller Mord
murder weapon U2/1	['mɜ:də 'wepən]	Mordwaffe
murderer U2/6	['mɜ:dərə]	Mörder/in
mystery MORE III	['mɪstrɪ]	Geheimnis

N

name U4/1	[neɪm]	(be)nennen
Native American MORE III	['neɪtɪv ə'merɪkən]	amerikanische/r Ureinwohner/in; indianisch
natural MORE III	['nætʃərəl]	Natur-
nearby EU/2	[nɪə'baɪ]	in der Nähe
necessary U1/1	['nesəserɪ]	notwendig
neck MORE II	[nek]	Hals; Nacken
necklace MORE III	['nekləs]	(Hals)kette
needle U9/1	['ni:dl]	Nadel
neither … nor U13/11	['naɪðə 'nɔ:]	weder … noch
neither (of us) MORE III	['naɪðə]	keine/r (von beiden)
nephew U2/2	['nefju:]	Neffe
newsagent U3/ME3	['nɪu:z'eɪdʒ(ə)nt]	Zeitschriftengeschäft, Trafik
nice try U8/D3	['naɪs traɪ]	netter Versuch!
nightmare MORE III	['naɪtmeə]	Albtraum
Nobel Peace Prize MORE III	[nəʊ'bel 'pi:s praɪz]	Friedensnobelpreis
nod your head U9/5a	[nɒd jə 'hed]	mit dem Kopf nicken
nonsense U8/ME2	['nɒns(ə)ns]	Unsinn, Quatsch
northeast MORE III	['nɔ:θ'i:st]	nordöstlich, Nordost-
not as far as I know U6/D3	['nɒt əz 'fɑ: rəz aɪ 'nəʊ]	Nicht so viel ich weiß.
not even MORE III	[nɒt 'i:vn]	(noch) nicht einmal
not on your life U8/D3	['nɒt ɒn jɔ: 'laɪf]	Nie im Leben!
note MORE II	[nəʊt]	Notiz
note MORE III	[nəʊt]	zur Kenntnis nehmen
notice MORE I	['nəʊtɪs]	bemerken
novel MORE III	['nɒvl]	Roman
nowadays U3/5	['naʊədeɪz]	heutzutage
nowhere U1/7	['nəʊweə]	nirgendwo
nurse U5/1	[nɜ:s]	Krankenpfleger/in
nutritious U6/7	[nju:'trɪʃəs]	nahrhaft

O

occasionally EU/2	[ə'keɪʒənəli]	ab und zu; hin und wieder
of all time U4/3a	[əv 'ɔ:l 'taɪm]	aller Zeiten
of course MORE I	[əv 'kɔ:s]	natürlich
offer MORE III	['ɒfə]	anbieten
office clerk U2/2	['ɒfɪs klɑ:k]	Büroangestellte/r
office worker U5/ME3	['ɒfɪs 'wɜ:kə]	Büroangestellte/r
official U1/3b	[ə'fɪʃl]	Schiedsrichter/in
official language MORE III	[ə'fɪʃl 'læŋgwɪdʒ]	Amtssprache
oh my goodness U7/8a	['əʊ maɪ 'gʊdnəs]	Du liebe Zeit!; Um Himmels willen…!
oil U11/1	[ɔɪl]	Öl
on horseback U8/10	[ɒn 'hɔ:sbæk]	zu Pferde
on the way MORE III	[ɒn ðə 'weɪ]	unterwegs
on the way up MORE III	[ɒn ðə 'weɪ ʌp]	auf dem Weg nach oben
opening night EU/ME3	['əʊpnɪŋ 'naɪt]	Premiereabend; Eröffnungsvorstellung
opera U8/3	['ɒp(ə)rə]	Oper
opinion MORE III	[ə'pɪnjən]	Meinung
option MORE III	['ɒpʃn]	Wahl; Möglichkeit
orange peel U10/ME3	['ɒrɪndʒ pi:l]	Orangenschale
orbit U13/1	['ɔ:bɪt]	Umlaufbahn
other MORE II	['ʌðə]	weitere/r/s
otherwise MORE III	['ʌðə'waɪz]	andernfalls, sonst
ouch MORE III	[aʊtʃ]	aua, autsch
ought U3/ME1	[ɔ:t]	sollte/n
ourselves U12/G	[aʊə'selvz]	sich (amüsieren)
(the) outback U8/8	['aʊtbæk]	Hinterland Australiens
out of town U14/6	['aʊt əv 'taʊn]	verreist; nicht zu Hause
out-foxed U1/9	['aʊt 'fɒkst]	ausgetrickst
outside MORE I	[aʊt'saɪd]	außen, außerhalb
over MORE III	['əʊvə]	mehr als
over the top MORE III	['əʊvə ðə tɒp]	übertrieben
over there MORE III	['əʊvə 'ðeə]	dort drüben
overcome U11/4	[əʊvə'kʌm]	bezwingen, überwinden
overweight U6/11	[əʊvə'weɪt]	übergewichtig
own MORE III	[əʊn]	besitzen
the only one MORE III	[ði 'əʊnli 'wʌn]	der/die/das Einzige

P

(be in) panic MORE III	[bi ɪn 'pænɪk]	panische Angst haben
pack MORE II	[pæk]	packen
package MORE III	['pækɪdʒ]	Paket
painful U3/9a	['peɪnfəl]	schmerzhaft
pal(ly) U12/7	['pæl(ɪ)]	Kumpel
palm U9/5a	[pɑ:m]	Handfläche
panic MORE III	['pænɪk]	in Panik geraten; Panik
paper(s) MORE III	['peɪpə(z)]	Dokument(e), Schriftstück(e)
paralysed, paralyzed (AE) U7/8b	['pærəlaɪzd]	gelähmt
park MORE III	[pɑ:k]	parken
pass sth on U12/2	['pɑ:s 'ɒn]	etwas weitergeben
passenger U13/ME3	['pæsɪndʒə]	Fahrgast; Passagier/in
pathetic U13/D3	[pə'θetɪk]	erbärmlich
pathway U7/4	['pɑ:θweɪ]	Pfad
patient U8/8	['peɪʃənt]	Patient/in
pay attention to MORE III	['peɪ ə'tenʃn tə]	Acht geben; aufpassen
peacock U1/9	['pi:kɒk]	Pfau
people MORE I	['pi:pl]	Leute, Menschen
per person MORE III	[pɜ: 'pɜ:sən]	pro Person
perfectly U7/2	['pɜ:fektlɪ]	perfekt
perform U12/5	[pə'fɔ:m]	aufführen
permission MORE III	[pə'mɪʃən]	Erlaubnis
personal U4/G	['pɜ:sənl]	persönlich
pesticide U11/1	['pestɪsaɪd]	Pestizid, Insektenbekämpfungsmittel
photograph MORE III	['fəʊtə'grɑ:f]	fotografieren
photographer MORE III	[fə'tɒgrəfə]	Fotograf/in
phrase MORE III	[freɪz]	Satz; Ausdruck, (Rede)wendung
pick up sth MORE III	['pɪk 'ʌp]	aufheben, abholen; hier: nehmen
piece of cake U1/D3	['pi:s ə 'keɪk]	ein Kinderspiel
pierced U9/1	[pi:əst]	durchstochen, gepierct
plan MORE II	[plæn]	planen
plant MORE III	[plɑ:nt]	pflanzen
plaque U13/1	[plæk]	Tafel
plastic MORE III	['plæstɪk]	Plastik, Kunststoff
plate MORE III	[pleɪt]	Teller
play a role U3/2	['pleɪ ə 'rəʊl]	eine Rolle spielen
playboy U2/2	['pleɪbɔɪ]	Playboy; Lebemann
pleasant U7/7	['pleznt]	angenehm
please MORE III	[pli:z]	eine Freude machen, erfreuen
Pleased to meet you. U9/D3	['pli:zd tə 'mi:t jʊ]	Angenehm!
pleasure MORE III	['pleʒə]	Freude, Vergnügen
plenty MORE III	['plenti]	eine Menge
plumber U10/9	['plʌmə]	Klempner/in, Installateur/in
poetry U3/G	['pəʊɪtri]	Dichtung, Lyrik
point MORE III	[pɔɪnt]	Punkt
polite MORE III	[pə'laɪt]	höflich
political U7/8b	[pə'lɪtɪkl]	politisch
pollution U11/8b	[pə'lu:ʃn]	Verschmutzung
poor U2/4	[pɔ:]	schwach
pop up U13/13	['pɒp 'ʌp]	plötzlich erscheinen
population U1/2	[pɒpjʊ'leɪʃn]	Bevölkerung
port U4/5	[pɔ:t]	Hafen
porter U5/ME3	[pɔ:tə]	Gepäckträger/in
position U2/3	[pə'zɪʃn]	Position, Stellung
possibility U9/G	[pɒsə'bɪlɪtɪ]	Möglichkeit
possible MORE II	['pɒsɪbl]	möglich
post sth MORE III	['pəʊst]	etwas (per Post) verschicken
postman (pl -men) U10/F	['pəʊstmən, 'pəʊstmen]	Postbote, Briefträger
practise MORE I	['præktɪs]	üben; Übung
pray MORE III	[preɪ]	beten
prefer sth MORE III	[prɪ'fɜ:]	etwas vorziehen, etwas bevorzugen
primarily U1/2	[praɪ'mərɪli]	hauptsächlich
primary school U1/2	['praɪmərɪ sku:l]	Grundschule
prison warden U5/ME3	['prɪzn 'wɔ:də]	Gefängniswärter/in
prize MORE III	[praɪz]	Preis, Gewinn
probably MORE II	['prɒbəbli]	wahrscheinlich
problem solving U3/6	['prɒbləm 'sɒlvɪŋ]	Konflikt lösen
produce MORE III	[prə'dju:s]	erzeugen; hier: hervorbringen
producer MORE III	[prə'dju:sə]	Hersteller, Produzent
product MORE III	['prɒdʌkt]	Produkt, Erzeugnis
profession U5/1	[prə'feʃn]	Beruf
promise MORE II	['prɒmɪs]	versprechen; Versprechen
prompt MORE III	[prɒmpt]	Hilfe
proper U1/4	['prɒpə]	richtig
protect MORE II	[prə'tekt]	schützen
protection U10/5	[prə'tekʃn]	Schutz
protest MORE III	['prəʊtest]	Protest-
protest MORE III	[prə'test]	protestieren
proud MORE I	[praʊd]	stolz
prove U2/7	[pru:v]	beweisen
provide U6/6a	[prə'vaɪd]	bereitstellen, hergeben
province U1/3b	['prɒvɪns]	Provinz
pub U1/5	[pʌb]	Kneipe
public MORE III	['pʌblɪk]	Öffentlich
public transport U1/6	['pʌblɪk trænspɔ:t]	öffentliche Verkehrsmittel
pull MORE I	[pʊl]	ziehen
Puritan U4/3b	['pjʊərɪtn]	Puritaner/in
push MORE II	[pʊʃ]	schieben, drücken
put down U1/3b	[pʊt 'daʊn]	ablegen; hier: (einen Aufstand) niederschlagen
put down U11/4	[pʊt 'daʊn]	schlecht behandeln
put forward U13/8	[pʊt 'fɔ:wəd]	vorschlagen
The penny's dropped. U12/D3	[ðə 'penɪ z 'drɒpt]	Der Groschen ist gefallen.

Q

queue MORE III	[kju:]	(Warte)schlange, Reihe
quite a while U1/6	['kwaɪt ə 'waɪl]	eine ganze Weile

R

racial U7/8b	['reɪʃəl]	Rassen-
racism U11/4	['reɪsɪzm]	Rassismus
racist U11/4	['reɪsɪst]	rassistisch
radio advert U13/5	['reɪdɪəʊ 'ædvɜ:t]	Radiowerbung
rare U10/1	[reə]	selten

rather	U1/7	['rɑ:ðə]	lieber
rattlesnake	U8/1	['rætlsneɪk]	Klapperschlange
ray	U7/7	[reɪ]	Strahl
re-enter	U13/G	[rɪ'entə]	wieder eintreten
reach	MORE III	[ri:tʃ]	erreichen
react	MORE II	[ri'ækt]	reagieren
reader	U12/2	['ri:də]	Leser/in
reason	MORE II	['ri:zn]	Grund
rebellion	U1/3b	[rɪ'beliən]	Aufstand
rebellious	U9/1	[rɪ'beliəs]	rebellisch
recall	U1/5	[rɪ'kɔ:l]	sich erinnern; sich entsinnen
recently	MORE III	['ri:sntli]	kürzlich, vor kurzem, neulich
receptionist	U5/1	[rɪ'sepʃənɪst]	Person am Empfang
recommend	MORE III	['rekə'mend]	empfehlen
record	U4/3a	['rekɔ:d]	Rekord
reference book	U12/5	['refərəns 'bʊk]	Nachschlagewerk
refuse	MORE III	[rɪ'fju:z]	ablehnen
regularly	U6/11	['regjʊləlɪ]	regelmäßig
relationship	MORE III	[rɪ'leɪʃnʃɪp]	Beziehung
relative	U2/4	['relətɪv]	Verwandte/r
relax	MORE III	[rɪ'læks]	sich entspannen
relaxation	U4/1	['ri:læk'seɪʃn]	Entspannung
release	MORE III	[rɪ'li:s]	freilassen; hier: veröffentlichen
religious	U9/1	[rɪ'lɪdʒəs]	religiös
remove	U10/5	[rɪ'mu:v]	entfernen
rent sth	MORE III	['rent]	etwas mieten
repeat	MORE II	[rɪ'pi:t]	wiederholen
reply	U5/9	[rɪ'plaɪ]	Antwort
reply	U12/ME4	[rɪ'plaɪ]	erwidern, antworten
report	U2/ME6	[rɪ'pɔ:t]	Bericht erstatten
Republic of Ireland	U1/2	[rɪ'pʌblɪk əv 'aɪələnd]	Republik Irland
research	MORE III	[rɪ'sɜ:tʃ]	Forschung
research sth	U7/7	[rɪ'sɜ:tʃ]	etwas erforschen; etwas recherchieren
rest	U13/ME3	[rest]	(Ruhe)pause
retire	U2/4	[rɪ'taɪə]	in Pension gehen
reverend	U8/8	['revrənd]	Pfarrer
review	MORE III	[rɪ'vju:]	Überprüfung; hier: Kritik, Rezension
rhythm	MORE III	['rɪðəm]	Rhythmus, Takt
right	MORE III	[raɪt]	in Ordnung, okay
right now	MORE III	[raɪt 'naʊ]	jetzt, sofort, gleich
ripe	EU/6	[raɪp]	reif
risk	U9/1	[rɪsk]	Risiko
rocket	U13/8	['rɒkɪt]	Rakete
rollercoaster	U12/ME4	['rəʊlə'kəʊstə]	Achterbahn
route	MORE III	[ru:t]	Strecke, Route
row (AE)	MORE III	[rəʊ]	Reihe
royal	MORE III	['rɔɪəl]	königlich
rubbish	MORE II	['rʌbɪʃ]	Müll
rubbish bin	U10/ME3	['rʌbɪʃ 'bɪn]	Mülleimer
rude	MORE III	[ru:d]	unhöflich
run	MORE III	[rʌn]	hier: fließen
run away	MORE III	['rʌn ə'weɪ]	weglaufen
run out of	MORE III	[rʌn 'aʊt əv]	ausgehen

S

safe	MORE II	[seɪf]	sicher
sailor	U2/15	['seɪlə]	Matrose
saint	U1/4	[seɪnt]	Heilige/r
sale	U5/3	[seɪl]	Verkauf
salesman	U2/2	['seɪlzmən]	Verkäufer
save	MORE I	[seɪv]	retten
save	MORE III	[seɪv]	sparen
scary	MORE I	['skeəri]	furchterregend; unheimlich
school dinner	U6/6a	[sku:l 'dɪnə]	Mittagessen in der Schule
scratch	U1/3a	[skrætʃ]	kratzen
scream	MORE II	[skri:m]	schreien; kreischen
screaming	MORE III	['skri:mɪŋ]	schreiend/e/es/er
seafood	U4/1	['si:fu:d]	Meeresfrüchte
search	MORE III	[sɜ:tʃ]	durch-, absuchen
second-hand	U3/ME1	[seknd'hænd]	gebraucht
secret	MORE II	['si:krət]	geheim; Geheimnis
secretary	U5/1	['sekrətrɪ]	Sekretär/in
section	U3/ME1	['sekʃn]	Abschnitt
see	MORE III	[si:]	hier: wissen, verstehen
see sb	MORE III	['si:]	jdn treffen
See you. (informal)	MORE III	['si: jə]	Bis bald.
seeker	U3/1b	['si:kə]	Suchende/r
select	U11/1	[sɪ'lekt]	auswählen
send out sth	MORE III	[send 'aʊt]	etwas versenden, verschicken
set off	U13/11	[set 'ɒf]	aufbrechen
settlement	U8/8	['setlmənt]	Siedlung
shade	MORE III	[ʃeɪd]	Schatten
shall	MORE III	[ʃæl]	sollen
shorten	U9/5b	['ʃɔ:tən]	kürzen
shorts	MORE III	[ʃɔ:ts]	kurze Hose, Shorts
shout at sb	U7/8a	['ʃaʊt ət]	jdn anschreien; jdn rufen
shout (out loud)	U3/1a	['ʃaʊt aʊt laʊd]	laut rufen
be sick	MORE III	['bi: 'sɪk]	erbrechen, spucken
sidewalk	U4/1	['saɪdwɔ:k]	Bürgersteig
sigh	U9/5b	[saɪ]	seufzen
sight	MORE III	[saɪt]	hier: Anblick
sign sth	MORE III	['saɪn]	etwas unterschreiben
signpost	U14/ME3	['saɪnpəʊst]	Wegweiser; Schild
silver	MORE III	['sɪlvə]	Silber
similar	MORE III	['sɪmɪlə]	ähnlich
simply	U13/11	['sɪmplɪ]	einfach
since then	MORE III	['sɪns 'ðen]	seitdem, seither
since/for	MORE III	[sɪns fə]	seit
sitting room	U9/5b	['sɪtɪŋ ru:m]	Wohnzimmer
slave	MORE II	[sleɪv]	Sklave/Sklavin
slavery	U11/4	['sleɪvrɪ]	Sklaverei
sleeping pill	U7/8a	['sli:pɪŋ pɪl]	Schlaftablette
smoked trout	U6/ME4	['sməʊkt traʊt]	geräucherte Forelle
soar	U13/9	[sɔ:]	zum Himmel hochsteigen
society	U7/8b	[sə'saɪəti]	Gesellschaft
soft drink	U11/3a	['sɒft 'drɪŋk]	Limo
sole	U9/5a	[səʊl]	Sohle
solution	MORE III	[sə'lu:ʃn]	Lösung
solve	MORE II	[sɒlv]	lösen
somebody	MORE I	['sʌmbədi]	jemand
someone	MORE II	['sʌmwən]	jemand

someone else MORE III	['sʌmwʌn 'els]	jemand anders
something MORE I	['sʌmθɪŋ]	etwas
sometimes MORE I	['sʌmtaɪmz]	manchmal
son-in-law U11/4	['sʌnɪn lɔ:]	Schwiegersohn
space travel U13/2	['speɪs 'trævəl]	Raumfahrt
spacecraft U13/5	['speɪskrɑ:ft]	Raumfahrzeug
speak out U3	['spi:k aʊt]	seine Meinung deutlich sagen
speciality U4/1	[speʃiælɪti]	Spezialität
spicy U6/ME5	['spaɪsɪ]	scharf gewürzt; würzig
spider's web U9/5b	['spaɪdəz web]	Spinnwebe
spiky U9/5b	['spaɪkɪ]	stachelig
spoon U1/3a	[spu:n]	Löffel
spot sth/sb MORE III	['spɒt]	jdn/etwas entdecken
spring MORE III	[sprɪŋ]	Frühling
stadium U4/3a	['steɪdɪəm]	Stadion
staff U1/9	[stɑ:f]	Angestellte, Personal
stairs MORE III	[steəz]	Treppe
stand still EU/4	['stænd 'stɪl]	still stehen
starve U1/3b	[stɑ:v]	verhungern
statement MORE III	['steɪtmənt]	Äußerung
stay in MORE III	['steɪ 'ɪn]	zu Hause bleiben
stay on U1/D3	['steɪ'ɒn]	bleiben
steel U7/2	[sti:l]	Stahl
sterile U9/1	['steraɪl]	steril
stinking rich U3/3	['stɪŋkɪŋ rɪtʃ]	stinkreich
store U3/ME1	[stɔ:]	Laden; Geschäft
stream U14/ME3	[stri:m]	Bach
stud MORE III	[stʌd]	Niete, Stecker; hier: Nasenstecker
stuff (informal) MORE III	[stʌf]	hier: solche Sachen
stuff oneself U6/11	['stʌf wʌnself]	sich vollstopfen
success U4/3a	[sək'ses]	Erfolg
successful MORE III	[sək'sesfəl]	erfolgreich
such MORE II	[sʌtʃ]	solch/er/es; so
suggest U1/D2	[sə'dʒest]	vorschlagen
suggestion MORE II	[sə'dʒestʃn]	Vorschlag
suit MORE III	[su:t]	Anzug
summarise U12/10	['sʌmə'raɪz]	zusammenfassen
summary MORE III	['sʌməri]	Zusammenfassung; Inhaltsangabe
suncream U7/ME4	[sʌnkri:m]	Sonnenschutz-creme
sunrise U13/2	['sʌnraɪz]	Sonnenaufgang
sunset U13/1	['sʌnset]	Sonnenuntergang
supervillain U7/1	['su:pəvɪlən]	Superbösewicht
support MORE III	[sə'pɔ:t]	unterstützen
surfboard MORE III	['sɜ:f'bɔ:d]	Surfbrett
surfer MORE III	['sɜ:fə]	Surfer/in
surprised MORE III	[sə'praɪzd]	überrascht
surround U1/9	[sə'raʊnd]	umgeben
survey MORE II	['sɜ:veɪ]	Umfrage
survive MORE III	[sə'vaɪv]	überleben
suspect U2/1	['sʌspekt]	Verdächtige/r
swallow U7/7	['swɒləʊ]	schlucken
swan U4/1	[swɒn]	Schwan
switch (on/off) U13/13	[swɪtʃ]	ein-/ausschalten

T

table MORE III	['teɪbl]	Tabelle; Liste, Verzeichnis
take MORE III	[teɪk]	hier: dauern
take care MORE III	[teɪk keə]	Pass auf dich auf!
take over U2/4	['teɪk'əʊvə]	übernehmen
take place U4/1	['teɪk 'pleɪs]	stattfinden
talk U14/10	[tɔ:k]	Vortrag, Rede
taste MORE III	[teɪst]	Geschmack
tasty U6/7	['teɪstɪ]	lecker
taxes U4/5	['tæksɪz]	Steuern
tea bag U10/9	['ti: bæg]	Teebeutel
teddy bear U2/D2	['tedɪ beə]	Teddybär
telephone booth U7/3	['telɪfəʊn 'bu:ð]	Telefonzelle
tent MORE III	[tent]	Zelt
term MORE II	[tɜ:m]	Semester; Schuljahresabschnitt
territory MORE III	['terətri]	Gebiet, Territorium
That's right. MORE III	['ðæts 'raɪt]	Das stimmt.; Das ist richtig.
That's settled. U9/D3	['ðæts 'setld]	Das ist also klar.
theatre MORE III	['θɪətə]	Theater
themselves MORE III	[ðem'selvz]	sich; (sie) selbst
thief (pl thieves) MORE II	[θi:f, θi:vz]	Dieb/in
thin MORE III	[θɪn]	dünn
think of (sb/sth) MORE III	['θɪŋk 'əv]	an (jdn/etwas) denken; sich ausdenken
think sth of sth MORE III	['θɪŋk əv]	etwas von etwas halten; eine Meinung zu etwas haben/äußern
thirst MORE III	[θɜ:st]	Durst
thrilling MORE III	['θrɪlɪŋ]	aufregend
throat MORE II	[θrəʊt]	Hals
through MORE II	[θru:]	durch
throughout the year MORE II	[θru:'aʊt ðə 'jɪə]	im ganzen Jahr
throw MORE I	[θrəʊ]	werfen
throw a party MORE III	['θrəʊ ə 'pɑ:ti]	eine Party geben
throw sb out U14/1	['θrəʊ aʊt]	jdn hinauswerfen
throw up U6/11	[θrəʊ 'ʌp]	erbrechen
thumb U9/5a	[θʌm]	Daumen
ticket MORE III	['tɪkɪt]	Eintrittskarte
tiny U10/5	['taɪnɪ]	winzig
(be) tired of sth MORE III	['taɪəd əv]	etwas satt haben
tiring U3/ME1	['taɪərɪŋ]	ermüdend
title MORE III	[taɪtl]	Titel
top-class U4/1	['tɒp 'klɑ:s]	erste Klasse
topic MORE III	['tɒpɪk]	Thema
totally MORE III	['təʊtəli]	völlig, total
tough EU/4	[tʌf]	hart, schwierig
tournament EU/4	['tʊənəmənt]	Turnier
track U8/10	[træk]	Weg, Pfad
tracker U8/9	['trækə]	Fährtenleser/in
traffic MORE III	['træfɪk]	Verkehr
tragedy U10/5	['trædʒədɪ]	Tragödie
tragic U10/5	['trædʒɪk]	tragisch
trail MORE III	[treɪl]	Weg, Pfad
train MORE III	[treɪn]	Zug
tram MORE III	[træm]	Straßenbahn, Tram
transport MORE III	['trænspɔ:t]	Transport, Beförderung
travel MORE II	['trævl]	reisen
travelling MORE III	['træv(ə)lɪŋ]	Reisen; Wander-
tree bark U8/4	['tri: bɑ:k]	Baumrinde
trendy U9/1	['trendɪ]	modisch; schick
trial U4/1	[traɪəl]	Prozess

troubled MORE III	['trʌbld]	besorgt, beunruhigt
truck U8/ME1	[trʌk]	Lastwagen
trust U7/4	[trʌst]	vertrauen
try MORE III	[traɪ]	Versuch
tune MORE III	[tju:n]	Melodie
turn MORE III	[tɜ:n]	werden
turn into MORE III	[tɜ:n 'ɪntu:]	(sich) verwandeln in
turn up U10/1	[tɜ:n 'ʌp]	erscheinen
typical U1/ME3	['tɪpɪkl]	typisch

U

ugly MORE II	['ʌgli]	hässlich
unclean U9/5a	[ʌn'kli:n]	unsauber
uncomplicated U13/9	[ʌn'kɒmplɪkeɪtɪd]	unkompliziert
underground MORE III	['ʌndə'graʊnd]	unterirdisch
undernourished U6/10	[ʌndə'nʌrɪʃt]	unterernährt
understanding MORE III	['ʌndə'stændɪŋ]	verständnisvoll
unemployed U5/6	[ʌnɪm'plɔɪd]	arbeitslos
unlock U2/4	[ʌn'lɒk]	aufschließen
until MORE II	[ən'tɪl]	bis
unusual MORE I	[ʌn'ju:ʒʊəl]	ungewöhnlich
upon MORE I	[ə'pɒn]	auf, an
upset U2/D2	[ʌp'set]	verstört
urban U1/9	['ɜ:bən]	städtisch
useful U3/ME1	['ju:sfl]	nützlich
usually MORE I	['ju:ʒʊəli]	gewöhnlich, normalerweise

V

(in) vain U1/5	[ɪn 'veɪn]	vergebens; umsonst
valley MORE III	['væli]	Tal
vegan U6/D1	['vi:gən]	Veganer/in
vegetarian U6/5	[vedʒɪ'teərɪən]	Vegetarier/in
veggie U6/D1	['vedʒɪ]	vegetarisch
version MORE III	['vɜ:ʒn]	Version, Fassung
victim MORE III	['vɪktɪm]	Opfer
victory U9/5a	['vɪktərɪ]	Sieg
view MORE III	[vju:]	Sicht; (Aus)blick, Aussicht
visitor MORE III	['vɪzɪtə]	Besucher/in
vitamin U6/6a	['vɪtəmɪn]	Vitamin

W

the worst MORE III	[ðə 'wɜ:st]	der/die/das Schlimmste
wake sb U4/D2	['weɪk]	jdn aufwecken
walk out U12/ME4	['wɔ:k 'aʊt]	gehen
walk the dog U2/ME4	['wɔ:k ðə 'dɒg]	den Hund ausführen
want sb to do sth MORE III	[wɒnt tə 'du:]	wollen, dass jemand etwas tut
warehouse U5/ME3	['weəhaʊs]	Lager
wash-off U9/5b	['wɒʃ'ɒf]	abwaschbar
wastepaper bin U2/5	[weɪst'peɪpə bɪn]	Papierkorb
waterhole U8/10	['wɔ:təhəʊl]	Wasserloch
waterproof EU/1	['wɔ:təpru:f]	wasserdicht
wave MORE III	[weɪv]	Welle
way MORE III	[weɪ]	Art, Weise
way MORE III	[weɪ]	Weg
weak MORE III	[wi:k]	schwach
weapon U2/1	['wepən]	Waffe
wedding U5/8a	['wedɪŋ]	Hochzeit
wedding dress U9/5b	['wedɪŋ dres]	Hochzeitskleid
wedding suit U9/5b	['wedɪŋ su:t]	(Hochzeits)anzug
what MORE III	['wɒt]	welche/r/s
What a nerve! U1/D3	['wɒt ə 'nɜ:v]	Was für eine Frechheit!
What are you up to? U4/D3	['wɒt ɑ: jʊ 'ʌp tʊ]	Was führst du im Schilde?
What's ... like? MORE III	['wɒts 'laɪk]	Wie ist …?
what's wrong U14/1	['wɒts 'rɒŋ]	Was ist los?
whatever U1/D3	[wɒt'evə]	was auch immer
wheelchair U7/8b	['wi:ltʃeə]	Rollstuhl
whenever U6/11	[wen'evə]	wann auch immer
wherever MORE II	[weə'revə]	wo(hin) auch immer
while MORE II	[waɪl]	während
whistle U1/9	['wɪsl]	Pfeife
who MORE III	[hu:]	der/die/das
wilderness MORE III	['wɪldənəs]	Wildnis
wildlife MORE III	['waɪld'laɪf]	Natur-
wine MORE III	[waɪn]	Wein
wish MORE III	[wɪʃ]	Wunsch; sich wünschen
witch trial U4/1	['wɪtʃ 'traɪəl]	Hexenprozess
within U13/5	[wɪð'ɪn]	innerhalb
wooden MORE I	['wʊdn]	Holz-, hölzern
world record U13/ME1	['wɜ:ld rɪ'kɔ:d]	Weltrekord
world-famous U6/6b	['wɜ:ld'feɪməs]	weltberühmt

Y

(31)-year-old MORE III	[jɪə 'əʊld]	(einundreißig) jährig, (einundreißig) Jahre alt
yeah (informal) MORE III	[jeə]	ja(wohl)
yet MORE III	[jet]	schon
You're welcome. MORE III	[jə 'welkəm]	Nichts zu danken., Keine Ursache., Gern geschehen.
youth MORE I	[ju:θ]	Jugend
youth club MORE III	['ju:θ 'klʌb]	Jugendzentrum

IRREGULAR VERBS

be	*was/were*	*been*	sein (war/waren) (MORE I)
beat	*beat*	*beaten*	schlagen (MORE III)
become	*became*	*become*	werden) (MORE I)
begin	*began*	*begun*	beginnen (MORE I)
blow	*blew*	*blown*	blasen (MORE II)
break	*broke*	*broken*	brechen (MORE I)
bring	*brought*	*brought*	bringen (MORE II)
build	*built*	*built*	bauen (MORE II)
burn	*burnt / burned*	*burnt / burned*	brennen (MORE III)
buy	*bought*	*bought*	kaufen (MORE I)
catch	*caught*	*caught*	fangen (MORE I)
choose	*chose*	*chosen*	(aus)wählen (MORE I)
come	*came*	*come*	kommen (MORE I)
cut	*cut*	*cut*	schneiden (MORE I)
dig	*dug*	*dug*	graben (MORE I)
do	*did*	*done*	tun, machen (MORE I)
draw	*drew*	*drawn*	zeichnen (MORE I)
dream	*dreamt (dreamed)*	*dreamt (dreamed)*	träumen (MORE II)
drink	*drank*	*drunk*	trinken (MORE I)
drive	*drove*	*driven*	fahren, treiben (MORE I)
eat	*ate*	*eaten*	essen (MORE I)
fall (asleep)	*fell (asleep)*	*fallen (asleep)*	fallen (MORE I)
feed	*fed*	*fed*	fressen; füttern (MORE III)
feel	*felt*	*felt*	fühlen (MORE I)
fight	*fought*	*fought*	kämpfen (MORE II)
find	*found*	*found*	finden (MORE I)
flee	*fled*	*fled*	flüchten (MORE III)
fly	*flew*	*flown*	fliegen (MORE I)
forget	*forgot*	*forgotten*	vergessen (MORE I)
get	*got*	*got*	bekommen, werden (MORE I)
get up	*got up*	*got up*	aufstehen (MORE I)
give	*gave*	*given*	geben (MORE I)
go	*went*	*gone*	gehen, fahren (MORE I)
grow	*grew*	*grown*	wachsen (lassen); züchten, anbauen (MORE I)
hang	*hung*	*hung*	hängen (MORE I)
have	*had*	*had*	haben (MORE I)
hear	*heard*	*heard*	hören (MORE I)
hide	*hid*	*hidden*	(sich) verstecken (MORE I)
hit	*hit*	*hit*	schlagen (MORE I)
hold	*held*	*held*	(fest)halten (MORE I)
hurt	*hurt*	*hurt*	(sich) verletzen, schmerzen (MORE I)
keep	*kept*	*kept*	(be)halten (MORE III)
know	*knew*	*known*	wissen, kennen (MORE I)
lay	*laid*	*laid*	legen (MORE I)
learn	*learnt (learned)*	*learnt (learned)*	lernen (MORE I)
leave	*left*	*left*	verlassen (MORE I)
let	*let*	*let*	lassen (MORE I)
lie	*lay*	*lain*	liegen (MORE I)
lose	*lost*	*lost*	verlieren (MORE II)
make	*made*	*made*	machen (MORE I)
meet	*met*	*met*	treffen (MORE I)
put	*put*	*put*	geben, setzen, stellen (MORE I)
read	*read*	*read*	lesen (MORE I)
ride	*rode*	*ridden*	reiten, fahren (MORE I)
ring	*rang*	*rung*	läuten (MORE I)
run	*ran*	*run*	laufen (MORE I)
say	*said*	*said*	sagen (MORE I)
see	*saw*	*seen*	sehen (MORE I)
send	*sent*	*sent*	senden, schicken (MORE I)
set	*set*	*set*	setzen (MORE III)
shake	*shook*	*shaken*	schütteln (MORE III)
shine	*shone*	*shone*	scheinen (MORE II)
shoot	*shot*	*shot*	schießen (MORE II)
show	*showed*	*shown (showed)*	zeigen (MORE I)
sing	*sang*	*sung*	singen (MORE I)
sink	*sank (sunk)*	*sunk*	untergehen, sinken (MORE II)
sit	*sat*	*sat*	sitzen, sich setzen (MORE I)
sleep	*slept*	*slept*	schlafen (MORE I)
smell	*smelt (smelled)*	*smelt (smelled)*	riechen (MORE II)
speak	*spoke*	*spoken*	sprechen, sagen (MORE I)
spend	*spent*	*spent*	verbringen, ausgeben (MORE I)
stand	*stood*	*stood*	stehen (MORE I)
steal	*stole*	*stolen*	stehlen (MORE II)
swim	*swam*	*swum*	schwimmen (MORE I)
take off	*took off*	*taken off*	ausziehen (MORE I)
take	*took*	*taken*	nehmen (MORE I)
teach	*taught*	*taught*	lehren, unterrichten (MORE II)
tell	*told*	*told*	sagen, erzählen (MORE I)
think	*thought*	*thought*	denken (MORE I)
wake (up)	*woke (up)*	*woken (up)*	(auf)wachen (MORE I)
win	*won*	*won*	gewinnen (MORE I)
write	*wrote*	*written*	schreiben (MORE I)

CLASSROOM LANGUAGE

Can you understand your teacher?

We have plenty of time.
Have a go.
Have a guess.
Don't worry about your pronunciation.
Don't worry, it'll get better.
Maybe this will help you.
Can anybody correct this sentence?
That's very good.
Well done.
That's nice.
I like that.
You did a great job.
That's correct.
That's quite right.
Yes, you've got it.
That's much better.
That's a lot better.
You didn't make a single mistake.
Your pronunciation is very good.
You're getting better all the time.
Work in pairs/threes/fours/fives.
Work in groups of two/three/four.
Stand up and find another partner.
Have you finished?
Do the next activity.
Let's check the answers.
Come out and write it on the board.
Repeat after me.
Again, please.
Would you like to answer question 3?
Right. Now we will go on to the next exercise.
Have you finished?
Next one, please.
You have ten minutes to do this.
Your time is up.
Are you ready?
Any questions?
I'm afraid it's time to finish now.
We'll have to stop there.
Hang on a moment.
Just a moment, please.
One more thing before you go.
This is your homework.
Do exercise 9 on page 18 for your homework.
There is no homework today.

When you have a problem, say this:

Sorry? / Pardon?
Can you help me, please?
What's … in English, please?
I don't understand this.
Sorry, I've forgotten my …
Sorry, what's our homework?

ENGLISH SOUNDS

[ɑ:] **ar**m
[ʌ] f**u**n
[e] d**e**sk
[ə] **a**, an
[ɜ:] g**ir**l, b**ir**d
[æ] **a**pple
[ɪ] **i**n, **i**t
[i] ever**y**
[i:] **ea**sy, **ea**t
[ɒ] **o**range, s**o**rry
[ɔ:] **a**ll, c**a**ll
[ʊ] l**oo**k
[u] Febr**u**ary
[u:] f**oo**d
[aɪ] **eye**, b**uy**
[aʊ] **ou**r
[eə] th**ere**
[eɪ] t**a**ke, th**ey**
[ɪə] h**ere**
[ɔɪ] b**oy**
[əʊ] g**o**, **o**ld
[ʊə] y**ou're**
[b] **b**ag, club
[d] **d**uck, car**d**
[f] **f**ish, lau**gh**
[g] **g**et, do**g**
[h] **h**ot
[j] **y**ou
[k] **c**an, du**ck**
[l] **l**ot, sma**ll**
[m] **m**ore, **m**u**m**
[n] **n**ow, su**n**
[ŋ] so**ng**, lo**ng**
[p] **p**resent, to**p**
[r] **r**ed, **r**ight
[s] **s**i**s**ter, cla**ss**
[t] **t**ime,ca**t**
[z] no**s**e, dog**s**
[ʒ] televi**si**on
[dʒ] oran**ge**
[ʃ] **s**ure, Engli**sh**
[tʃ] **ch**ild, **ch**eese
[ð] **th**ese, mo**th**er
[θ] **th**ink, mou**th**
[v] **v**ery, ha**v**e
[w] **wh**at, **w**ord

Acknowledgements

Illustrated by Roberto Battestini, Christian Bendelari, Giovanni Da Re, Pietro Dichiara, Michele Farella, Svjetlan Junaković, Giovanni Giorgi Pierfranceschi, Cristiano Lissoni, Valentina Mai, Lorenzo Sabbatini, Fabio Sardo, Nicola Zanni.

The publishers would like to thank the following for their kind permission to reproduce the following photographs:

Alamy p42, p53 (miner; prison warden; porter), (CD: Ultimate Food; Food Icons) p54 (yoghurt; milk; orange juice; beef; chips; cheese; bread; crisps), (CD: Food icons; Ultimate Food) p63 (mineral water; coffee), p84 (Ötzi), p102 (Honduras woman with child), p103 (Brazil worker picking coffee), (CD: Food icons) p119 (pizza), p128 (Graf Zeppelin), p147 (tennis tournament; school fete), p148, p149, p151 (Tovalu), p155; **Andy Hay rspb-images.com** p96 (The egg collection with the RSPB); courtesy of **Barbara Wuertz www.issiweb.com** p35 (Salem Witch Museum), p38; **Bloomsbury** cover image of Harry Potter and the Half-Blood Prince by J.K. Rowling p112; **Boyds Mills Press, Inc.** A Step from Heaven by An Na, jacket designed by Helen Robinson (Front Street, an imprint of Boyds Mills Press, 2001) p112; **CANNON/DC COMICS / THE KOBAL COLLECTION** p64 (Superman), p65 (Superman); **COLUMBIA/MARVEL / THE KOBAL COLLECTION** p64 (Spiderman); **Corbis** p10 (The Cranberries), p57 (young Somali girl holding starving boy), p64, p68 (Christopher Reeve; Halle Berry in Catwoman), p105, p144 (trooping the colour); **David Loftus** p55 (Jamie Oliver); **Dkimages** p150; **Dreamstime** p15 (portraits of two girls and one boy), p36, p55, p122; **Fotolia** p33 (newsagent), p46 (travel agent; website designer), p58, p100; **Getty Images** p142 (Wimbledon logo); copyright **Guardian News & Media Ltd** 2006 p96 (The day Britain's most notorious egg collector climbed his last tree); **Gary Braasch** p151; **HarpersCollins Publishers** cover image of Away laughing on a fast camel by Louise Rennison p114; **Helbling Languages** p54 (pizza; tomatoes), p84 (belly piercing), p86 (boy giving pen to another boy), p98 (tea bags); **©iStockphoto.com** p6 (Croagh Patrick), p8 (The Ha'penny Bridge; Anna), p11, p26, p27, p29, p33 (baker's; chemist's), p34, p35 (Swan Boats), p42 (Greg; Emily), p46 (soldier; shop assistant; teacher; waiter; flight attendant; bank clerk), p47 (Philip), p53 (aerobics teacher), p54 (eggs), p63 (couple at restaurant; cream of potato soup; smoked trout; sausages and beans; beef and potatoes; cola), p65, p72, p73 (Ryan and Amy; Rottnest Island), p74 (Ayers Rock; Broome), p81, p84 (tongue piercing), p86, p87, p93 (snowboard; diary), p96 (golden eagle), p102, p103, p104 (Martin; Jason), p109, p113, p119 (girl), p128 (tuk tuks), p140, p143 (Nayana), p144 (hurricane Katrina), p149, p152; **Margaret K McElderry Books** p112 (cover image of Blood Red Road by Moira Young); **NASA** p120, p123; **National Gallery of Ireland** p7 (The Battle of the Boyne by Jan Wyck); **National Library of Ireland** p7 (A starving Irish family from Carraroe; County Galway, during the Famine); **© Orion Books** p112 (cover image of Wolf Brother by Michelle Paver); **PlanetSpace** p122 (Canadian Arrow); **Shutterstock** p6, p8, p10, p15, p28, p33, p34 (lobster), p35, p36 (The Patriots), p46, p47 (Mandy), p53, p54, p56 (packed lunch; junk food), p63, p71, p72 (map), p73, p74 (Didgeridoo; view from the Harbour Bridge; Eve and Jeremy), p81 (girl), p84 (earring), p86 (hand; Asian girl), p88, p93, p98, p112, p117, p119, p120 (space shuttle; sunset), p128 (skytrain), p144, p147, p149, p153, p154; **© Simon and Schuster Inc.** p112 (cover image of Missing Me by Sophie McKenzie), p115 (cover image of Dead Girls Don't Write Letters by Gail Giles); **The Elliott/D'Errico Photo Library** p94 (types of sand); **The Hindu** p143; **The International Sand Collectors Society, Nick D'Errico ISCS/PG Director** p94; The **Random House** Group Ltd cover images of The Illustrated Mum by Jacqueline Wilson, The curious incident of the dog in the nighttime by Mark Haddon, The boy in the striped pyjamas by John Boyne, Noughts and crosses by Malorie Blackman p112, Kiss by Jacqueline Wilson, The stuff of nightmares by Malorie Blackman p114; **United States Library of Congress' Rare Book and Special Collections Division** p37 (W.D. Cooper, Boston Tea Party); **United States Library of Congress' Prints and Photographs Division** p104 (Martin Luther King); **Wikimedia Commons** p7 (Dublin memorial to the Great Famine), p21 (Edgard Allan Poe), p37, p75 (EU flag), p120 (Challenger explosion), p128, p142 (Wimbledon); **123rf** p8 (Phoenix Park), p56 (dinner ladies; cookery lesson), p104 (Hannah; Amy), p141, p142 (James); **20TH CENTURY FOX / THE KOBAL COLLECTION** p64 (X-MEN).

Commissioned Photography & Production by Charlotte Macpherson pp 14, 24, 32, 52, 62, 70, 80, 92, 100, 108, 118, 130, 131, 132, 133, 136, 146.